THE LAWYER'S GUIDE TO
LexisNexis®
CaseMap®

BY DANIEL J. SIEGEL

T0175327

© 2010 American Bar Association. All rights reserved.
Printed in the United States of America.

Library of Congress Cataloging-in-Publication Data
The Lawyer's Guide to LexisNexis CaseMap. Daniel J. Siegel: Library of Congress Cataloging-in-Publication Data is on file.

13 Digit ISBN: 978-1-61632-099-7

12 11 10   5 4 3 2 1

Discounts are available for books ordered in bulk. Special consideration is given to state bars, CLE programs, and other bar-related organizations. Inquire at Book Publishing, American Bar Association, 321 N. Clark Street, Chicago, Illinois 60654.

Contents

CHAPTER 5
Case Tools   181

About the Author

Daniel J. Siegel, Esquire

Mr. Siegel is the founder of Integrated Technology Services, LLC, a consulting service for attorneys, and the principal of the Law Offices of Daniel J. Siegel, LLC, both located in Havertown, Pennsylvania. He has used CaseMap in his practice for over a decade, and has been certified to train and support CaseMap and TimeMap since 2005. Mr. Siegel is also certified to train and/or support numerous other software and technology products, including Time Matters, Legal Files, Concordance and Worldox.

Mr. Siegel authors the "Technology" column in *The Philadelphia Lawyer*, the quarterly magazine of the Philadelphia Bar Association, and "Tech Brief," the Technology column in *Trial*, the monthly magazine of the American Association for Justice (formerly the Association of Trial Lawyers of America). A nationally-known writer and lecturer, Mr. Siegel has served as a writer, lecturer and course planner on technology, civil litigation, workers' compensation, ethics and professional responsibility, non-profit law, personal injury and other matters for the American, Pennsylvania, and Philadelphia Bar Associations, the Pennsylvania Bar Institute, and the American, Philadelphia, and Pennsylvania Trial Lawyers Associations. A past Co-Chair of the Philadelphia Bar Association Law Practice Management Division, Mr. Siegel serves on various Bar Association committees, and is a member of the Editorial Boards of *The Philadelphia Lawyer* and *The Legal Intelligencer,* Philadelphia's daily legal newspaper. He received his law degree from Temple University in 1984 and his bachelor's degree from Franklin and Marshall College (with honors) in 1981.

Acknowledgments

I can still remember purchasing my first computer in 1986, nearly two years after graduating from law school. Since then, it is difficult to believe just how much technology has become a part of my life, my law practice, my business and law firms. In that time, many colleagues have supported and encouraged my interest in technology, and to all of them I offer my thanks.

But the most important thank you must go to my wife, Eileen, and to my sons, Bradley and Douglas, who have unceasingly supported me and encouraged me to follow my passion. I cannot imagine where I would be without them, and thank them for allowing me to complete one of my dreams, to write a book.

Introduction

Welcome to LexisNexis CaseMap. For those lawyers, paralegals, and other support persons who have never used CaseMap, you are in for a treat. LexisNexis CaseMap is a product unlike any other. CaseMap is a computer program that makes analyzing cases easier and allows you to do a better job for your clients in less time. Designed to be a litigation dashboard, CaseMap is extremely easy-to-use and remarkably versatile.

Why CaseMap

CaseMap is also a collaborative tool, allowing lawyers to share information with co-counsel or facilitating production of limited information to assist in negotiation, trial, and settlement. Users of CaseMap do not need to know how to use fancy computer programs. To the contrary, the skills required to use CaseMap effectively are the ability to type a few letters at a time and the ability to analyze information, a skill that is central to all lawyers.

Traditionally, lawyers prepare cases with a variety of very basic means. Many use a trial notebook, organized into sections such as chronology, documents, research, and evidence. Others use Microsoft Word or Corel WordPerfect tables, while many create Microsoft Excel spreadsheets or a Microsoft Access database to organize their case information to show the who, what, and where for each item within a case. In this mode, as cases proceed through discovery, litigators refer to their spreadsheets, note cards, or legal pads to determine what information they have and what information they need, and to try to determine how best to prepare for trial. All of these methods provide simple functionality. CaseMap expands exponentially on this capability. With CaseMap, all of this information, the same information lawyers have compiled for years, is at your fingertips, without the need to shuffle papers, without the need to go from spreadsheet to spreadsheet, or from index cards to legal pads, and to do so more quickly and far more efficiently.

As a database, CaseMap allows you to organize critical knowledge in your cases about facts, people (the cast of characters), and the issues in your case. Facts are simply that—information about anything and everything involved in the case. If a fact is necessary to prove or disprove any matter in a case, or may be used for purposes of examination, cross-examination, or impeachment, it should be included in the CaseMap database. People, organizations, and other data are the building blocks on which your case is constructed. Documents, along with other forms of evidence, are the sources used to prove, disprove, or question all of the facts. Issues are those matters that you are seeking to prove or disprove in the case. The key to CaseMap is organizing this information, along with other data, so that you can analyze your case more quickly and more effectively than with traditional methods.

Lawyers who use CaseMap, and who learn the ins and outs of the product, swear by it. It is to many users a religion. Lawyers who have not used it wonder what the product can do, while lawyers who use it wonder how they lived without it. With CaseMap, you can analyze the entire case, one aspect of the case, or various issues with your case, simply with one click of a mouse. Reports appear with such ease that users tend to take them for granted, but they are veritable fountains of information.

Consider a simple automobile case in which plaintiff had six months of soft-tissue treatment. Traditionally, there was a limited amount of evidence, and the lawyers would prepare for trial in a rudimentary fashion. But at trial, or even at deposition, the plaintiff would often be cross-examined about his or her treatment, including why there were gaps and why the treatment progressed as it did. There may be other questions about prior medical history or the frequency with which the plaintiff took the prescribed medication for his or her injuries. And what would happen? The plaintiff and his or her counsel would often be surprised, because they had no easy way of analyzing any gaps in the treatment easily or effectively.

Alternatively, consider a large pharmaceutical case or a class action replete with documents, witnesses, and a variety of other materials. One mass tort with which I was involved contained over 30 million separate documents. Through group collaboration made simple with CaseMap, we compiled a database of 477 "hot documents" and a list of every witness so that we were able to see every key piece of information relating to every witness, including documents, all by clicking a mouse. When it was time to depose the corporate executives, we did not have to scramble to discover which facts and which documents were crucial to their depositions. All we needed to do was click a button to see the information and click a couple of more buttons to get our reports.

In today's cases, there is a far greater emphasis on motions practice, and motions for summary judgment have become commonplace. Lawyers regularly devote hours, if not days, reviewing transcripts and documents (that they had reviewed earlier in the case) to prepare or defend against these motions. With CaseMap, and its ability to analyze the issues in a case (what parties want to prove or what parties want to disprove), determining which issues are ripe for summary judgment is simple. Conversely, determining which issues are unripe for summary judgment is just as easy. Unlike any other product, CaseMap offers a Summary Judgment Wizard, a way of using the database to create a report that can be easily sent to your word processor, so that drafting the motion or answer becomes far easier and the results far better.

CaseMap has been on the market for many years and has built a loyal following. The product is easy to use, although it does require some training, and continues to improve. The product links with a wide range of other tools, such as LexisNexis TimeMap, LexisNexis TextMap, LiveNote, Sanction, CT Summation, LexisNexis Concordance, and many others. These integrations allow CaseMap to be far more versatile than merely a case-analysis tool. They allow CaseMap to be the central dashboard around which litigation revolves.

For years, my colleagues have claimed that I am a cheerleader for Case Map. That is true only in the sense that I cheer a product that makes being a lawyer easier and allows me to create a better product with ease. I hope this book lets you do the same for your clients.

Expectations and Objectives

Learning any piece of software takes time, and becoming an effective CaseMap user takes time as well. It is unlikely that most people will simply sit down and read this book from cover to cover. Rather, this book explains how to use all of CaseMap's features or, if you prefer, provides guidance on specific features when the situation arises, with step-by-step instructions and illustrations. And for veteran CaseMap users, there are practical tips to help you use the product more effectively.

Each chapter focuses on a different aspect of CaseMap. More important, there is no legalese and no geek-speak. My goal is to avoid using technical terms, computer jargon, or other confusing language.

The early chapters address what you see on the screen when you start to use the program. This means navigating the program's spreadsheets, and learning the basic keystrokes and commands needed to perform basic operations. From there, you will learn how to enter data and analyze it efficiently and effectively. Next, the book explains how to work with and link data, one of the keys to unlocking the value of the program. The later chapters cover many advanced features that you may want to take advantage of as your CaseMap skills develop.

You do not need to be a sophisticated computer user to use CaseMap. You need to be willing, however, to do some things a little bit differently at times from how you may have done them in the past. But when you do so, you will be rewarded with a robust database that makes you a better client advocate.

Remember, CaseMap also has its own internal Help function, the company's Web site provides excellent information for users, and registered licensed customers are generally entitled to free customer support.

Repetition

If you read the book and notice that certain commands are repeated, you are correct. In CaseMap, many of the steps to do one thing are the same for many others.

The Theory of CaseMap

CaseMap is a versatile product that can be used to analyze virtually any case, regardless of whether you are representing the plaintiff or the defendant. It also enables you to analyze specific data within a case to determine the validity of theories of liability and damages, as well as affirmative defenses, such as comparative negligence and mitigation of damages.

What many users of CaseMap do not readily recognize, however, is that there is a "theory" about using CaseMap, and users who embrace its theory recognize how the software revolutionizes their practices. You could use CaseMap without recognizing and embracing the theory, but doing so would be the equivalent of buying a computer and using it only for e-mail. Once you understand how CaseMap works, and why it is important to think the way CaseMap "thinks," its advantages become more evident.

Handling any case effectively generally involves telling a story. The best trial lawyers, regardless of whom they represent, know that the key to effectively presenting a case—whether it is at a pretrial hearing, at arbitration, at a settlement conference, to a jury, or even on appeal—is telling a story. Thus, if you represent someone who was injured in a motor vehicle accident, the story is the accident, the resulting treatment, and how the accident affected the plaintiff's life and work.

When preparing a CaseMap database, the most effective CaseMap users recognize that they must tell a story, and do so in minute snippets. They understand the need to separate each fact, and why each fact must stand alone. In any case that you place into CaseMap, you not only need to tell the complete story, but you also need to be able to analyze the story's components to determine their strengths and weaknesses and whether they are worth pursuing.

Once you have created your story, you understand why the little bits and pieces matter. Building your narrative is no different from building a skyscraper. It so requires a strong framework: a solid foundation, sturdy girders, windows, elevators, the roof, etc. But what about the smaller things, such as the nuts and bolts that keep the girders attached, the glue that is used to keep the windows in place, all of those components? Just as you would not have a sturdy building if you did not have the big things and the little things, so too you will not have an effective CaseMap database if you do not include all of the big things and little things.

Telling a story seems easy, but when a user starts working with CaseMap, he or she frequently loses focus on that. CaseMap allows you to enter each fact, and, when the facts are read in their entirety, it is as though every portion of the story has been put together completely.

For the soft-tissue car accident case, on page 2, you could simply create a fact within CaseMap that the plaintiff received treatment from one date to another. But by doing so, you lose the ability to analyze and determine the number of visits, what was said and evaluated on each visit, which medications were prescribed on each visit, what tests were performed on each visit, and what diagnoses were made at each visit. Consequently, lumping all of the treatment together results in one fact that is difficult to analyze. Thus, if there were thirty-six office visits over a two-month period, it would be easy to determine that the plaintiff went to the doctor approximately four times per week over that two-month period.

Conversely, if the plaintiff went to the doctor four times during that two-month period, there would be no easy way to differentiate that plaintiff from the plaintiff who went more frequently, because lumping all of the dates together simply doesn't help the analysis. It also would not show, in this example, that the plaintiff went three times during the week following the accident and did not go to another office visit for eight more weeks. Clearly, these are very important facts.

While those facts themselves are important, the analysis that flows from them is more significant. The analysis tells us that the person who went thirty-six times went regularly and presumably had more serious injuries than the person who went four times with a nearly two-month gap. Knowing this information in advance of a hearing, and being able to analyze, explain, and address it thoroughly, is where CaseMap provides a user with a tremendous advantage.

In a global analysis, CaseMap becomes even more versatile. As cases grow in scope, there are more parties, witnesses, documents, and information. When the information is coded in a way that makes reading and analyzing it easy, evaluating the case becomes simpler.

CaseMap not only catalogs all of the information in a case, but also focuses a lawyer's thinking and analysis on the entire matter, not just on one section or portion. This means that every piece of information that a lawyer needs to analyze his or her case is available at the click of the mouse. CaseMap is able to accomplish this because, unlike other programs, it puts together the facts, people, documents, issues, and research, so that a lawyer can examine how all of these elements interrelate to the case's issues (items that need to be proven or disproven) and to other matters, such as research and the law. With this process, a lawyer can easily see which areas in the case have strengths, which have weaknesses, and which need further development. In addition, a lawyer can also verify what areas of the case may warrant a motion or warrant further discovery, while being able to determine where an opponent may also be proceeding with his or her case.

In essence, CaseMap is a database on steroids. It contains everything in one place. Traditionally, lawyers have viewed a case as a group of facts that have to be proven, disproven, or neutralized in a courtroom. In contrast, CaseMap looks at the facts as information developed by both sides and provides tools that allow lawyers to analyze those facts. For example, a lawyer may have facts that tend to show that the defendant in a car accident case disregarded a red light, entered an intersection, and caused a collision. CaseMap can help establish that there is no evidence to support those facts, because the police report has no information relating to what the parties did, the plaintiff did not see the defendant, and there are no witnesses other than the defendant himself, who claims to have had a green light. This lack of proof will therefore require the lawyer to muster additional facts, witnesses, perhaps even video surveillance of the intersection, or other information to strengthen that critical aspect of the liability case. Similarly, a defendant may be able to develop evidence to show that the plaintiff's claims that he received regular physical therapy are unfounded, because the plaintiff was only treated for a short period of time with large gaps. A timeline that can be made into a visual graphic in TimeMap with just a few clicks of the mouse can demonstrate this very effectively.

CaseMap also focuses lawyers on the issues in the case—i.e., the things that must be proven. The issues are any matters or legal theories necessary for a case. At their simplest, common issues are liability and damages. In a complex pharmaceutical case, for example, the issues may also include what information was disclosed to or withheld from the U.S. Food and Drug Administration. They may include what information was known to researchers on behalf of the pharmaceutical company and what information the pharmaceutical company disclosed or failed to disclose to those researchers. Each of these may be issues either central to the case or to a particular witness or entity that has direct relevance to a case. Thus, if a pharmaceutical company's expert does not know that significant information about adverse reactions was not provided during his research and testing, that relevant piece of information could be analyzed in CaseMap both through the Issues and Facts spreadsheets.

In addition, CaseMap organizes all of the people in a case so that a user can easily see who was involved in the case and what role he or she played. With merely a mouse click on that person's name, a user can easily see every fact that has been developed in CaseMap relating to that person (or organization or other object). This can be critical. If you are preparing for the deposition of Mr. Jones, one click of a mouse will create a report that not only lists all of the key facts relating to him, but that also shows the documents and other items that support those facts, disprove those facts, or have any relevance to those facts. In essence, the CaseMap report is the initial outline of the deposition or trial questioning because it addresses every fact or event in the case related to Mr. Jones.

The "practice" of CaseMap is also different from how other programs work. In fact, loyal CaseMap users discover that the program revolutionizes the way they prepare their cases. With just a simple query (question), lawyers can see how different entities, persons and issues relate to each other and view instant reports, allowing them to analyze those areas of a case on which they need to put further emphasis. Finally, CaseMap creates a practical work product that can be used to help prepare cases for trial and/or settlement or as a basis for discussing the case with a client to highlight its strengths and weaknesses.

In essence, using CaseMap aims a new magnifying glass at every aspect of a case. When you use CaseMap, the difference between this product and others is the global way in which it contains and provides information to lawyers and staff. In other words, CaseMap can be looked at like a globe. From a distance, a globe simply shows everything. But when you move in more closely, you can examine the rivers, oceans, and countries. Yet you can also do more. You can examine the way the rivers intersect or bisect a country and how that affects the land around it. CaseMap is no different. In its global representation of a case, you can look at the people and issues independently, but when you start to look at them more closely, you can see how each relates to the other. Just as the lack of proper damming could clause a flood, the lack of data about particular facts, or about a particular event, could make it impossible or easy for the other party to disprove.

Another value of CaseMap is how it facilitates the sharing of information among counsel and with clients. In this age in which more and more cases are handled cooperatively, there remain few easy ways for lawyers to share information without having lengthy conferences, etc. As cases become more disparate geographically, it is not as easy for lawyers to meet with co-counsel and to share information. CaseMap facilitates the sharing of information through the use of replicas and reports. Its easy-to-create, easy-to-read reports show the case through a variety of lenses, so that each person involved in the case can examine it with a critical eye. In addition, lawyers can create replicas that allow them to share information in a case and work together to create a global work product. For example, in various mass tort litigation, lawyers work together using CaseMap to create global databases. In the Vioxx litigation in New Jersey, for example, approximately fifteen law firms cooperated to create a CaseMap database showing all of the issues relating to liability against the drug manufacturer. They regularly shared documents, analyzed their information, entered relevant information, and added documents to the database using replicas. When the replicas were complete or at a point at which the information could be synthesized, the lawyers would send the replicas to the law firm that held the master, and that law firm would then synchronize all of the replicas and send the latest information to all of the lawyers. As a result, every law firm involved in the case had the same up-to-date information, and, when the firms determined who would conduct the various depositions, those lawyers could easily see all of the relevant information relating to a particular witness or party.

Finally, clients are highly impressed with the nature of CaseMap's reports. These allow a client to see what information has been developed in the case, what information the client may not have provided, and what information needs to be augmented to strengthen a case. The "Mark Me Up" report, for example, allows clients to work with their lawyers in CaseMap in an easy way that does not require any technological skills. Similarly, the Jumpstart Intake Interview Wizard allows clients to provide a host of information to their lawyers in a way that facilitates the client's thinking about a case and often elicits more information than is likely to be gleaned from meetings. The Interview Wizard contains a wealth of information the client can fill in and return to the lawyer, who can immediately integrate it into the CaseMap database.

About CaseMap 9

With the release of CaseMap 9, LexisNexis has added the capability to store CaseMap data on a Microsoft SQL Server® database, i.e., CaseMap 9 provides centralized, secure remote access so that users may use the SQL server environment to create and manage cases with large or long-lived databases, and across offices. By allowing the use of SQL, users have additional security and flexibility, which will permit different users to use different sets of features as they work on the cases.

Although CaseMap 9 has been "tuned" to work better in the Windows 7 environment and runs on 64 bit Windows® Vista and Windows® 7 systems, from a functional standpoint, there are no differences between CaseMap 8.5 and CaseMap 9. Thus, CaseMap users who are familiar with using CaseMap's earlier versions will not have to learn any new features—the only thing that has changed is the flexibility of creating some cases that may be unusually large or long-lived for the CaseMap SQL server environment.

While there are some minor differences in CaseMap SQL administrations, all examples in this book refer to the Windows-based version of the program.

CaseMap 9 Case File Types

CaseMap 9 allows users to create SQL or "local" cases.

SQL Cases: These case databases are created by an administrator using a special CaseMap Admin Console. Designated case staff are then assigned to cases by the administrator.

Local Cases: These traditional case databases are exactly the same as the pre-CaseMap 9 cases and may be created by any user and saved to/stored on a designated network folder. Authorized users may edit the case staff.

CaseMap 9 SQL Administration

Firms that use the CaseMap 9 SQL version can centrally control the creation of new SQL cases and assign users to the cases. Using the CaseMap Admin Console, a CaseMap administrator can assign specific permissions for individual case staff. For example, some users may be able to enter data but not able to create or delete custom fields. The CaseMap Server must be installed on a local hard drive and cannot be run from a network server. In addition, a user must be logged on with administrator rights in order to install CaseMap Server.

Getting Started

2

Logging On

To start CaseMap, double-click on the LexisNexis CaseMap short-cut (a blue icon) that was placed onto your Windows desktop when you installed the product (see Figure 1). If the icon is missing, go to Start>All Programs>LexisNexis CaseMap Suite and click on the CaseMap icon. To create a shortcut on your desktop, highlight the program's icon and right-click, then select Send To>Desktop (Create Shortcut).

Figure 1

When the program opens, you will be at the Getting Started with CaseMap screen (see Figure 2). From this screen, you can open an existing case, open the demo case (the Hawkins case), learn more about the program, or create a new case. If you have previously worked on a case, it will be listed under Open a Case on the right side of the program's Welcome screen (see Figure 3). If the case is not listed, just click on More Cases and locate

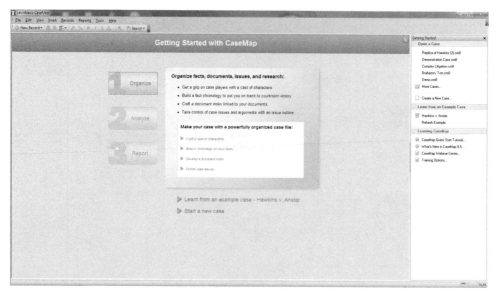

Figure 2

Figure 3

the case you are looking for on your computer or on your network using Windows Explorer.

When you open a case, you will be asked to log in (see Figure 4). Every CaseMap user should have a separate login and, if used at your firm, a password. By requiring every user to have a separate login, it will be easier if you or someone else needs to track or review another user's work. When you log

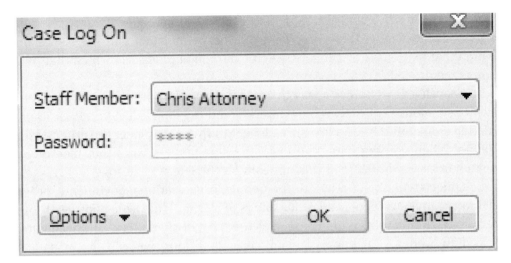

Figure 4

in to CaseMap, the program will return you to the last spreadsheet and view on which you had worked in that particular case. That is all you need to do, and you are ready to work.

Basic Terms

Throughout this book, you will see certain terms that appear regularly. It is important to understand what those terms represent and how they assist you in utilizing CaseMap.

Spreadsheet—A spreadsheet is a working area in CaseMap that is visible to the user. You can access spreadsheets using the shortcut buttons on the left side of the screen. The view (the way the spreadsheet appears) on the screen is the same view that would appear in the default instant report for that spreadsheet.

Field—Each column in a spreadsheet is known as a field. For example, the Source field stores information specifying where the information in that record came from and the Date & Time field stores the date and time when each fact or event occurred. Each record is made up of multiple fields, most of which are not displayed by default.

Record—This is the information in a case file that describes a particular fact, object, issue, question, or research item in a record. Records appear in a spreadsheet as rows running from left to right. You will frequently need to use the navigation bars on the bottom and right of your screen to view all of the information in a particular record.

Cell—A cell (or box) is the place on a spreadsheet into which you type data. It is the location at which a field and a record intersect.

Link—This is a connection between two different elements or aspects of a case. For example, there may be a link between a fact and the issues on which that fact bears or a link between a person and a fact in which that person is mentioned.

Search—Searching is a way to explore case information. CaseMap offers two basic methods for searching: filtering and tagging. When you filter information, you limit the rows in a spreadsheet to those that meet the criteria you define. When you tag data, you mark the spreadsheet rows that meet your search criteria with an icon that appears on the left of each row.

Object—An object refers to the people, organizations, documents, other demonstrative evidence, and other things in a case. Thus, when you read "object," you should think of things such as the "cast of characters" or documents.

Full Names—Full names (sometimes called "long names") are the names of people and documents displayed in spreadsheets. All objects must have full names. If, as is strongly recommended, you use short names, you never again have to type a full name after you create the item's short name.

Short Names—Short names, which are the critical feature in CaseMap that enable data linking, are "special" names (really shortcuts for full names) that either you or CaseMap assigns to each object and issue in a case. If you do not create short names, you will not be able to link various data from the different spreadsheets, and your ability to analyze information will be dramatically reduced.

The Demo Case ("Hawkins")

The best way to learn CaseMap (or any other software program) is to "play" with it. "Playing with CaseMap" means trying all of its features, clicking every button, reading every menu, and just figuring out all of the things the program can do.

Throughout this book, we will use the *Hawkins v. Anstar* case, a hypothetical employment matter included with CaseMap as a reference. Although you are free to create another example case, it is recommended that you use the Hawkins case because it is designed to demonstrate all of CaseMap's features; in addition, the designers of the program have integrated the case seamlessly with other products in the CaseMap Suite (such as TextMap and TimeMap), making it an excellent way to learn not only CaseMap, but all of the products in the suite. Finally, because the Hawkins case is fictitious, you will also not have to worry about accidentally changing or deleting any data from a real case.

The default user in the Hawkins case is Chris Attorney, although you can log in as one of the five other users or create additional users. Otherwise,

Never Work with Real/Live Data

There is nothing worse than losing data or destroying your case information. As a result, it is strongly recommended that you never train or practice using CaseMap (or any other software program) while using real/live data.

Instead, before you attempt to customize CaseMap—or if you are unsure how a particular feature works and just want to be sure—it is strongly recommended that you do so using the Hawkins case, because you cannot destroy the Hawkins case. You can, however, destroy data within your own case, even accidentally, and the results could be disastrous, especially if you haven't backed up the program.

As a result, remember: Never play with real data; always play with demo data.

there is no difference between Hawkins and any other case. You can add or delete data and test the program's features as much as you want, without any concerns.

The Hawkins case, which appears on the right side of the opening screen, appears under the heading "Learn from an Example Case" and is entitled *Hawkins v. Anstar* (see Figure 3). If you double-click on *Hawkins v. Anstar*, CaseMap will open the case in the same status that it was when you last worked on the case. If you have never worked on the case, the Hawkins case will open in its original form. You can also restore the Hawkins case to its original form (and permanently remove all of the changes you have made) simply by clicking on Refresh Example (just below *Hawkins v. Anstar*). When you refresh the example case, CaseMap informs you that "The example case has been refreshed" and asks "Open it now?" When you answer "Yes," CaseMap reopens the Hawkins case in its original (unchanged) condition.

Remember, once you click Refresh Example, all of the changes you have made in the Hawkins case are permanently lost.

Creating a New Case

To create a new CaseMap case, you will use the New Case Wizard (see Figure 6). You access this Wizard by clicking on the Create a New Case icon on the Getting Started panel on the right side of CaseMap (see Figure 5), by clicking on "Start a new case" at the bottom of the Getting Started with CaseMap screen, or by selecting File>New from the menu bar at the top of the screen.

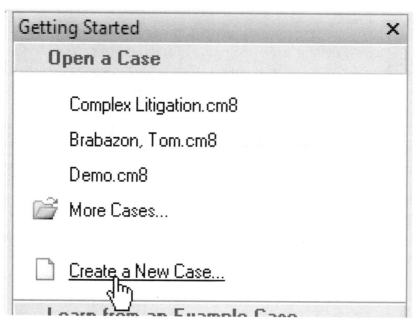

Figure 5

Selecting File Locations

When creating a case in CaseMap, it is important to carefully choose the location where the case file will be stored and where the documents and other objects to be used will be located. Although you can store documents and other objects in any location accessible to CaseMap users, you should avoid this method of linking. Instead, and consistent with best practices, many CaseMap users create a dedicated location on their computers or their networks to store all of their CaseMap databases. In addition, they generally create a separate directory/folder to store the documents and other items that will be linked to the CaseMap database.

By using dedicated directories for CaseMap databases and files, you will find it much easier to work with your data and your objects. In addition, replication will be simpler, even if you do not use a document-copying process when creating a replica. More important, as discussed in the document-review section of the book (page 185), there are significant advantages when working with Adobe and the CaseMap Doc Previewer to splitting documents into multiple components.

The first thing CaseMap asks for is the name of the new case (see Figure 7). You should enter the name of the case as descriptively as possible. CaseMap next asks for the time zone in which most of the facts in the case occurred (the default time zone). This is important because CaseMap will record

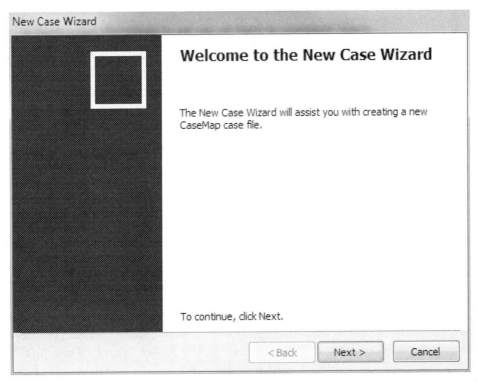

Figure 6

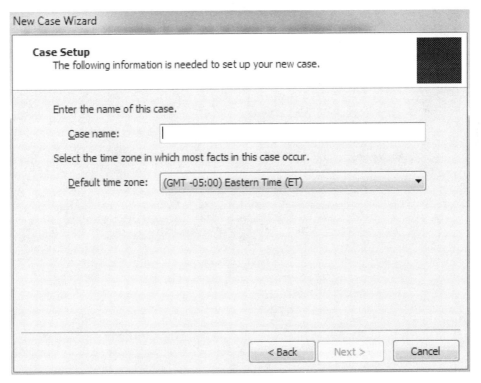

Figure 7

case facts based on the time and time zone/location where they occurred. Thus, if something happened at 3 p.m. in New York and another event took place at 12 noon in California, the events would have occurred at the same time, and CaseMap will know that when compiling the chronology of events.

The Wizard will then ask you to select a template for your case (see Figure 8). You can use the default CaseMap template (as most users do), which provides the basic CaseMap fields and other information. You can also create custom templates so that you do not have to enter all of the objects, issues, staff names and other information common to all of your cases. Once you create a custom template, you can simply apply that template to any new case and avoid additional unnecessary data entry.

Custom templates can be very handy, whether to eliminate entering the names of all of your staff or when handling repetitive types of litigation. For example, if your practice involves mass tort litigation and you regularly represent individuals who took a particular drug, there will be certain objects and issues common to all of your cases. This could also apply to automobile accident cases, medical malpractice cases, etc. The New Case Wizard also allows you to remember which templates you have created when you check "Remember my selections" at the bottom of the Select Template window. On the next screen, you will be asked to enter your name and the name of your

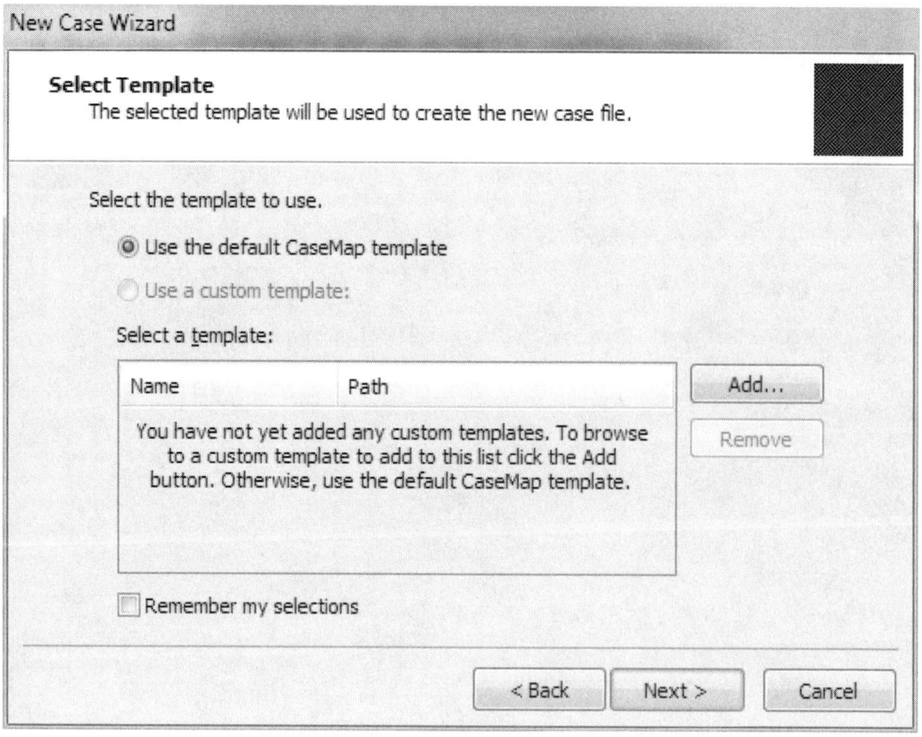

Figure 8

Only Add the Data You Need to CaseMap

CaseMap is intended to be a repository for all information relating to the critical aspects of your case, not necessarily a container for every piece of data you have. Despite this, some users link every document and code every fact (no matter how insignificant) in CaseMap, while others only store those documents that they intend to use during discovery, at trial, or for some other purpose. Doing the latter allows you to build a dedicated database containing only the essential documents and makes it easier to locate linked files than if there are hundreds or thousands of unnecessary files linked to your database. Remember, the goal of CaseMap is to allow you to analyze your data efficiently. Data overload can be counterproductive to that purpose.

firm or organization (see Figure 9). Because this information will appear when you generate reports, you must enter it at the beginning of every case; by default, CaseMap remembers the firm name for the last case created and will insert it into the dialog, although you may change the name at any time.

You may also create logins for additional staff members at this preliminary stage; you can also do so later by using the Manage Case Staff option on the Tools menu. On the next screen, CaseMap asks where to store/save the case file on your computer or network (see Figure 10). By default, CaseMap stores the case file at the location specified at Tools>Options>File Locations. Unless you restrict this option (which must be done on each user's computer), you can create a case in a different location by browsing to it and saving the case there. CaseMap will remember this information for your case without the need for you to navigate to it every time you open the case.

After selecting the location for the case, select Finish and your case is ready to use (see Figure 11). At this point, you can also use the Case Jumpstart Wizard, if you so desire. The Case Jumpstart Wizard is one way of building your cast of characters and entering information when creating a new

Make Copies of Files Before Using Them in CaseMap

Because you may annotate or make other changes to the documents and other items linked to your CaseMap database, you should only work with *copies* of the original files stored on your computer or network. The best practice is to copy any documents or other items to be linked to CaseMap to the specific case's CaseMap directory. This will avoid any accidental changes to the original files.

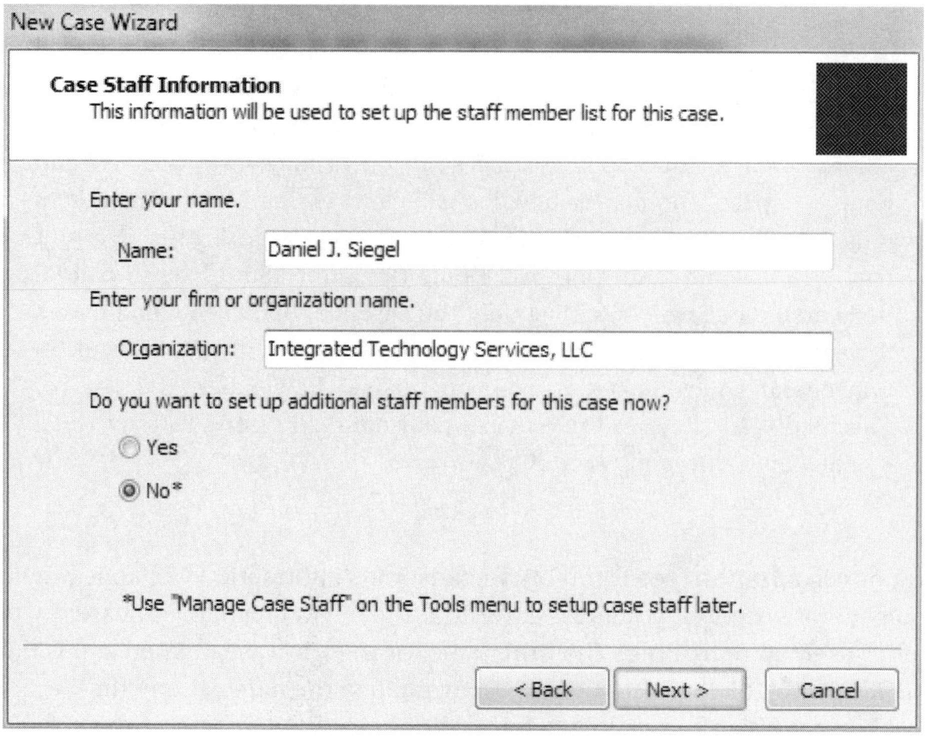

New Case Wizard

Case Staff Information
This information will be used to set up the staff member list for this case.

Enter your name.

Name: Daniel J. Siegel

Enter your firm or organization name.

Organization: Integrated Technology Services, LLC

Do you want to set up additional staff members for this case now?

○ Yes

◉ No*

*Use "Manage Case Staff" on the Tools menu to setup case staff later.

[< Back] [Next >] [Cancel]

Figure 9

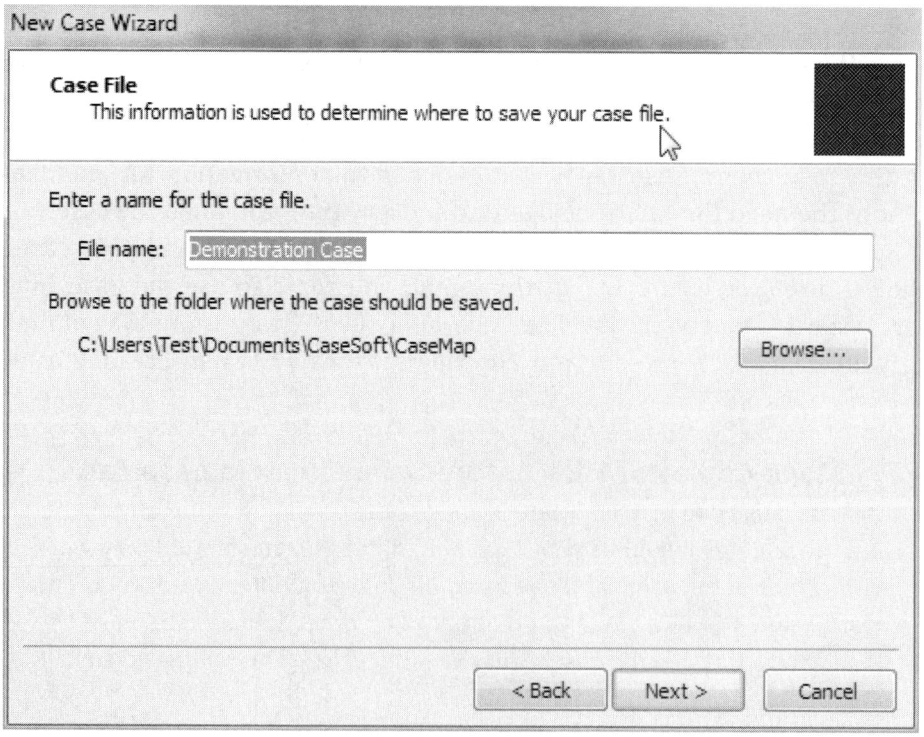

New Case Wizard

Case File
This information is used to determine where to save your case file.

Enter a name for the case file.

File name: Demonstration Case

Browse to the folder where the case should be saved.

C:\Users\Test\Documents\CaseSoft\CaseMap   [Browse...]

[< Back] [Next >] [Cancel]

Figure 10

Figure 11

case. The Wizard allows you to identify and create objects for the various people and organizations in your case, including litigants, judges, counsel, witnesses and others. The Wizard displays a check mark next to those categories for which you have entries, although you do not have to enter information in every category. You can cancel the Wizard at any time, but if you do so before clicking Finish, your data will not be saved. In addition, the Wizard does not check for duplicate information that may have already been entered into CaseMap. You can access the Case Jumpstart Wizard at any time by going to Help>Case Jumpstart Wizard.

CaseMap Windows & Toolbars

When you open CaseMap, it can look a little bit confusing because CaseMap stores and displays information on multiple spreadsheets. But once you are used to working with the program, you will welcome the ability to switch easily between different views at any time. If you have opened the Hawkins case to its original format, you will see a screen that looks like the one displayed in Figure 12.

At the top left of the screen on the blue bar will be the name of the case that you have logged into. This is called the title bar (see Figure 12).

Figure 12

On the second row is the menu bar (see Figure 12), which contains the standard File, Edit, and other menus found in most Windows programs; the menu bar also contains dropdown menus designed specifically for CaseMap. The menu bar runs from left to right at the top of the screen, just below the title bar. Each word on the menu bar (File, Edit, View . . .) opens a dropdown menu with various options related to the spreadsheet you are viewing. Just click on an option to execute a command. Many commands have (and display) related keyboard shortcuts that make it easy to perform routine actions without using your mouse. As discussed in the Customizing CaseMap section on page 43, you can add or remove menus and options from the menu bar by adding a toolbar on the Tools>Customize menu or by right-clicking and selecting the Customize option.

The third row is the CaseMap toolbar (see Figure 12), with icons that allow you to perform various common tasks in CaseMap. Every button on the toolbar, except the B, I, U, and A buttons, has corresponding options on the menu bar. The B button allows you to turn on or off bold text formatting in description fields. The I button allows you to italicize information in description fields. The U button allows you to underline text in description fields. The A button lets you format text in description fields in a wide variety of colors. To use the B, I, U and A features, select the text you desire to format, and click on the appropriate button or buttons. The buttons will be highlighted when the format is applied and will be off (not highlighted) when there is no formatting on the text. You can also customize this toolbar by adding or removing features using the Tools>Customize menu or by right-clicking and selecting the Customize option. Adding these shortcuts will make CaseMap even more efficient.

The fourth row is called the spreadsheet title bar (see Figure 13), which displays the name of the spreadsheet you are viewing and allows you to view every spreadsheet in your case. The left side of the bar shows the title of the current spreadsheet. The right side of the bar displays the number of records in the current spreadsheet. If the right side of the bar says "Filtered: X of Y," CaseMap is informing you that you have used a filter (Search) that is displaying some, but not all, of the records in the spreadsheet. In addition, when you run a filter, the Search Results bar will appear in the row below and specify

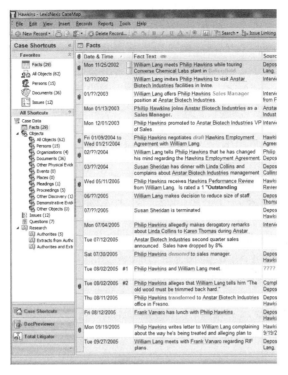

Figure 13

the parameters of the current filter. To remove the filter, click Cancel Search; or select Save to save the filter for use again. You can also right-click anywhere in the data and select Cancel Search to make all of the records visible again.

To the side of the spreadsheet title bar is the navigation bar (see Figure 13), which runs vertically on the left-hand side of the screen when you open a case in CaseMap. You can also hide the navigation bar by clicking on the arrow at the top (see Figure 13). The navigation bar is divided into three sections: Case Data, Objects, and Research. The Case Data section contains the Facts spreadsheet, the Objects section contains the various Objects spreadsheets, and the Research section includes three spreadsheets designed to allow you to integrate your case research with the Facts and Objects spreadsheets.

By default, this pane shows an expanded Case Shortcuts section and buttons at the bottom to access the DocPreviewer or Total Litigator panes. The Case Shortcuts section is divided between Favorites (Facts, All Objects, Persons, Documents, and Issues) and All Shortcuts, which are the spreadsheets you use most frequently. The numbers (in parentheses) to the right of the name of each spreadsheet indicate the number of records/entries on the spreadsheet. As with most other aspects of CaseMap, you can customize the Favorites section to include each of the spreadsheets that you use most frequently. Below the Favorites is the All Shortcuts section, which lists all of the different shortcuts in the program. You can view all of your case shortcuts by clicking on the All Shortcuts bar.

The Total Litigator bar at the bottom left of the screen contains links with both Litigation Tasks and Litigation Tools, most of which require you to subscribe to the particular LexisNexis service. To use these features, click on tasks such as Early Case Assessment, Discovery, and Research or use the Litigation Tools menu to launch programs such as TimeMap, TextMap, Concordance, CourtLink, and File and Serve.

It is important to note, for example, that you will see Case Shortcuts highlighted on the bar below the list of spreadsheets when you are looking at the Case Shortcuts. This allows you to know which of the different sidebars you are viewing. If you click on DocPreviewer, for example, you will see that an entirely different group of icons appears. If you click on Total Litigator, a feature that allows CaseMap to work seamlessly with a variety of LexisNexis research and litigation tools, the program displays the related options. You can also display and configure fewer or more buttons on the Navigation bar depending upon your preferences.

Viewing Files

With CaseMap, you do not have to switch from one program to another to view the document or other source of the information on display. Rather, by clicking on the black paperclip icon on the left column on any row displaying it in the Facts spreadsheet (see Figure 14), or by highlighting and right-clicking a short name in the Source cell and clicking Open Linked File or by right-clicking on a file name in the Linked File Field, you seamlessly view the source file(s) for any fact, etc. Because CaseMap does not have its own file viewer, it

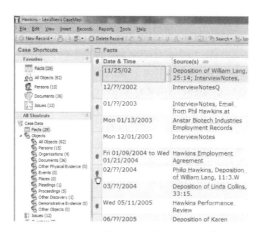

Figure 14

will open the source/linked file in whatever program is associated with the file on your computer.

Spreadsheets (Overview)

CaseMap organizes your case using spreadsheets. Because CaseMap allows you to create links—i.e., relationships—between the data in your spreadsheets, it is far easier to analyze your information. Linking spreadsheet data also offers users powerful new and innovative ways to explore your case information. Finally, by linking items on the spreadsheets, you will be able to see your results, including the linked documents and other items, with the click of the mouse, rather than moving back and forth from one program to another and searching for information.

CaseMap comprises five primary spreadsheets, which represent the major types of information entered and organized in a case. When you create a case from scratch, CaseMap automatically creates blank Fact, Object and Issues spreadsheets, as well as spreadsheets for questions and organizing research. One of CaseMap's advantages is that it is flexible, making it easy to start, enter or modify information, and simple to come back to later. Another helpful feature of the program is that once you learn how to do a task on one spreadsheet, you will have learned how to do it on all of the spreadsheets, because tasks are done in a predictable manner from sheet to sheet.

When you look at the various spreadsheets, you will see little icons/indicators that allow you to sort or otherwise understand what the column on the spreadsheet means. If you look carefully at the Date & Time column on the Facts spreadsheet, you will see a little arrow. This arrow indicates that the data in that column can be sorted in either ascending or descending ("A to Z" or "Z to A") order. When you click on the Fact Text column, you will see that it has a little chain-link icon next to the words Fact Text (see Figure 15). This means that the fields with information in the Facts Text column can link to other information in other spreadsheets. The Source column also has a link icon on the top, which means that it also links to other data in other spreadsheets within the program.

The Material and Status columns contain a plus sign (+) icon, which indicates that the information in that column may be evaluated based on a variety of criteria set up either by the program or by the user. If you go to the All Objects spreadsheet, for example, you will see that it has similar abilities to sort and evaluate information.

📎	Date & Time /	Fact Text ⊕	Source(s) ⊕	Material +	Status +	Linked Issues ⊕	Evaluation
📎	11/25/02	William Lang meets Philip Hawkins while touring Converse Chemical Labs plant in Bakersfield.	Deposition of William Lang, 25:14.	Yes	Disputed b Us		◀ ↘ ▾
	12/??/2002	William Lang invites Philip Hawkins to visit Anstar	InterviewNotes	No	Prospective	Wrongful Termination	↓

Figure 15

When you look at data within the program, for example, by clicking on any row in the Fact spreadsheet, you will notice a dark paper clip displayed on the far left column of some rows. The dark paper clip means that the data or the fact is linked to one or more sources. In fact, you can link facts to many sources and are not limited by any one source or any one type of source. Your only limitation is that each source must be a separate object within CaseMap. If you click on the row for 11/25/02 in the Facts spreadsheet of the Hawkins case, you will also see a box with three ellipses in the Date & Time cell. When you click on the ellipses, it will open up the CaseMap Date Stamper, which allows you to enter dates and times in very specific detail. Similarly, throughout CaseMap, whenever you enter a cell with the three ellipses in it, you can click that icon to instantly view whatever facts or objects are associated with it.

When you click into the Fact Text box (see Figure 16), you may notice that some of the entries, such as William Lang and Philip Hawkins's names, suddenly change in appearance from William Lang and Philip Hawkins to LangW and HawkinsP. These names, LangW and HawkinsP, are called short names, and the use of short names is essential to getting the most out of CaseMap. If you click into the Material or Status columns, you will note that there is a down arrow that provides you with options of how to evaluate information within a particular field.

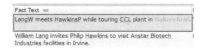

Figure 16

Facts Spreadsheet

Most CaseMap users spend the majority of their time working with the Facts spreadsheet, which comprises the individual facts that tell the story of your case. Because you will spend so much of your time working with the Facts spreadsheet, it is important to understand what the spreadsheet shows and how many of the navigational items on the Facts spreadsheet are common to other spreadsheets.

The far left column of the Facts spreadsheet has a paper clip at the top. Any fact row that has a black (darkened) paper clip visible in this column is linked to a document or other source. When you click on the paper clip, CaseMap will display a list of all files linked to that fact (see Figure 17). If you highlight and left-click the item displayed, CaseMap will open that item. For example, if the link is to a PDF, the document will open in Adobe Acrobat or another PDF reader.

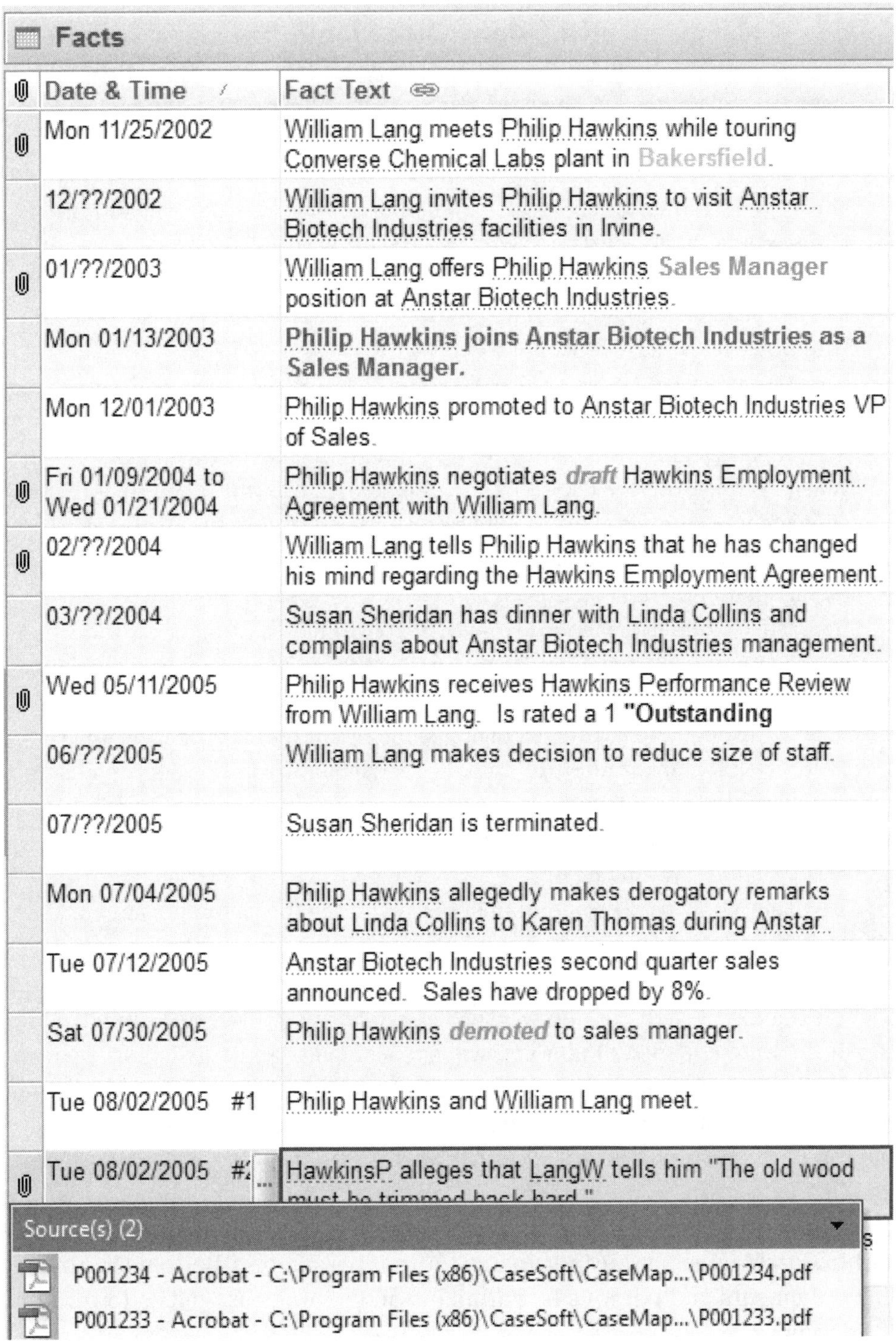

📎 **Facts**	
📎 **Date & Time** /	**Fact Text** ⊝
📎 Mon 11/25/2002	William Lang meets Philip Hawkins while touring Converse Chemical Labs plant in Bakersfield.
12/??/2002	William Lang invites Philip Hawkins to visit Anstar Biotech Industries facilities in Irvine.
📎 01/??/2003	William Lang offers Philip Hawkins Sales Manager position at Anstar Biotech Industries.
Mon 01/13/2003	**Philip Hawkins joins Anstar Biotech Industries as a Sales Manager.**
Mon 12/01/2003	Philip Hawkins promoted to Anstar Biotech Industries VP of Sales.
📎 Fri 01/09/2004 to Wed 01/21/2004	Philip Hawkins negotiates *draft* Hawkins Employment Agreement with William Lang.
📎 02/??/2004	William Lang tells Philip Hawkins that he has changed his mind regarding the Hawkins Employment Agreement.
03/??/2004	Susan Sheridan has dinner with Linda Collins and complains about Anstar Biotech Industries management.
📎 Wed 05/11/2005	Philip Hawkins receives Hawkins Performance Review from William Lang. Is rated a 1 **"Outstanding**
06/??/2005	William Lang makes decision to reduce size of staff.
07/??/2005	Susan Sheridan is terminated.
Mon 07/04/2005	Philip Hawkins allegedly makes derogatory remarks about Linda Collins to Karen Thomas during Anstar
Tue 07/12/2005	Anstar Biotech Industries second quarter sales announced. Sales have dropped by 8%.
Sat 07/30/2005	Philip Hawkins *demoted* to sales manager.
Tue 08/02/2005 #1	Philip Hawkins and William Lang meet.
📎 Tue 08/02/2005 #: ...	HawkinsP alleges that LangW tells him "The old wood must be trimmed back hard."

Source(s) (2)	▼
📄	P001234 - Acrobat - C:\Program Files (x86)\CaseSoft\CaseMap...\P001234.pdf
📄	P001233 - Acrobat - C:\Program Files (x86)\CaseSoft\CaseMap...\P001233.pdf

Figure 17

The Right-Click Menu

There is probably no better time-saving feature in CaseMap than the right-click dialog menu. Just try it anywhere in CaseMap and see how many options it provides.

If you right-click on a cell almost anywhere in the Facts spread-sheet, for example, a dialog pops up highlighting your selection and providing you with an option to filter and tag or cancel a search (instead of clicking the red funnel). Equally important are some of the other features in this menu. The Send To dialog allows you to send the current record (the row in which your cursor is sitting) to LexisNexis TimeMap, NoteMap, Microsoft Word, Corel WordPerfect, a Web browser, Microsoft Excel, or LexisNexis Total Litigator.

Right-clicking can also bring up the Link Assistant (see Figure 18). When you use the Link Assistant in this context, it will begin by either showing you a list of all of the links starting with the first one alphabetically, or, if there is a selection entered into the selection field, it will begin by highlighting that selection to allow you to review or modify the selection. This right-click menu also allows you to add an object on the fly, change the object detail, or open any file that is linked to that CaseMap fact. If you had highlighted a particular word or phrase, you would be able to, through the right-click dialog, copy or cut that information and to paste it elsewhere in the program. If you right-click in the Source field, you could open any linked file that is properly linked in CaseMap.

Similarly, right-clicking on any other spreadsheet generates a number of similar time-saving options. When it comes to saving time, or if you are unsure how to do something in CaseMap, try the right-click menu.

At the top of each column, you will see different icons. For example, at the top of the Date & Time column you will see a small triangle facing up or down. The up or down triangle means that the Date & Time field can be sorted in either ascending or descending order. To change the sort order, simply click on the top of the column and select either Sort Ascending or Sort Descending.

If a field displays a chain link, such as the Fact Text or Source fields, this means that a user may link information within that column to other data within CaseMap using the short name for that person or other object. You can link documents and persons to both facts and sources as well as to other information.

Any column that displays a plus sign at the top indicates that the column is a sortable evaluation column—i.e., the user can evaluate the data in that fact based on various criteria.

Workflow in CaseMap

There is no right or wrong way to create a case in CaseMap. Some users begin by entering facts while others begin by entering objects and others start with the issues. In most cases, as long as the data are entered, it does not matter how or in what order you do so, but the following guidelines help outline the purpose of these spreadsheets:

- Use the **Objects** spreadsheets to create and organize your "cast of characters"—i.e., the people, documents, organizations, and other items in your case.
- Use the **Issues** spreadsheet to organize and explore the claims, defenses, legal theories and arguments in your case.
- Use the **Facts** spreadsheet to create the chronology of all of the relevant facts in your case.

Objects Spreadsheet

The Objects spreadsheet is used to create the "cast of characters," the list of all of the key people, organizations and other things involved in your case. In reality, CaseMap includes numerous "objects" spreadsheets, including spreadsheets for Persons, Organizations, Documents, Other Physical Evidence, Events, Places, Proceedings, Pleadings, Other Discovery, Demonstrative Evidence, and Other Objects. Each of the objects spreadsheets contains certain data fields common to all objects, along with data fields that specifically relate only to the type of information relevant to a particular object. Thus, Gender is listed only on the Persons spreadsheet.

All Objects Spreadsheet

The All Objects spreadsheet displays all of the objects in a particular case. However, because this spreadsheet includes all objects, it only displays the fields common to all objects. The All Objects spreadsheet can also be customized to show or hide documents, depending on the number of documents in a case, a particularly helpful feature as cases grow in size.

The following fields are common to all objects: Description, Full Name, Linked File, Linked Issues, Related Files, Role In Case, Object Type, Short Name.

Persons Spreadsheet

The Persons spreadsheet is the main spreadsheet where the names of all persons involved in the case should be listed, with both a full name and a short name. While some users do not list all persons involved in a case on this spreadsheet and instead write their names in a traditional method (i.e., in

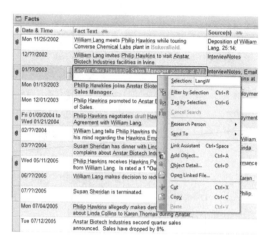

Figure 18

long form), it is highly desirable to list every person in your case on the Persons spreadsheet. By giving each person a unique full and short name, you are better able to determine the relationships between different persons and events, and, should an individual become highly relevant later on in the case, including him or her on the Persons spreadsheet facilitates analyzing information about that person. In addition, by creating both a full and a short name for every person, you can enter facts more efficiently.

Making the All Objects Spreadsheet More User-Friendly by Not Displaying Documents

By default, the All Objects spreadsheet displays all of the objects in a particular case, including documents. This view is generally acceptable, but it can become far less helpful or very frustrating to use if your case has numerous documents. With a simple change in your settings, CaseMap allows you either not to show documents when the All Objects spreadsheet is open or only to show documents when there are fewer than the number you specify. To limit the number of documents that appear, go to Tools>Options>Documents on the Menu bar (see Figure 19). Under the All Objects Spreadsheet section of this tab, you can choose either to "Always show documents in the All Objects Spreadsheet" or to "Hide documents in the All Objects Spreadsheet once the number of documents exceeds" the number you specify. If you enter 0 into the latter option, no documents will appear on the All Objects spreadsheet. This case-specific setting requires you to close and reopen the case before it becomes effective.

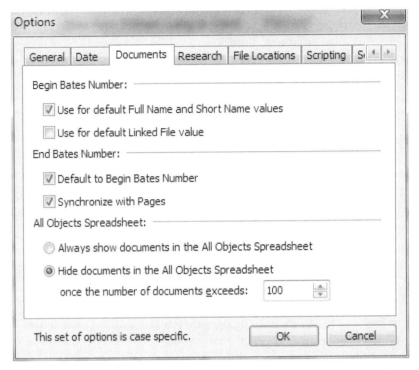

Figure 19

The following fields are unique to the Persons spreadsheet: Addresses, Address: E-mail, At Trial, Calling Party, Counsel, Deposition Date, Deposition Status, Gender, Phone Numbers, Title, Works For.

Organizations Spreadsheet

Organizations are the companies, businesses, and other entities involved in a case. Like other objects, organizations have both a full name and a short name.

The following fields are unique to the Organizations spreadsheet: Address: Business, Address: E-mail, Phone Numbers.

Documents Spreadsheet

Documents include all of the documents (in whatever format, such as PDF, TIFF, etc.) in your case. They can also include videos, sound files, or virtually any other type of item. The Document spreadsheets can contain a wealth of information about a particular document, far more than will normally be needed in any case. However, it is important to enter all the information that is or is likely to be relevant to avoid the need to reenter data later.

The following data fields are unique to the Documents spreadsheet: Author, Bates—Begin, Bates—End, Copied To, Date, Depo Ex. #, Mentioned In, Producing Party, Recipient(s), Sent Via, Trial Ex. #, Type.

Other Physical Evidence Spreadsheet

This general spreadsheet can include a variety of other objects. For example, it could include the names of medications in a personal injury case or the name of a pharmaceutical drug in a pharmaceutical class action. In a criminal case, it could refer to the various pieces of evidence. The name is generic and items that are placed in the Other Physical Evidence spreadsheet could often be placed in the Demonstrative Evidence spreadsheet, which looks virtually identical to the Other Physical Evidence spreadsheets and the Other Objects spreadsheet.

The following fields are unique to documents and items of Other Physical Evidence: Bates #, Trial Ex. #.

Events Spreadsheet

The Events spreadsheet is designed to include all key incidents that are likely to have numerous facts relating to them and differ from individual facts, which should be included on the Facts spreadsheet as part of the chronology. For example, in a car accident case, you should create the accident as an event; or, in a contract claim, you might set up the meeting between client and defendant as an event because numerous case-related facts transpired; conversely, a phone call is more likely to be an individual fact.

The following fields are unique to the Events spreadsheet: Attendees, Begin Date & Time, End Date & Time, Location.

Places Spreadsheet

The Places spreadsheet is for specific locations of relevance in your particular case. If, for example, your case involved a claim of medical malpractice, places might include the emergency room, the operating room, and other locations within the hospital.

There are no fields unique to the Places spreadsheet.

Pleadings Spreadsheet

The Pleadings spreadsheet is designed to include all of the different pleadings in a case. These are often listed, although they may not always appear in the Facts spreadsheet. Some pleadings could also appear as documents because, as noted above, there is no right and wrong way to enter this information into CaseMap.

The following fields are unique to the Pleadings spreadsheet: Date, Type.

Proceedings Spreadsheet

The Proceedings spreadsheet is designed to include all court hearings, trials, grand jury hearings, depositions, and other proceedings-related matters in a case. If you link deposition and other transcripts from TextMap with CaseMap, you must first create the deposition as a proceeding within CaseMap.

The following fields are unique to the Proceedings spreadsheet: Attendees, Date, Notice Date, Subpoena Served, Status, Type.

Other Discovery Spreadsheet

The Other Discovery spreadsheet could include documents other than pleadings, although there is no limitation as to the type of item listed on this spreadsheet. For example, in the Hawkins case, interview notes are listed as an example of "other discovery."

The following fields are unique to the Other Discovery spreadsheet: Response Date, Response Received, Service Date, Type.

Demonstrative Evidence Spreadsheet

The Demonstrative Evidence spreadsheet is designed to include the various pieces of evidence that may or will be used as exhibits or evidence at trial, depositions, hearings, etc.

The following fields are unique to the Demonstrative Evidence spreadsheet: Estimated Cost, For Use By, Mission Statement, Production Status, Trial Ex. #, Type.

Creating Proceedings

CaseMap categorizes all court hearings, trials, grand jury hearings, depositions, and other related matters as "proceedings." While in CaseMap, you create proceedings the same way you would create any other object, including the creation of Full and Short Names. If you are working in TextMap, for example, and wish to link a deposition or other TextMap transcript with CaseMap, you must first create the deposition as a proceeding within CaseMap. In TextMap, the first time that you attempt to send a transcript annotation to CaseMap, you will be required to create the CaseMap object. The dialog will first ask whether you wish to categorize the proceeding as a Document, Pleading, Proceeding, Research Authority, or Other type. Generally, you should select Proceeding and create a full name and a short name. This dialog appears only during the first instance in which you attempt to send an annotation to CaseMap (see Figure 20).

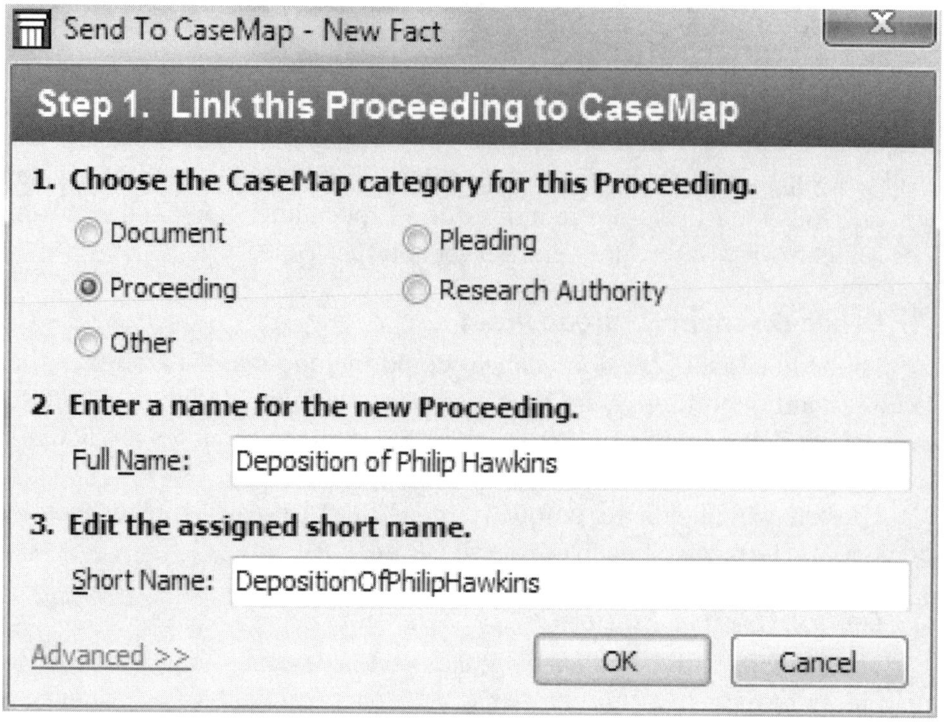

Figure 20

Other Objects Spreadsheet

The Other Objects spreadsheet is the place to include any other objects that do not fall within the various other spreadsheets.

There are no fields unique to the Other Objects spreadsheet.

Issues

One of the most important aspects of CaseMap is the creation of an issues outline and utilizing that outline to analyze the data in your spreadsheets. Generally, issues are the equivalent of the legal theories and burdens of proof required to establish, prove, or disprove a legal theory or element of a cause of action. When examined at their most basic level, issues are those items that a party is attempting to prove or disprove. While there is no formula for creating issues, they can be critical not only for analyzing case data, but also for using CaseMap features such as the Summary Judgment Wizard (to file or defend against motions for summary judgment).

Issues can be as basic as duty, breach of duty, negligence, and damages in a simple personal injury case. Or, in a class action, they could include the elements of a class action: numerosity, commonality, typicality, adequate representation, common questions of law or fact, common questions predominate over questions affecting only individual members, and superiority of class action. Of course, there may also be subparts to each issue. Issues can also include affirmative defenses, matters subject to pretrial and posttrial motions, or virtually any other item you can think of. For example, in the Hawkins case, the issues reflect four causes of action: wrongful termination; age discrimination; retaliation and deserved termination. In addition, there is a fifth issue relating to damages.

Or consider a products liability case in which a bystander is injured. The issues under "products liability" could include manufacturer, distributor, end user, purchaser, and foreseeable victim, the latter for those circumstances in which a bystander is injured by the product, because in some states a bystander's ability to recover damages is limited.

Creating the Issues spreadsheet is therefore one of the most critical stages in the birth and development of a CaseMap outline. The most difficult aspect of issue creation is coming up with the "right number" of issues. Most new CaseMap users tend to either create too many issues or too few issues. When there are too many issues, they tend to be so specific that virtually every fact is assigned to its own issue. On the other hand, creating an issue outline that merely specifies the causes of action, without subissues, might assign too many facts to too few issues, leading to an inability to effectively analyze your data. Striking the correct balance is the key, and it takes time and experience to learn how to do so.

One method of creating issues is to confer with staff and other counsel to arrive at a preliminary list of the issues in your case. Thus, in a claim that a manufacturer improperly marketed a pharmaceutical product, one of the claims may be that although the drug had been approved by the United States Food and Drug Administration (FDA), the manufacturer failed to supply the FDA with sufficient information for it to properly analyze the efficacy and safety of the drug. Because the FDA approval process requires multiple steps, and is preceded by numerous studies by the manufacturer, an issue outline could include issues specific to each stage of the process.

Creating and Working with Issues

Creating issues in CaseMap is simple. First, go to the Issues spreadsheet. If there are no issues, simply type in the first issue in your case, which is the issue's full name. As soon as you create the issue, CaseMap gives the issue its short name (to use as a link elsewhere in the program). If you want, you can change the short name to something easier to remember, or leave it with the CaseMap default. You can always change the full name and/or the short name. CaseMap automatically numbers issues 1, 1.1, 1.1.1, etc. and does not offer you the ability to change the outline style.

When creating an issue, you can include a description and other information. By clicking on the Record Detail icon (Ctrl+F2) (see Figure 21), you

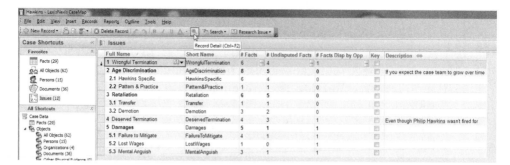

Figure 21

can add additional details, called traits, about the issue. Once staff members have created links to the issue, you can view not only the issue's traits, but also how the issue has been evaluated by other staff, a summary of all of the other CaseMap entries to which the issue links, and the history of who updated the issue and when (see Figure 22). To create another issue, just hit the

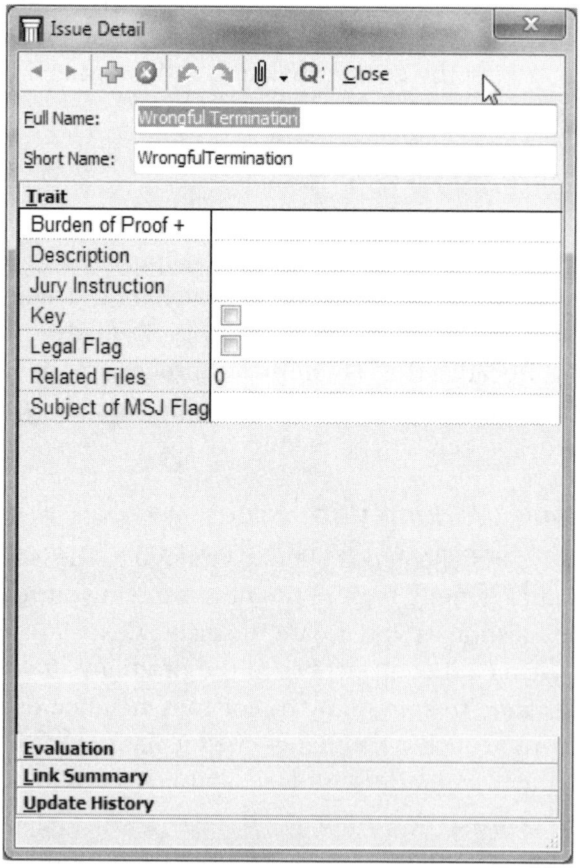

Figure 22

You Cannot Delete Issues When a Replica Is Outstanding

Although you can make numerous changes to the CaseMap database while replicas are outstanding, there are certain limitations. For example, you cannot delete case issues when a replica is outstanding because another user may be creating links to the issues you intend to delete. Thus, you must wait until all replicas are synchronized or until all replicas have been removed from the synchronization history before deleting issues.

Insert key or New Record>Insert or Insert>New Record>Issue (see Figure 23). CaseMap will create the new issue at the same level of hierarchy as the previous one. To demote (make the issue a sub-issue) the issue or change its location or to promote the issue (make the issue higher in the issues outline), just click on the little compass arrows in the row header to the left of the selected issue and move the issue to the desired location (see Figure 24).

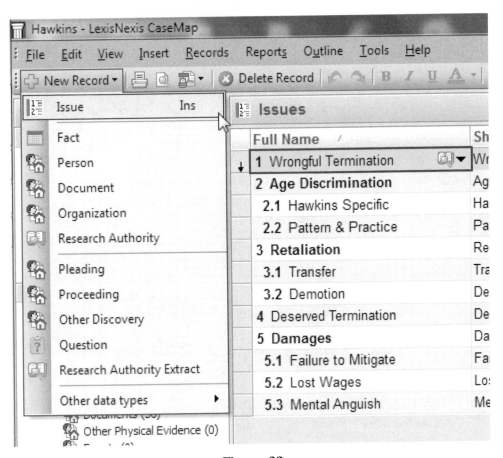

Figure 23

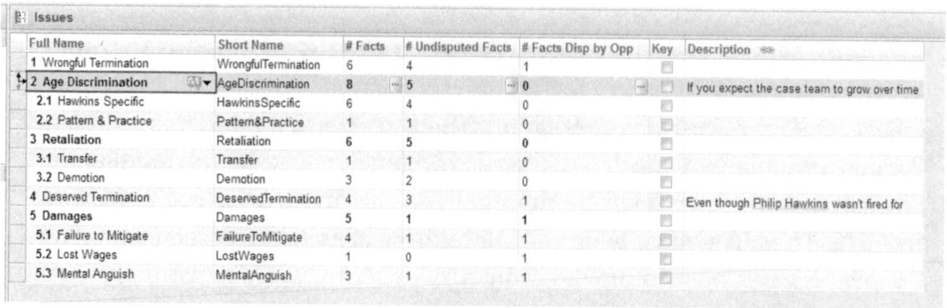

Full Name	Short Name	# Facts	# Undisputed Facts	# Facts Disp by Opp	Key	Description
1 Wrongful Termination	WrongfulTermination	6	4	1		
2 Age Discrimination	AgeDiscrimination	8	5	0		If you expect the case team to grow over time
2.1 Hawkins Specific	HawkinsSpecific	6	4	0		
2.2 Pattern & Practice	Pattern&Practice	1	1	0		
3 Retaliation	Retaliation	6	5	0		
3.1 Transfer	Transfer	1	1	0		
3.2 Demotion	Demotion	3	2	0		
4 Deserved Termination	DeservedTermination	4	3	1		Even though Philip Hawkins wasn't fired for
5 Damages	Damages	5	1	1		
5.1 Failure to Mitigate	FailureToMitigate	4	1	1		
5.2 Lost Wages	LostWages	1	0	1		
5.3 Mental Anguish	MentalAnguish	3	1	1		

Figure 24

With CaseMap, issues can have as many sublevels as you need. You can also revise issues, change their level of hierarchy, etc., at any time. Creation of issues takes time, and issues can and should be refined throughout the development of a case. For firms who handle similar cases frequently, the issues can be exported by using CaseMap's Template feature, which allows you to create new cases while using those aspects of other cases common to the new case.

Other Shortcuts

The Navigation bar also contains shortcuts to the Questions and Research spreadsheets. These spreadsheets permit users to enhance their case outlines with case law, statutes, and other authorities and provide an opportunity to record questions raised by the case and any answers to those questions.

Research Spreadsheets

CaseMap includes three research-related spreadsheets—Authorities, Extracts from Authorities, and Extracts and Authorities—which are located on the All Shortcuts portion of the CaseMap sidebar.

CaseMap contains a section designed to include all of your case-related research in one location. The three research-related spreadsheets are highly integrated; provide an easy means of viewing information relating to cases, statutes, regulations, articles, and other relevant items; and are designed to allow you to link your case-related research with relevant facts and objects throughout your case file. In addition, if you also perform research using LexisNexis or Total Litigator, there are additional tools that allow you to instantly determine whether your research is current.

Research Authorities Spreadsheet

The Authorities spreadsheet is the place to store case law, statutes, rules, jury instruction, regulations, law review articles, and any other items that you intend to cite or refer to in your case. When you open the Authorities spreadsheet, it will display the fields for Name, Jurisdiction, Type, Citation, Description, Notes, Linked Issues, Linked File, and # Extracts. Jurisdiction and Type are "+" fields—i.e., they are open-ended dropdown lists that allow you to add values to the menu by merely typing them in and clicking Yes at the prompt.

To add a new research item, just click New Record>Research Authority or Insert>New Record>Research Authority. You can also use the Issue Linking Tool to link authorities with issues; just click on the Issue Linking button to open the Issue Linking Tool panel on the right-hand side of the spreadsheet, select the issue or issues you want to link with the authority, and you are done.

If you are using LexisNexis or Total Authority for research, the Research Authority button on the toolbar allows you to view the current citation, get the document, Shepardize the document, or set up a Shepard's Alert. You can also use the Send to CaseMap feature by right-clicking on the authority while in Lexis (see Figure 25) to link the authority into CaseMap. When you do, the Jurisdiction and Citation fields will automatically be populated with the relevant information. A Shepard's Signal will appear, which can automatically update itself if you are online when you open your case file. You can also update an authority by going to Tools>Case Tools>Update all Shepard's Signals now

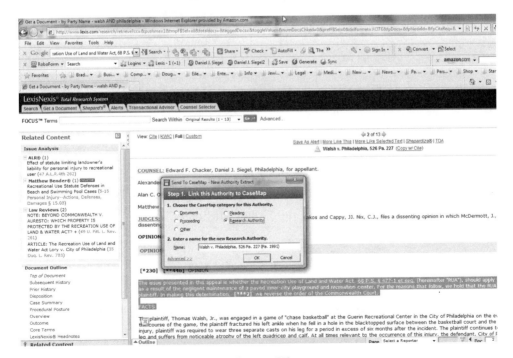

Figure 25

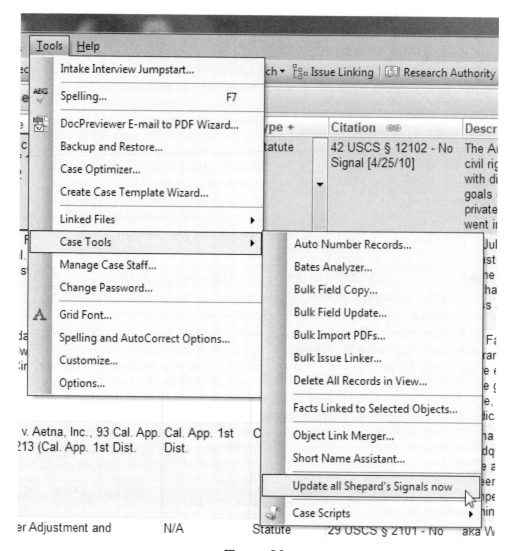

Figure 26

(see Figure 26), if you have been working on a case file since the wee hours of the morning, and you want to update a key authority before you stop work on the case in the afternoon.

Extracts from Authorities Spreadsheet

The Extracts from Authorities spreadsheet is where you store the relevant text or subsections from the Authorities spreadsheet. As soon as you create a new authority, it is available as an authority name on this spreadsheet; you can also create a new authority here that will then appear on the Authorities spreadsheet. By default, this spreadsheet displays the Authority Name, Extract Text, Description, Notes, Linked Issues, and Linked File fields, but like other spreadsheets, you can display other fields or remove those you do not need.

To add an extract, just click New Record>Research Authority Extract or Insert>New Record>Research Authority Extract. You can also use the Issue Linking Tool to link extracts with issues; just click on the Issue Linking button to open the Issue Linking Tool panel on the right-hand side of the spreadsheet, select the issue or issues you want to link with the extract, and you are done.

If you are using LexisNexis or Total Authority for research, the Research Authority button on the toolbar allows you to view the current citation, get the document, Shepardize the document, or set up a Shepard's Alert. You can also use the Send to CaseMap feature to link the extract into CaseMap. After entering the name of the authority, you would generally enter the text of the extract to which you are linking and any other data you need; you can also link the extract to any relevant issue or issues using the Issue Linking Tool.

Authorities and Extracts Spreadsheet

The Authorities and Extracts spreadsheet displays a compilation of the information on the authorities and the extracts from Authorities spreadsheets. By default, this spreadsheet displays all authorities and extracts. By using the Authority filter (a dropdown menu), you can view extracts from one particular authority. You can create a new authority using the New Authority button, or you can add a new extract by clicking on New Record>Research Authority Extract or Insert>New Record>Research Authority Extract. As with the other research spreadsheets, you can also use the Issue Linking Tool to link extracts with issues.

LexisNexis

LexisNexis continues to improve CaseMap's integration with other LexisNexis products through the Total Litigator feature. The LexisNexis Total Litigator bar at the lower left corner of the CaseMap screen links to both Litigation Tasks and to Litigation Tools. A user can click the bar to link to tasks such as Early Case Assessment, Discovery, and Research. Or, a user may utilize the Litigation Tools menu to launch programs such as TimeMap, TextMap, Concordance, Court Link, and File & Serve. Beginning with CaseMap 7.0, the program's Internet Explorer integration included two context menus—i.e., right-click menus that allow easy entry of information appearing in Internet Explorer to be added to CaseMap. Each of these entries is called Send to CaseMap, but each has different functionality depending on whether text is selected. In addition, the functionality will depend on the Web site, page, and context of the information to be included.

For example, when utilizing Lexis.com, case summary documents and briefs, pleadings, and motions can be sent to CaseMap as an authority. To do so, highlight the selected text and right-click to send the text to CaseMap as an extract along with the page as an authority.

Utilizing LexisNexis File and Serve, a user can go to the Case History page and send the selected document links to CaseMap as a pleading.

Utilizing Total Litigator, various items may be sent directly to CaseMap simply by right-clicking and using the Send to CaseMap entries.

Similarly, a user may select and right-click a citation in the Research Authorities spreadsheet of CaseMap. The shortcut menu will allow the user to obtain a copy of the citation in LexisNexis Total Litigator. The user may also Shepardize the citation or obtain and print a copy of the case using only a few clicks of the mouse (see Figure 27).

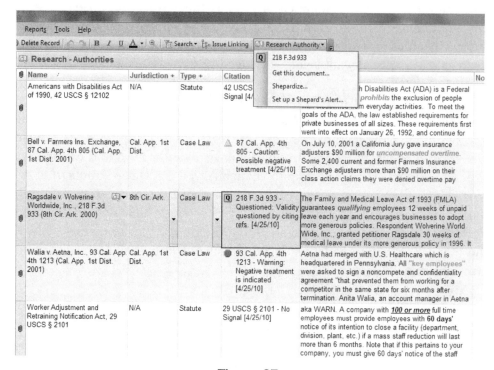

Figure 27

Question Fields

CaseMap contains a separate Questions spreadsheet that appears in the All Shortcuts window of the Case Shortcuts section of CaseMap sidebar. The Questions spreadsheet is used to capture information about questions that arise in a case. To create a new question, just press the Insert key or New Record>Question or Insert>New Record>Question and type the question. A question can contain information linked to other information (remember to use short names), such as names and organizations. You can also include a due date for the question, the name of the CaseMap user to whom the question is assigned, the criticality (importance) of the question, the answer to the question, and the answer's status. Other fields may also be included—Research Notes, Answered On (date), etc.

Because users can evaluate the importance of a question, its relevance to other facts, etc., questions are an area of CaseMap for which evaluations may be particularly helpful. As with other entries, users can view all of a question's traits, evaluations, and links by clicking on the Record Detail icon or Ctrl+F2. You can also add custom Trait fields to augment the ones CaseMap automatically sets up.

Update History Fields

By default, CaseMap spreadsheets do not display the six Update History fields—Creation Author, Creation Scribe, Creation Time Stamp, Last Update Author, Last Update Scribe, and Last Update Time Stamp. These fields, which can be very important but cannot be modified by individual users, are used to track the names of the users who created and updated information and when they did so. CaseMap automatically captures this information whenever you enter or update any cell on any spreadsheet.

Customizing CaseMap

Most CaseMap users are eager to jump in and get started. I suggest, however, that you take a step back and wait. In addition to having training to gain familiarity with the program, you will benefit from customizing the software so that it works the way you want it to.

The Customize Menu

It is important to understand how to customize CaseMap and, later on, how to make additional changes so that you get the most benefit from the program. The simplest way to customize CaseMap is to right-click on any of the toolbars and click Customize (see Figure 28). When you do, it will bring up the Customize menu (see Figure 29). You can also reach this menu by clicking on Tools>Customize (see Figure 30). The Tools>Customize menu allows you to

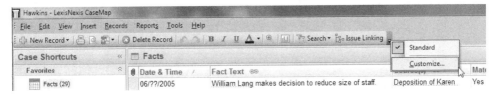

Figure 28

Figure 29

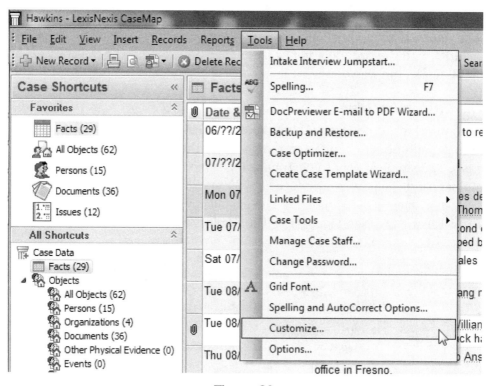

Figure 30

Adding Commands to the Toolbar or a Dropdown Menu

It is extremely helpful, and a time-saver, to include any commands you frequently use on the CaseMap toolbar or on a dropdown menu. To do so, go to Tools>Customize and select the Commands tab, which allows you to view all of the program's available commands, sorted by category, and add them to the program's global toolbars and menus. To place any command on the toolbar, locate the command on the Commands tab (see Figure 31), then left-click and drag the command to the toolbar and drop it where you want it to appear (see Figure 32). You can also drag the command and hover it over a menu. The menu will appear (see Figure 33), and you can then drop the command wherever you prefer it to appear on the menu.

Figure 31

modify how menus and other features of CaseMap appear, and it is one of the more versatile menus in CaseMap because it addresses true user preferences.

You can create your own toolbar from the Toolbar tab, although users rarely do so. On the other hand, when you click on the Commands tab, you can view all of the program's available commands, sorted by category, and can add them to the program's global toolbars and menus (see Figure 34). For example, if you click on the File category, you will see all of the commands

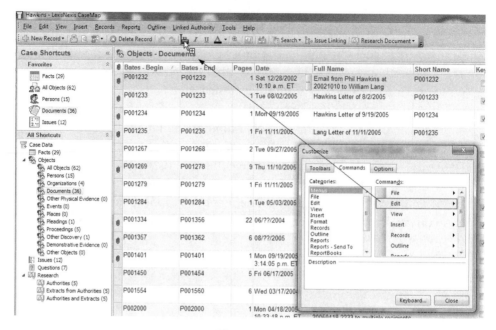

Figure 32

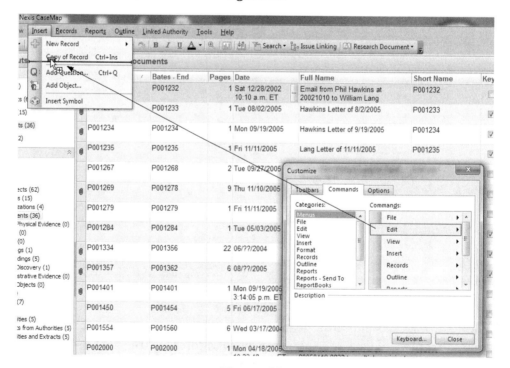

Figure 33

that appear on the File dropdown menu. To place one of those commands on a toolbar, just find the command, left-click and hold, and drag the command to the toolbar. Try it. You will discover how easy it is to do.

Figure 34

Many users like to include the Cut, Copy, and Paste commands on their toolbars, making them easier to access and use. If, on the other hand, you want to remove a command that you do not regularly use, click on Customize, then left-click on the unwanted command and drag it off the toolbar. When you do that, a little x will appear to confirm that you are deleting the command.

Although most CaseMap users do not customize their keyboards, CaseMap offers users the ability to assign specific functions to keys on your keyboard, the same type of customization available within other Windows programs.

When you select the Customize menu, the first tab is Toolbars, which allows you to select whether the Standard toolbar will be displayed along with the main toolbar. In addition, you can create additional toolbars with specific commands on them. You rarely have to do this, because the second tab, Commands, allows you to add virtually every CaseMap command to one of the program's toolbars.

If you desire to create a new toolbar, just click on New and name the toolbar. From there you can add commands using the Commands tab, which you can also access from View>Toolbars>Customize. If your toolbars seem to be missing information, or you have added too many commands, clicking the Reset button will restore the toolbars to their default status.

The Commands menu allows you to add (or remove) commands from any of the CaseMap toolbars. To add a command, locate the command under the appropriate category, and then left-click (do not double-click) and hold the command in the right column and drag the command to the place you want it to be on your toolbar. You can add numerous commands to the toolbars, thus saving keystrokes when you place frequently used commands on the toolbars. To remove a command, *with the Commands menu open*, left-click on the command you do not want to display and drag it off the toolbar, and it will disappear.

While the Command dialog is open, you can also right-click on any command and reset it, delete it, change its appearance, or add it to a group of commands. This function works identically to the way toolbars are revised in various Windows programs.

The third tab of the Customize menu is the Options menu (see Figure 35), which is different from the dialog box that appears under Tools>Options (see Figure 36). The top portion of this menu, Personalized Menus and Toolbars, allows you to change how the menus appear. If, when opening a menu, you want to see all available commands (such as the File, Edit, or View menus), uncheck "Menus show recently used commands first." If, on the other hand, you want to see the commands you use most frequently, check that box. If you make that

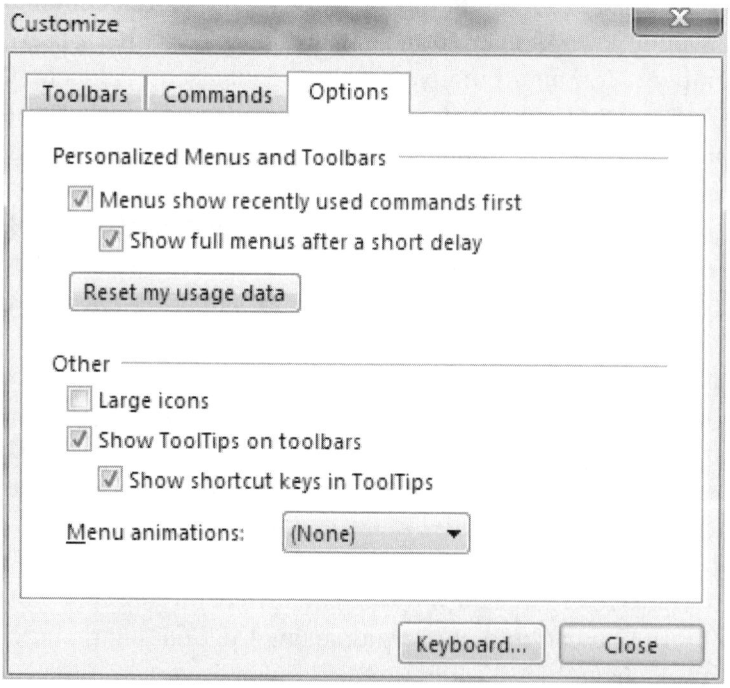

Figure 35

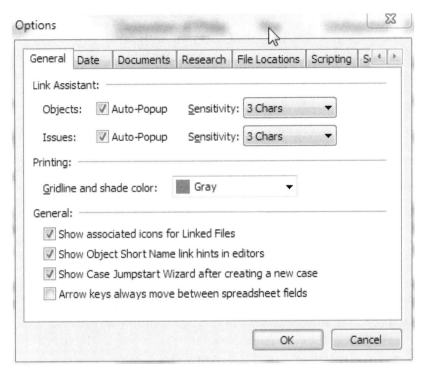

Figure 36

selection, you can also set whether CaseMap will automatically display the full menus after a short delay. Finally, you can reset your usage data, which will clear the program's memory of those commands you used most recently.

In the bottom section of the menu, you can choose whether you want the program to show larger icons, to display tool tips, and to permit shortcut keys to appear. You can also select the type of animations that appear for these menus. Finally, you can customize how your keyboard shortcuts and other keys work; generally, there is no need to change these settings, and if you intend to do so, you should be careful to be certain that your changes do not affect any other shortcuts or settings.

The Options Menu

CaseMap users can benefit from some of the features available on the Options menu, which allows you to customize many aspects of the program. To access this menu, go to Tools>Options.

General Options

The General Options tab allows you to customize how various features operate in CaseMap (see Figure 36). The top section of this tab, Link Assistant, de-

Keep the Link Assistant On

The Link Assistant is one of the most valuable features in CaseMap because it makes it easy to create links between various pieces of data. By turning off the Link Assistant (to do this, you would uncheck the Auto Pop-up boxes on the Tools>Options>General menu), you will have to manually make links, which is more tedious and will likely lead to less data being linked. Similarly, by increasing the number of characters that must be typed before the Link Assistant appears, users will type more information than may be necessary before consummating the links (see Figure 37).

termines how and if the Link Assistant will work for both objects and issues. By checking Auto-Popup, the Link Assistant will automatically appear when entering data in any CaseMap field that has a "link" at the top of the column. By default, the sensitivity is set at three characters for objects and issues. This means that the Link Assistant will appear as soon as the user types three characters that match a pattern found in a short name anywhere in the database. You can change the sensitivity to appear from anywhere between two and six characters.

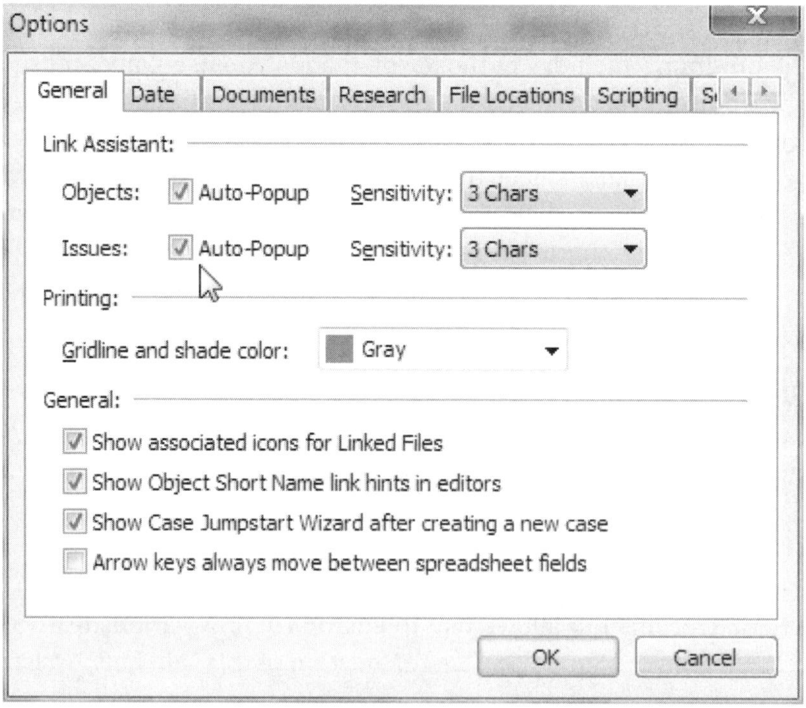

Figure 37

The Printing section of this tab specifies the default gridline and shade color that appear in CaseMap spreadsheets. These are the borders on the edges of spreadsheets when they are printing.

The bottom section of the General tab, General, customizes how certain features of the program operate. Although the default options are acceptable to most users, you may at times have a need to change these settings.

"Show associated icons for Linked Files" allows CaseMap to display the icon associated with the program that opens a linked file. Thus, when enabled, a PDF file linked to CaseMap will display the file name and the Acrobat icon.

"Show Object Short Name link hints in editors" allows the program to suggest ways to create effective short names. "Show Case Jumpstart Wizard after creating a new case" automates whether this Wizard appears when you create a new case. If you do not plan on using this feature regularly, you would deselect it; you can always manually access the Jumpstart Wizard by going to Tools>Intake Jumpstart Interview.

Finally, "Arrow keys always move between spreadsheet fields" allows you to use arrow keys to move between cells on a spreadsheet.

Dates

This tab displays how dates and times will appear in the case's spreadsheet (see Figure 38). This setting is case specific.

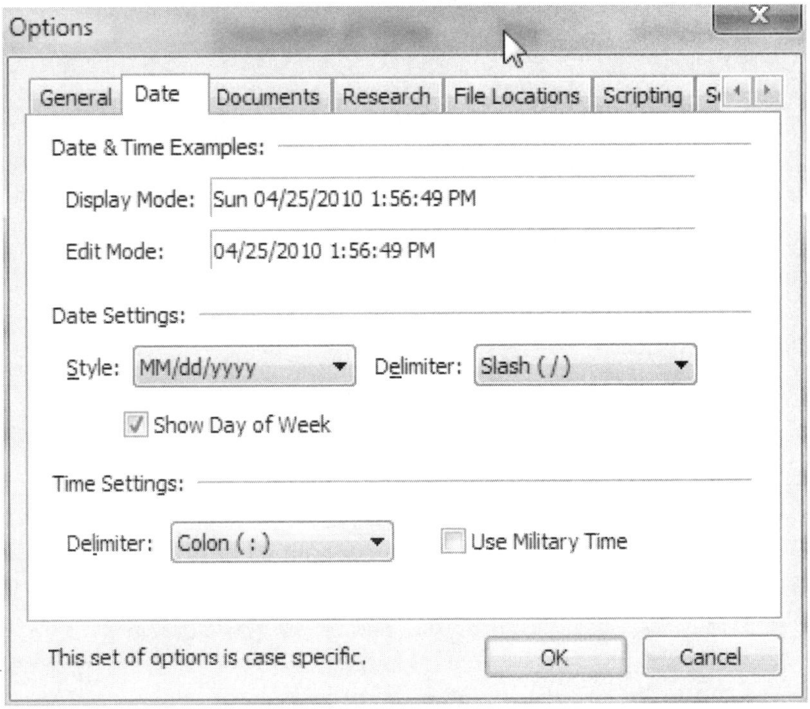

Figure 38

The center section, Date Settings, allows you to specify the style in which a date will display—e.g., 03/09/2009 (MM/dd/yyyy)—and whether the fields will be separated by a slash (/), dash (-) or period (.). Finally, the bottom Time Settings section specifies whether time will be separated by colons or periods and whether the time will display in standard or military time.

Documents

These case-specific settings outline how CaseMap creates the default values for documents in the program (see Figure 39). The top section, Begin Bates Number, specifies whether the beginning Bates number for a document (the Bates number on page 1 of the document) is the default value for defining a document's full name and short name. The second line specifies whether the beginning Bates number is the default value for linked files.

The second section of this tab, End Bates Number, determines whether the document name will default to the beginning Bates number and whether the ending Bates number will be synchronized.

The third section, All Objects Spreadsheet, can be very helpful, particularly in cases with large numbers of documents. If the first button is selected, all documents will always appear in the All Objects spreadsheet. If the second button is selected, CaseMap will display documents in the All Objects

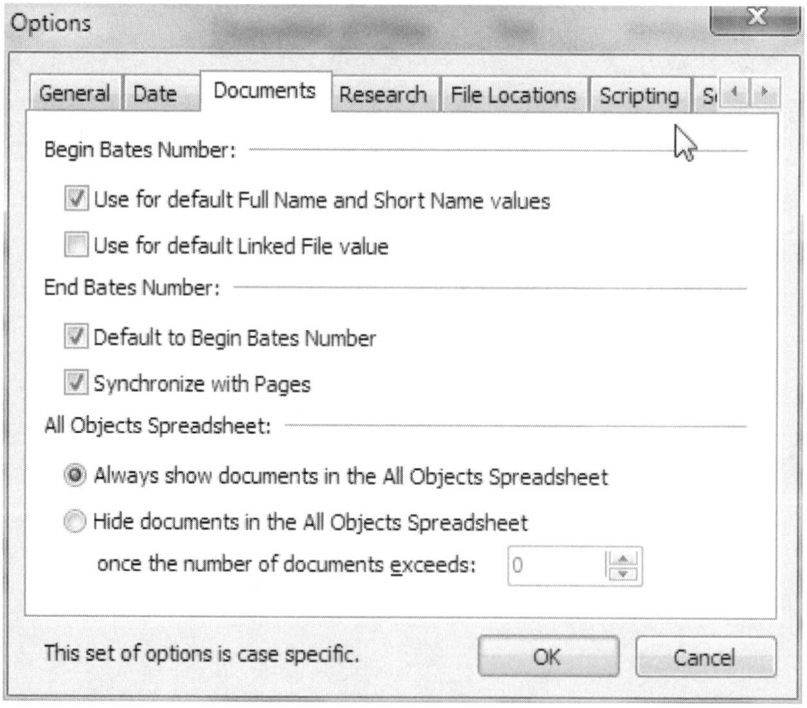

Figure 39

spreadsheet until the number of documents exceeds the number entered in the dialog box. Thus, for cases with many documents, you may wish to enter "0" and hide them in the All Objects spreadsheet; otherwise, users may have to scroll through many screens of documents to view any other types of objects.

Research

This tab customizes how or if a Research menu appears in CaseMap and also determines how CaseMap will interact with LexisNexis Shepard's Signals (see Figure 40). The top section, General, determines whether a Research menu appears on the main toolbar and how the Research menus appear in spreadsheets and right-click menus.

The second section, Shepard's Signals, activates the Shepard's Signals features. If you do not use Shepard's, then you may wish to deselect these options.

File Locations

This tab specifies the default locations for CaseMap files, including case files, case templates, case replicas, export files, import files, and linked files (see Figure 41). By highlighting a file type and clicking the Modify button, you can

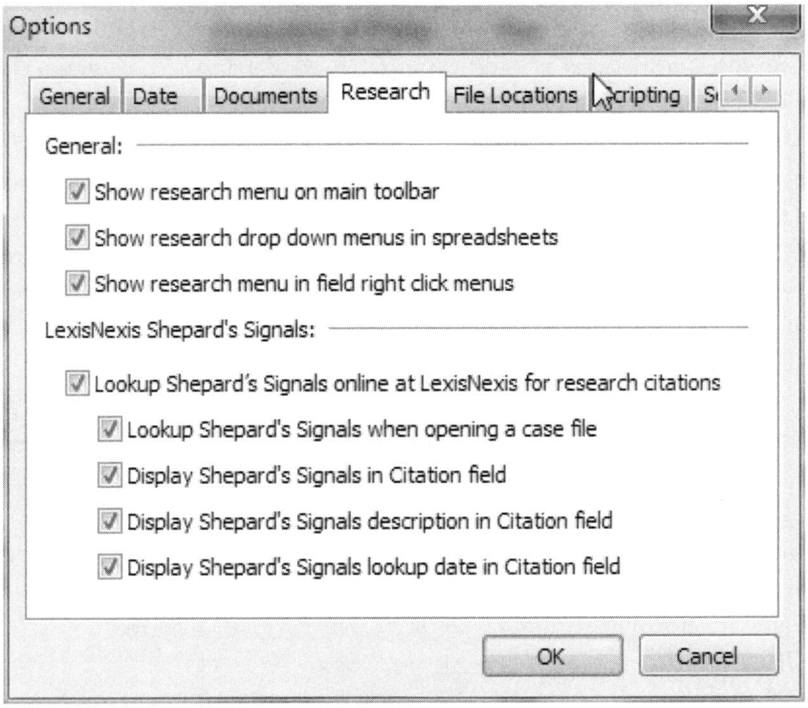

Figure 40

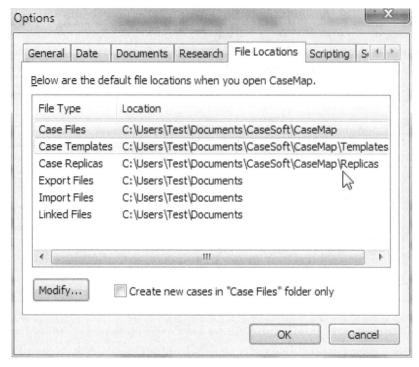

Figure 41

change the default file location for each type of file. By default, CaseMap stores files in its local directory on the user's computer. If you want files to be stored on a network, you should change these settings for every user when you install CaseMap locally on their computers (CaseMap is installed on each user's computer, not on a central server).

In addition, if you want to restrict where new case files are stored, you should check the box next to "Create new cases in 'Case Files' folder only," thus prohibiting users from creating new cases in any location other than the one specified in the File Locations dialog.

Scripting, Send to Plug Ins, and ReportBook Plug Ins

These three tabs relate how these features operate (see Figure 42). In general, most users will never change these settings or have any need to review them.

Accessibility

This tab determines how CaseMap operates for users who may need augmented features.

Changing Fonts

CaseMap allows users to change the appearance of fonts in a number of ways. The main toolbar includes dialogs to permit a user to add boldface, italics, and underlining or to change the color of a particular word, section, cell, etc.

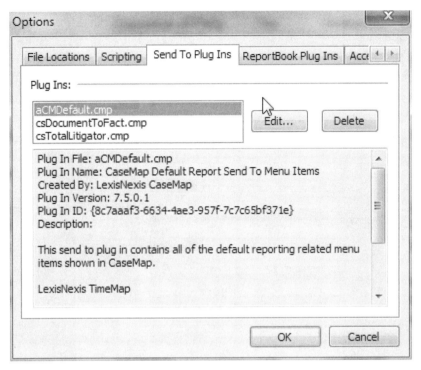

Figure 42

In addition, a user may wish to change the default font used to display all of the text in CaseMap. To do so, just go to Tools>Grid Font and select the default font and font size to be used in your case. Any changes made through this dialog will affect the way all of the contents appear in a CaseMap database.

Row Heights

By default, CaseMap data rows are two lines high. This is generally sufficient to view most facts, but, like other CaseMap features, the height of a row may be modified. To do so, move your mouse to the left-hand column within a particular spreadsheet. When you place your mouse between the lines, an up and down arrow (the Row Height dialog) will appear (see Figure 43). Simply left-click and drag the dialog up to reduce the size of the rows in your database or down to increase the number of rows that appear on a given spreadsheet. The minimum row height is one line and the maximum is fifty.

Remember, when you make this change it will affect the appearance of the spreadsheet on your computer and may change the appearance of the information when you print a report. If you have selected the Auto-Fit check box on the Print dialog box, the row height will be based on the largest amount of text found in a cell. If you unchecked the Auto-Fit check box on the Print dialog box, the row height for a printed spreadsheet will be based on the current row height setting of your on-screen spreadsheet, and information is likely to be truncated.

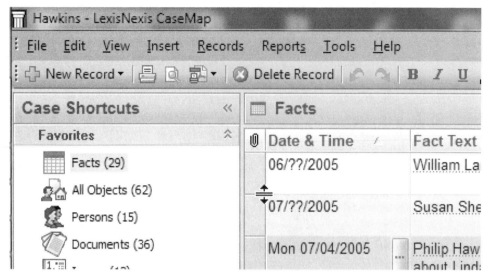

Figure 43

Views

A "view" is merely a way of looking at any particular spreadsheet. CaseMap allows you to create literally infinite numbers of views containing virtually any information you wish to display. The most effective way to examine and analyze case data is by creating different custom views for each way you wish to analyze the information. It is easy to do so. To begin, go to View>Current View, and another menu appears.

Default Views

By default, CaseMap includes various views for each spreadsheet. You can see the default views by clicking on the View menu and mousing your cursor over Current View (see Figure 44). Perhaps the most important series of views are those for the Facts spreadsheet because you will probably spend the vast majority of your time working with that spreadsheet. Depending on the nature of the case, you will probably create (define) various views to assist you in analyzing the information.

Create New Views in Addition to Default Views

CaseMap includes a number of default views. It is recommended that you do not change or delete these views because most users tend to like them and to use them. Rather, instead of changing or deleting a default view, you should add new views to the ones in the program. Thus, *before changing a view, remember to select New View, Rename View, or Copy View* from the View>Current View>Define Views menu.

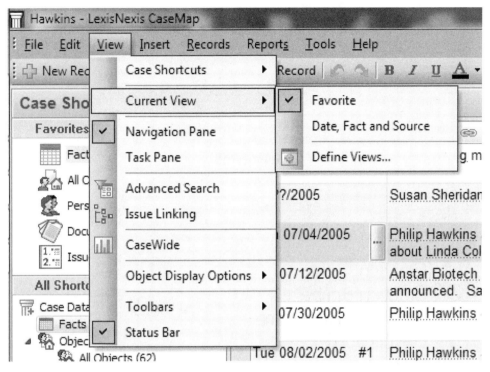

Figure 44

The default view in CaseMap is commonly known as Favorite (see Figure 45). The Favorite view in the Facts spreadsheet has columns named Date & Time, Fact Text, Source(s), Material, Status, Linked Issues, and Evaluation for the information for each fact. There are numerous other pieces of information that you could include with each fact. To get a sense of how much information is available, when you right-click on the Menu bar that includes the date and time and fact text, you will be given a variety of options, including Insert Fields. When you choose that option, the Select Field(s) to Insert dialog box appears, showing the list of available fields for the Facts spreadsheet (see Figure 46). When you right-click on any of the spreadsheets at the top of the data areas, you will see a similar dialog, albeit with the information necessary for that particular spreadsheet. As you can see on the Facts spreadsheet, you can include a wide variety of information, such as the date and time when the fact was created; a description; whether it is considered key; the name, date, and time when that fact was last updated; and a variety of other information. In addition, you can create new fields, although generally CaseMap contains fields that encompass almost any piece of information you would need.

You can change the view in CaseMap in many ways. If you have a predefined view, you can simply click on View menu, click on Current View, and highlight the name of any other view in the program. Thus, if you are on the Facts spreadsheet and highlight Current View and check "Date, Fact and

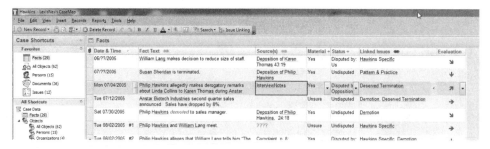

Figure 45

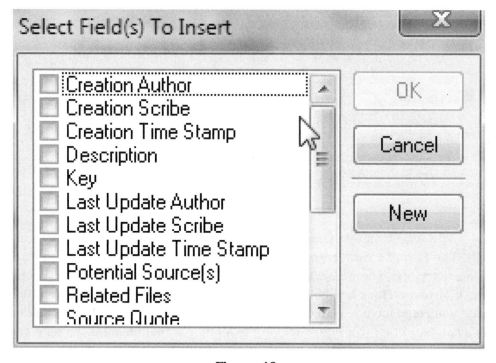

Figure 46

Source," you will see a spreadsheet with only three columns: the date and time, the fact text, and the source(s) of the information in the fact (see Figure 47). If you wish to add fields to any particular view, all you do is right-click at the top of the column where you want to insert a field or fields (see Figure 48). You can then highlight Insert Field, select a particular field (see Figure 49), and it will be inserted to the *left* of the column on which you right-clicked with your mouse (see Figure 50).

You can also rearrange the order in which fields appear simply by left-clicking on the title of the column and moving the title of the field to another place on the spreadsheet (see Figure 51). As you move the title, you will see

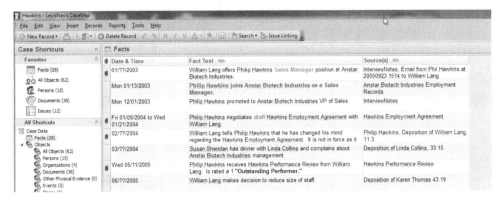

Figure 47

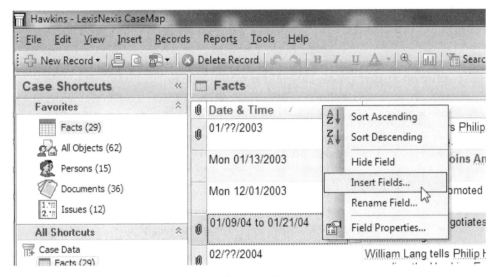

Figure 48

that it "moves" with you and that right and left blue arrows appear between the nearest column where you are dragging that title. If you drop the name between the arrows, the column will move. If you wish to remove a column, you would right-click on the name of the column and click Hide Field and the column will disappear (see Figure 52). This does not mean that the data in the column disappear, only that the column is not currently available for view.

Creating Views

There are two ways to create a new view: using the menu bar or after changing the displayed view to include the fields you want. To create a new view using the menu bar, go to View>Current View>Define Views (see Figure 53). This dialog box allows you to reorganize, rename, copy or modify or delete ex-

Hide Fields to Improve Your Printed Reports

If you want to print a particular spreadsheet but do not want to print all of the information in the current view, you can simply hide unnecessary fields on the spreadsheet. To hide a field in CaseMap, right-click on the title of the field, and select Hide Field.

Also, because reports print exactly as the data appear on the screen, and because different entries may sort differently, you should remember to sort your spreadsheet based on the criteria you desire before printing a report. Finally, always re-sort the Facts spreadsheet before printing it to ensure that new entries are properly sorted.

For example, on the default Facts spreadsheet in the Hawkins case, click View>Current View>Date, Fact and Source. Because you only want to see the Date and Fact Text, right-click on the top of the source column and click Hide Field. You should now only see two columns: Date and Time, and Fact Text. Next, place your cursor between the columns and you will see the little icon appear that allows you to widen or shrink the columns based on your preferences. Adjust the column width to meet your needs. After the two columns display the way you want them to, click the Print Preview button or File>Print Preview; both will provide the same view. When you look at the spreadsheet as it appears on pages 2 and 3 of the Print Preview screen, you can see how cleanly the information displays.

Now go back to the top of the Menu bar, right-click, and select Insert Fields. Select five or six fields and then click OK. Next, click the Print Preview button or File>Print Preview. When you look at the spreadsheet as it appears on the Print Preview screen, you can see how the content overflows the page and is difficult to review.

isting spreadsheet views as well as create new views from scratch. If you go to View>Current View, CaseMap displays all of the views available to you. There will be a check mark next to the view currently being displayed. By default, CaseMap uses the Favorite view (on the Facts spreadsheet), which displays Date & Time, Fact Text, Source(s), Material, Status, Linked Issues, and Evaluation. There are also views available for other spreadsheets.

To add additional views, simply go to Views>Current Views>Define Views. The dialog box will display the current view (see Figure 54), including the spreadsheet to which it applies. You should avoid changing the default views. Instead, the dialog provides you with the following options: New View, Copy View, Rename View, or Delete View. Select the option you prefer, and CaseMap will ask you to name the view. Choose a name and click OK. CaseMap

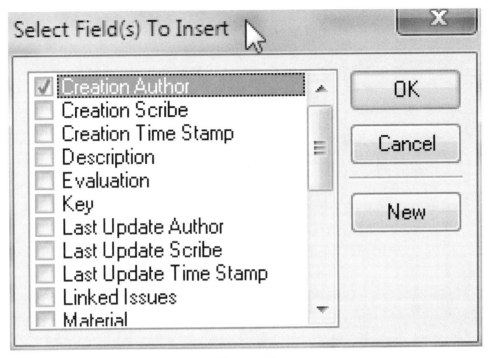

Figure 49

will then display a two-column dialog. On the left will be a list of all fields currently displayed in the view, and on the right will be the names of all fields that may be included in the view.

Next, select the fields you want to include in the view and highlight them. Then click on the left arrow and they will be moved to the right side of the dialog box. Continue adding fields until you have included all of the desired fields. To remove a field from the view, highlight it (on the left side of the dialog box) and click the right arrow. You can also move fields up or down (which moves them left or right in the displayed spreadsheet) and set the default sort order using the A/Z icon. To define the default sort order, click the A/Z icon and a dialog will appear that allows you to specify the fields you want to sort, provided it is a sortable field. If none of the fields is sortable, you will not be able to define a sort with a view. When you click Close, CaseMap will save the view, the dialog will close, and the newly defined view will display on the screen. To switch to another view, go to View>Current View and choose the view you wish to save.

Another way to create a new view is to make changes directly from the spreadsheet view. To do this, insert or hide whichever fields you want displayed or hidden. Next, go to the menu bar and select View>Current View>Define Views. Then copy the view and give it a new name, and your view will be

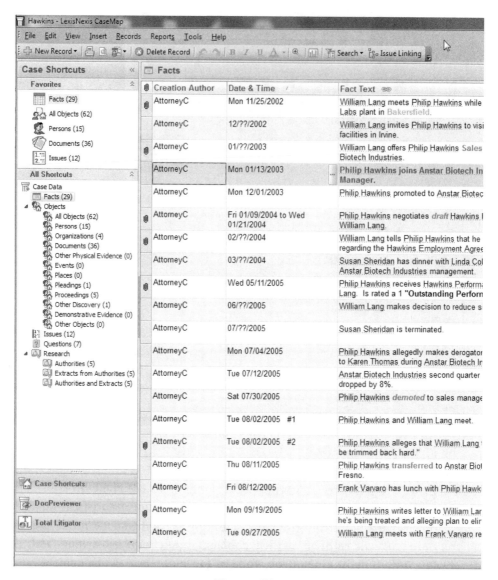

Figure 50

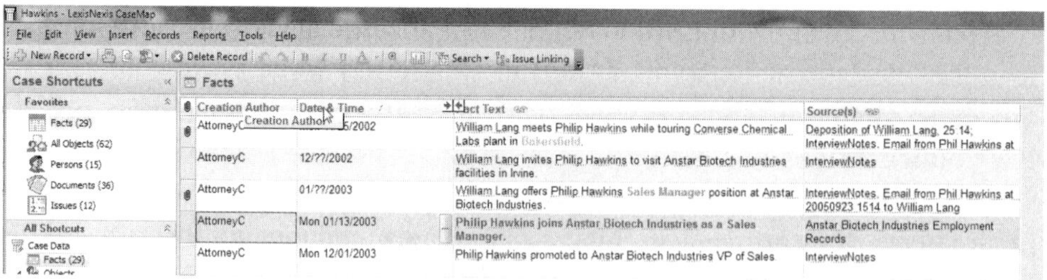

Figure 51

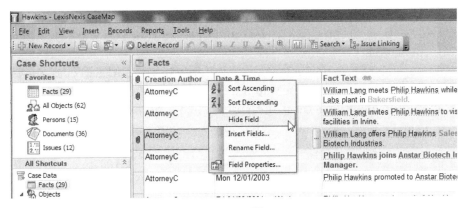

Figure 52

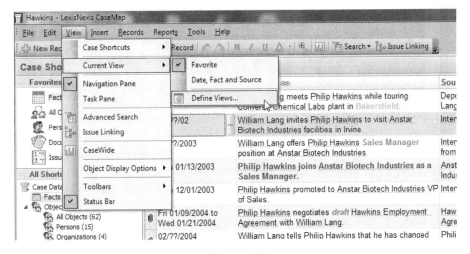

Figure 53

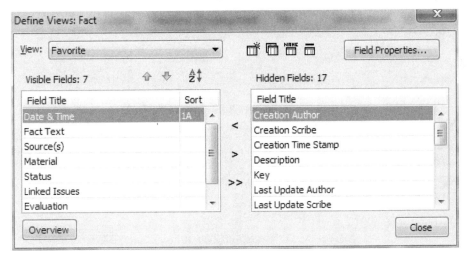

Figure 54

saved. Creating a view this way—and copying the view rather than saving or overwriting the current view—is fast and ensures that you will see the view before you save it.

If you wish to create a new view from scratch, you can also click the New View icon and, by default, CaseMap names it "Fact View 1" or "Object View 1" or some other name based on the spreadsheet you are viewing (see Figure 55). You can change the name to anything you want simply by deleting or typing over it in the name box. When you create a new view, there are no fields listed as visible.

Figure 55

To select the fields for your view, simply highlight the name of each field that you wish to move into the new view and then click the left arrow at the top in the middle. You can also rearrange the visible fields by highlighting a field and selecting the move-up or move-down green arrows. You can define the default sort order by selecting one of the fields, provided it is a sortable field. If the field itself is not sortable, CaseMap will allow you to use an advanced sort dialog based on whichever other fields in the report are sortable. If none of the fields is sortable, you will not be able to define a sort within the view. When you hit Close, CaseMap will save the view you have defined and display it on the screen. To switch to another view, simply go back to View>Current and choose the view you wish to see (see Figure 56).

Remember, because CaseMap turns all views into reports, changes you make to a view's layout using the Define Views dialog are the equivalent of redesigning your report.

Arranging and Manipulating Columns

The amount of information a CaseMap database could contain is enormous. Just look at the Object Detail (the magnifying glass icon on the toolbar or

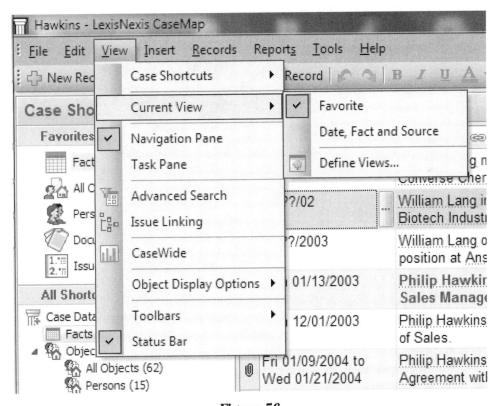

Figure 56

Ctrl+F2) for any object, and you will discover just how much information may be included about virtually any fact or object. In reality, you will only display the data most relevant to your case or the particular analysis you are performing. To accomplish this, you should arrange the information in the form most convenient for you. This is also important because if you want to print the displayed spreadsheet, printing is "What you see is what you get," and if you have too many columns, the printing will either take up multiple pages or will have to be condensed in a way that makes the information difficult to read.

Moving or rearranging columns of data is easy. And, as explained in the Views chapter, you can then save your custom format for future use.

As a result, revising the views for various spreadsheets is a highly effective way of arranging information in a way that you want to see it. There are a few options.

Hiding a column: To hide a column, right-click on the title of the column on the Navigation bar that you want to hide and select Hide Field (see Figure 57). The field no longer displays, although all of the data remains stored in the Object Detail.

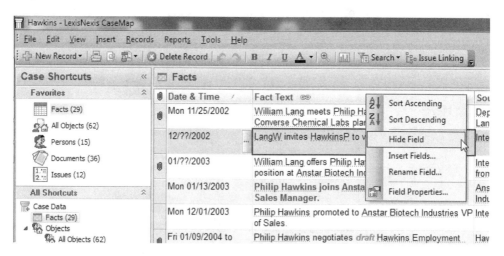

Figure 57

Inserting a column: To insert a column, right-click on the column on the Navigation bar to the right of the location where you want to display the column, and select Insert Fields (see Figure 58). CaseMap will display all of the available fields; check the field or fields you want to display and click OK (see Figure 59). The field will display to the left of the column on which you right-clicked.

Moving a column: To move a column, in the Navigation bar, left-click on the title of the column you want to move, and then drag it to where you want to move it (see Figure 60). When the left and right blue arrows display at the

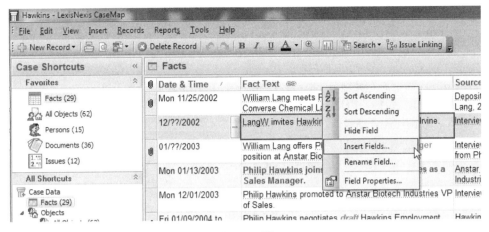

Figure 58

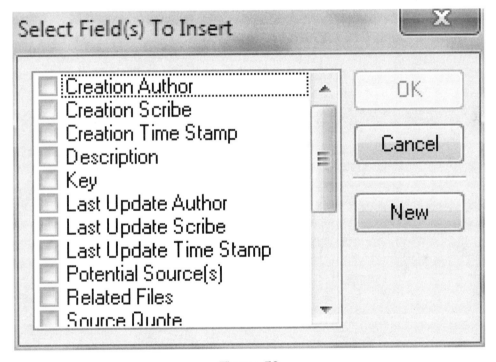

Figure 59

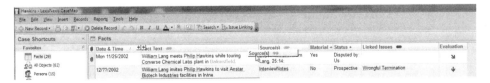

Figure 60

location you want to move the column to, release the left mouse button and the column will display in the new location.

Resizing a column (making it larger or smaller): On the Navigation bar, place your cursor between the column you want to resize and the column to the right or left (see Figure 61). A cursor will appear with two lines and arrows pointing left and right. Left-click at that location and drag the cursor to the right or left to resize the column.

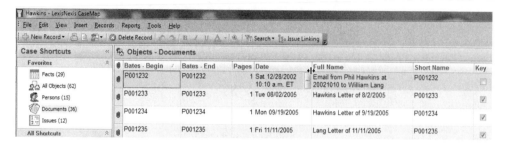

Figure 61

Entering Case Information

3

Introduction

Entering information into CaseMap—whether you are adding facts, objects or any other data—is a simple four step process:

- Open the spreadsheet into which you want to enter new information or update existing data;
- Open the spreadsheet view you want to use;
- Enter data—preferably using as many short names as possible;
- Link your data to other sources, including data, objects or documents and, if necessary, add the objects or sources to your CaseMap database.

In these few steps, you will have created a new entry or modified an old one, and linked the information to all of the relevant sources and objects. This chapter will explain how to create and enter the data.

The more effectively a user enters case information, the easier it will be to conduct further analysis throughout the litigation. Generally, information is entered or should be entered in its simplest forms and then analyzed in the spreadsheets.

Full Names and Short Names

All of the persons, documents and other objects in CaseMap have both full names (long names) and short names. While it is

Use Naming Protocols

A little advanced planning can be very helpful when using CaseMap. As a best practice, you should always create object naming protocols for each case so that all users who create objects do so in a consistent manner, thereby avoiding duplication and preventing confusion.

For example, by default, when you create an organization, CaseMap will create a short name from using the initials of the object. Thus, if you create Abington Memorial Hospital as an organization, by default, CaseMap will create "AMH" as the object's short name. In certain instances, short names such as this are not intuitive and, because other users may not recognize the short name when entering data, those users may instead create another object with a different short name that is more "logical" for that user. To avoid these situations, you should devise a naming protocol so that, for example, you name organizations using the full first name and the object's remaining initials. In the case of Abington Memorial Hospital, you could create "AbingtonMH" as the short name.

Equally important is creating a document-naming protocol so that all users can easily determine which documents are in the database and avoid entering duplicate documents into CaseMap. One method of naming documents, which is highly effective and avoids duplication, is to create full names for documents that begin with the date of the object—such as the date of the letter, the date of the e-mail, the date of the report, etc.—entered in the following format: YYYY-MM-DD, corresponding to the four-digit year, the two-digit month, and the two-digit day, where possible.

In other words, if a medical report was authored on May 12, 2010, its full name would be 2010-05-12 Medical Report of Dr. Jones, and CaseMap's corresponding short name would be 2010-05-12MedicalReportOfDrJon. You could then modify the short name to be 2010-05-12MedRepJones, which would enable other users to know that the May 12, 2010, report of Dr. Jones was already included in the database (see Document Naming Tips, p. 73).

not necessary to give an object a short name, because all of the information is linked by virtue of short names, if you fail to do so, you will lose one of the major benefits of CaseMap—the ability to link information throughout the spreadsheets. It is easy to know when a field allows linking, because at the top of the column for that field on any spreadsheet there will be a little chain-link icon. When a column has the chain-link icon, information entered into any of the cells in that column can link to other information throughout CaseMap.

Full Names

Creating effective names is critical to maximizing the benefits of CaseMap. Full names are relatively simple and self-explanatory: they are the complete names of the various persons, organizations, etc. in your case. If a person's name is William Jones, then his full name should be entered "William Jones." If a person went to Liberty Hospital, then the full name should be entered as "Liberty Hospital."

Short Names

Short names are the names used by CaseMap to link information. When you create a full name, CaseMap will create a default short name for that particular object. For persons, the short name will be the last name of the person and his or her first initial. Thus, if you create a person object for Mary Jones, her short name will be JonesM. Similarly, if you create a name for William Smith, MD, CaseMap will recognize that the MD is not part of the name and will create the name SmithW.

Use Short Names All the Time

Using short names is vital to effective use of CaseMap. That is why you should examine the short names CaseMap creates by default very carefully because you may have multiple persons with the same last name in your case, and some may have first names that begin with the same letter. You may also have businesses and other entities with similar names.

Although CaseMap's default names are generally acceptable, they are not always the best or most effective names to use. When you have Walter Smith and William Smith, for example, short names such as SmithW and SmithW2 are probably not the most intuitive because users may not remember whether William Smith is SmithW or SmithW2. Thus, it is always beneficial to examine the short name to be certain that, when persons are entering data and using the Link Assistant (the most common method of entering data in CaseMap), the short names provide a sufficient description for users to know that they have located the proper short name to link to a particular entry. Otherwise, you will have confusion and may have to go back through the database and make revisions that are time-consuming and not productive.

Creating and Naming Objects

When you create an object, you do so by using either the Insert key, the New Record button on the toolbar, or the menu item Insert>New Record, and then select the type of record to create. Virtually every record, other than those for questions and research, will have a short name and a full name. If you create a person with a first name and last name similar to another individual's, CaseMap will recognize this information. For example, if your database contains an entry for William Jones, his short name will be JonesW. This is also the information that will appear when you use the Link Assistant. If you then add Walter Jones as another person in your case, by default CaseMap will create the short name JonesW2. You can leave that short name as defined, or you can go back to the object and click into the Short Name cell and change the short name to SmithWalter. Another option is to go to the respective cells and change both names to SmithWilliam and SmithWalter.

You may also change a person's short name or any other short name by either clicking into the short name cell or clicking on the Object Detail, which will display the full name and short name at the top of the dialog box. When you change a short name, it will instantly update the short name through the entire database. You do not have to go back and revise the entire database. Similarly, if you discover that a person's name either was entered incorrectly or has been changed (through marriage, for example), when you change that name in the appropriate spreadsheet, CaseMap will update the short name and the entries in your spreadsheets automatically.

Merging Objects

CaseMap also contains a tool that allows you to merge objects that were inadvertently created and to merge duplicate objects. To perform this operation, go to Tools>Case Tools>Object Link Merger (see Figure 62). Initially, the tool asks you to select the objects that are duplicates and then to select which object should be deleted. The tool will then transfer the short name links from the object to be deleted to the object that is being retained. This utility only merges the short name links and does not transfer any other data from the deleted object record to the new object. Thus, if you merge two document records, the Bates-Begin value of the record being deleted is not transferred to the record being maintained. If you desire to maintain data from any of the cells of the record for the object being deleted, you should transfer the data into the other object's cells by either copying or retyping the data before running the Object Link Merger utility. This utility works on any object type that has a short name in the case. Another alternative is not to use the Object Link Merger and instead to copy the data you wish to preserve and manually delete the duplicate object.

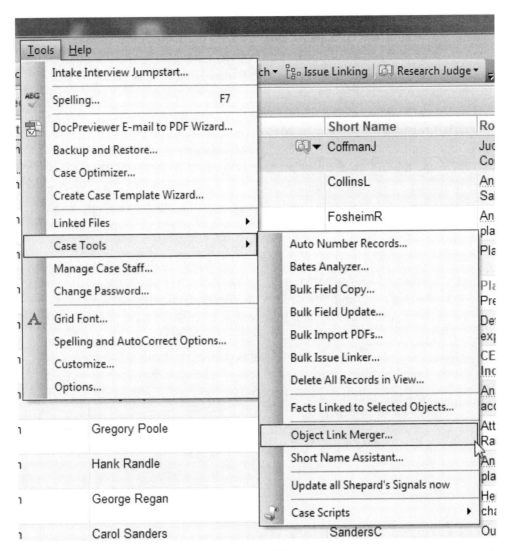

Figure 62

Document Naming Tips

Effectively naming documents and other objects is particularly important in CaseMap. As discussed elsewhere, by default, CaseMap will create a document's full name using the beginning Bates number for that document. While acceptable in certain cases, this is probably not the most effective way for naming your documents. Rather, most users will not recall or remember the Bates number for a particular document. In addition, as litigation grows larger, there is a distinct likelihood (a virtual certainty) that documents will appear multiple times in discovery. Thus, it is possible that a police report, for example, could appear with different Bates numbers depending on who produced the document and when.

Consequently, your full name should be highly descriptive and easy for any user to understand—i.e., avoid the use of confusing acronyms, Bates num-

Correcting or Changing Names and Other Objects

It is easy to make mistakes typing in names, organizations, and other objects. If you have done so, making corrections is easy. For example, in the Persons spreadsheet in the demonstration case, one of the people is William Lang. If, in fact, William Lang spelled his name "Langs," rather than "Lang," all you have to do is to go into the cell on the Object-Persons spreadsheet containing his full name and correct his name, in this case adding an *s*. As soon as that correction is made, the object's short name will be changed globally throughout the program. You can then view the facts linked to William Langs simply by clicking on the # Facts cell or by going to the Facts spreadsheet and confirming that his name has been changed throughout the program.

Another possibility is that you have created an object—for example, a person—but failed to enter that person's name or other object's name correctly (e.g., although you created an object for John Jones with a short name of "JonesJ," you typed John Jones in various facts on the Facts spreadsheet). Fortunately, you do not have to correct every one of these errors manually. Rather, all you have to do is perform a search-and-replace, replacing "John Jones" with "JonesJ"; as soon as the search-and-replace is completed, CaseMap will have made the changes and the facts will be linked to your person.

If CaseMap fails to automatically link all of the short names, that is not a problem. To correct this, just use the Short Name Assistant found at Tools>Case Tools>Short Name Assistant.

bers, and other names that are not intuitive to most people. To do so, establish a document-naming protocol before entering any case data so that all users can easily know which documents are in the database and can avoid entering duplicate documents and other objects into CaseMap. One method of naming documents, which is highly effective and avoids duplication, is creating full names for documents that begin with the date of the object—such as the date of the letter, the date of the e-mail, the date of the report, etc.—entered in the following format: YYYY-MM-DD, corresponding to the four-digit year, the two-digit month, and the two-digit day, where possible.

In other words, if a police report was created on June 2, 2009, its full name would be 2009-06-02 Police Report and CaseMap's corresponding short name would be 2009-06-02PoliceReport. If a document was created in June of 2009 (with the specific date unknown), its full name would be 2009-06 Document, and its short name would be 2009-06Document. By naming documents using the date first, and by putting the year first in the date, CaseMap views that information as text (as do computers generally), and will sort those documents in date order in the Name column on the appropriate Objects spreadsheets.

In addition, if all users name documents with this format, they will be prompted through the Link Assistant and consistently know whether other documents are in the database that were created on that same date. If that is the case, then the user will know to verify whether the document that he or she is creating is in fact a new document and not another copy of a document already included within CaseMap. Similarly, when CaseMap creates a short name by default, if the document was created with the method described above, then the document's short name will in fact begin with the date and show the relevant information.

Consider the following possibilities for a document that is Bates numbered C-000123 to C-000129, which is a witness statement given on June 2, 2009, by Mary Jones. If you would name this by its Bates number, it would appear in a CaseMap database as C-000123 and you would have to know that this witness statement was previously assigned a Bates number. Absent a chart to which users could refer, and absent the possibility that the witness statement appears multiple times, it would be very difficult for you or anyone else to know what the document is without seeking further information. If the document was named Witness Statement of John Smith June 2, 2009, any person entering the document or object into the database would have to continue to type until he or she first went through all of the witness statements and then arrived at the person's name who gave the statement, etc. If, as suggested, the document was named "2009-06-02 Witness Statement of Mary Smith," as soon as you began entering in the data with the date, it would prompt you to look and see whether other witness statements had been entered that were created on that date. If none appears, then you can confidently create that object with the understanding that it is probably a new entry in the database. This method avoids duplication and facilitates faster data entry when writing facts. While using Bates numbers to name documents is not recommended, it is important to continue to enter Bates numbers because they likely will be used at trial, at depositions, and in other proceedings.

The goal of CaseMap is to allow a user to enter as much helpful information as possible as quickly as possible. There are many ways to name documents, and there is no right or wrong way. Users should therefore become comfortable with whatever method they use in order to create documents and to name them. There are potentially numerous other methods of naming documents, and you should discuss document naming with other staff members to devise a system that will work for you. Every example has items that do not fit the mold. For example, undated documents could be named as "Undated" or "Unknown" so that people who are coding the information know that the document has no date.

Dates/Date Stamper

When you enter a new fact in CaseMap, the first piece of information you will generally enter is the date on which that fact occurred. There are two ways to enter dates in CaseMap: (1) typing the date into the cell and (2) using the Date Stamper, the versatile feature that allows you to enter dates and times to the split second.

Although you do not have to use the Date Stamper, and can enter dates directly in any of the date fields in CaseMap, it generally makes sense to type dates without times directly into the Date field and to use the Date Stamper to enter or edit more complex dates and times. For example, when you are merely entering a date without a time, it is quicker to enter the date by typing it in the cell. To enter a date, you can type it in completely, such as "3/9/2009." Or, you can enter "030909" and CaseMap will know that you meant March 9,

Changing Global Date Formats

CaseMap allows you to customize how dates are entered for a particular case—this is a global setting that applies to all users—by going to Tools>Options>Date (see Figure 63). With this tab, you can control how dates and times will display in your case.

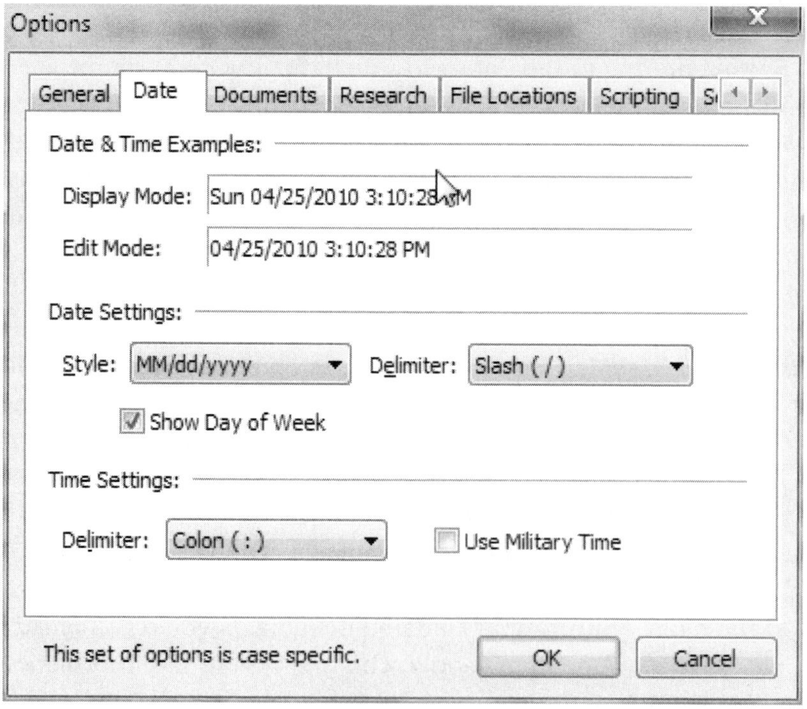

Figure 63

2009. Remember, however, to include the zeroes, where applicable. Otherwise, if you enter "3909," CaseMap will think you meant to enter the year 3909, not a more specific date.

When you enter a date that CaseMap does not recognize, it will display the Invalid Date dialog, which will prompt you to enter a correct date in the cell. Similarly, if you do not know the date, or no date is relevant, you can enter "NA" or "TBD" into the date cell. NA (not applicable) applies when there is no relevant date for the fact. TBD indicates that the date of the fact is to be determined. NA and TBD may be entered manually or from the Date Stamper.

On the other hand, if you need to be more specific with your date and time entry, or the dates are more complex, you will probably want to use the Date Stamper. You can access the Date Stamper from one of six fields: Date & Time for Facts, Deposition Date for Persons, Date for Documents, Begin Date and Time For Events, End Date & Time for Events, and Due Date for Question. Most users will access the Date Stamper from the Date & Time cell on the Facts spreadsheet. When you click into the Date & Time cell, you will see three ellipses at the right of the cell. When you click on those ellipses, you will open the Date Stamper (see Figure 64), which has Day, Time, and Time Zone tabs, from which you may enter specific times, the duration of the event, and the time zone in which the event occurred (regardless whether it is inside or outside the United States).

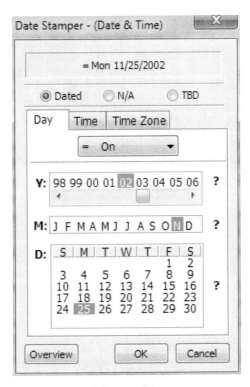

Figure 64

The Date Stamper allows you to indicate whether a fact is "dated," or "not applicable" (NA) or "to be determined" (TBD). From the initial Date Stamper window, you can also specify whether dates, through the dropdown, are "around" a certain date, before, on or before, on, on or after, or after a particular date. You can also indicate the year, the month, and day of the particular fact.

From the time tab of the Date Stamper (see Figure 65), you can indicate whether a particular time (hour in the day) is relevant or not applicable. The Date Stamper box allows you to enter or update the values of date and time fields. You can not only create a day and time, but you can also select the appropriate time zone through the Date Stamper options. The Date Stamper can also be used to edit the time zone abbreviations, something that is only done when a case has facts that occurred outside the United States.

The Time Zone tab is used to indicate the time zone in which a fact or event occurred (see Figure 66). In most cases, you will not have to enter this information because all of the events will have occurred within the default time zone, specified when you initially created the case. When certain facts occur in different time zones, you will need to use the Time Zone tab to reflect that information. You will also use the Time Zone tab to edit the short name of time zones when your case has facts that occurred outside the United States.

The Date Stamper also allows you to create fuzzy dates and fuzzy times, which are time ranges with incomplete details. For example, you could indicate

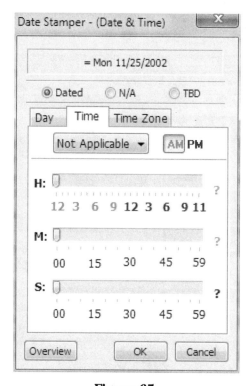

Figure 65

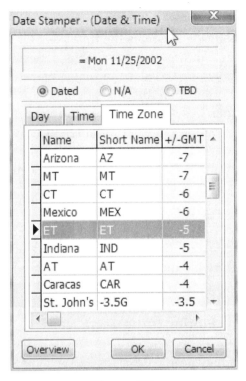

Figure 66

that an event occurred in March 2008 and place question marks for the date because you are unable to confirm the date or the date is missing for that event.

Times

Here are some examples of how to enter times into CaseMap (if not using the Date Stamper):

For This Time	Enter This
June 1, 2009, 12 a.m.	060109 12 am
June 1, 2009, 1 a.m.	060109 01 or 060109 1
June 1, 2009, 12 p.m. (noon)	060109 12
June 1, 2009, 3 p.m.	060109 3 pm or 060109 15
June 1, 2009, 3:15 a.m.	060109 0315
June 1, 2009, 3:15:05 p.m.	060109 3:15:05 pm or 060109 151505 or 060109 031505 pm
June 1, 2009, 3:15:05 a.m.	060109 031505

You can include times within date ranges. These can be very helpful in cases where split seconds can make a difference in determining what happened and when.

Time Zones

CaseMap automatically specifies the time zone for each date you create, based on the case's default time zone (which is determined when the case is opened). Thus, you only need to select a time zone when a fact or event occurred in a time zone other than the case's default one. When sorting spreadsheets by date and time, CaseMap considers the time zone in which an event occurred, so that events that occurred in different time zones appear in correct chronological order.

Here are some examples of how to enter times occurring in different time zones into CaseMap (if not using the Date Stamper):

For This Time	Enter This
June 1, 2009, 12 a.m. Eastern time	060109 12 am et
June 1, 2009, 12 a.m. Pacific time	060109 12 am pt

Editing Time Zone Names

You can use the DateStamper to edit the short names of time zones. Generally you will only need to edit time zone short names for facts or events that occurred outside the United States.

You can include time zones within date ranges.

Date Ranges

CaseMap provides a variety of ways to enter date ranges. You can enter specific dates ("June 1, 2009, to July 3, 2009") or fuzzier dates ("June 2009 to July 2009"), and virtually every other alternative you can imagine. The following are examples of how to enter date ranges into CaseMap:

For This Date	Enter This
Around June 1, 2009	~060109
After June 1, 2009	>060109
Before June 1, 2009	<060109
On or before June 1, 2009	=<060109
On or after	=>060109
June 1, 2009 (exact date)	060109
05/01/2009 to 06/22/2009	050109 – 062209
06/01/2009 to 06/22/2009	050109 – 062209
06/10/2009 to 06/22/2009	050109 – 062209

Date Ranges

When entering date ranges, it is important to either use the word *to* or a dash between dates, being certain to leave a space before and after *to* or the dash. If you do not do so, CaseMap will not accept the dates and will generate an error message.

You could have also entered June 1, 2009, as "06/01/09" or "06/01/2009" or "06-01-09" or "06-01-2009."

When sorting dates, CaseMap will sort these dates in the following order (ascending):

Range (start date before other dates)	05/01/09 – 06/22/09
Around	~06/01/09
Before	<06/01/09
On or before	=<06/01/09
Exact date	06/01/09
Range (start date same as other dates)	06/01/09 – 06/22/09
On or after	=>06/01/09
After	>06/01/09
Range (start date after other dates)	06/10/09 – 06/22/09

The order will be reversed when sorting in descending order.

Fuzzy Dates

You will not know the date and/or when every event occurred in your case. CaseMap addresses this situation through the use of "fuzzy dates." This feature allows you to enter question marks for the portions of a date you do not know. As a result, if you know that an event occurred in June 2009 but do not know on which date it occurred, you can use a fuzzy date. The feature works in a variety of ways and is even included in the CaseWide Timeline, which includes an extra month (a fuzzy month) and an extra day (a fuzzy day) to handle these dates.

The following are examples of fuzzy dates:

6/??/2009
??/??/2009
??/??/????

Here are some examples of how to enter fuzzy dates into CaseMap:

For This Date	Enter This
??/??/2009	09
??/??/1998	98
03/??/2009	3/99
??/??/????	?

You can also use fuzzy dates with date ranges. But if you know that an event occurred throughout the month of March 2009, you should not use the fuzzy date feature, but should instead use the exact date range for the event, such as 06/01/09–06/22/09 for an event that occurred from June 1, 2009, to June 22, 2009.

Date Sequencing

When multiple events occur on the same date, but you either cannot separate them in time or cannot determine a more specific time, CaseMap offers users an optional date sequencing feature, which works in the Date & Time field on the Facts spreadsheet. This feature is helpful when you want to place facts in a specific order.

To add sequencing, just type a sequence number along with the date. Just type "#" followed by your desired sequence number (e.g., "060209 #1"), and CaseMap will use this sequence number when sorting your facts. Consider the following example:

Date & Time	Fact Text
06/02/09 #1	Accident occurs
06/02/09 #2	William Lang ejected from car
06/02/09 #3	Philip Hawkins arrives at scene and calls police
06/02/09 #4	Police arrive at scene
06/02/09 #5	Tow truck arrives at scene and moves vehicles
06/02/09 #6	William Lang taken by EMS to hospital
06/02/09 #7	Police cannot recreate accident because vehicles were moved and William Lang is not present to provide statement
06/02/09 #8	Police leave accident scene

An entry with a date that is sequenced will appear after an entry with the same date that does not have the sequencing number. If you plan to have numerous sequenced events on a particular date, you may wish to use two digit numbers, e.g., 01, 02 . . . 10, etc.

Date Navigator

The Date Navigator is a mini-calendar that allows you to quickly enter dates. When you right-click on any date field, such as the Date & Time field on the Facts spreadsheet, one of the options is the Date Navigator (see Figure 67). Selecting the Date Navigator brings up a calendar that displays dates from 1910 to 2050. Just click on a date on the calendar and it will be entered in the spreadsheet.

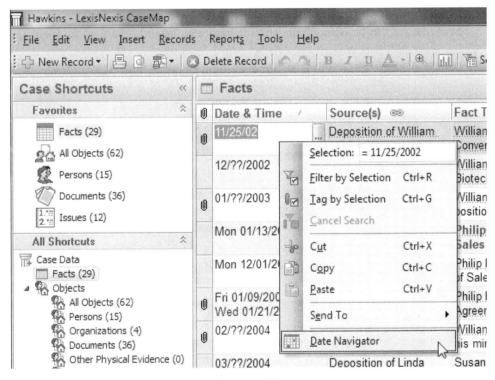

Figure 67

Entering Facts and Data into a Spreadsheet

The primary way to enter information into a CaseMap file is to enter it directly into a spreadsheet. To enter a new item, click on the New Record button at the top of the toolbar (see Figure 68). There are other ways to perform the same operation. You can also click on the Insert menu and select "New Record" and then select the type of record you want to add (see Figure 69). Perhaps the most commonly used shortcut is the Insert key on your keyboard. When you use the insert key, CaseMap adds a new row to any spreadsheet—just as if you had stopped, clicked on your mouse, and clicked the New Record button. Generally speaking, it is faster to insert new data by using the Insert key on your keyboard than by any other means.

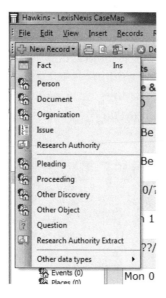

Figure 68

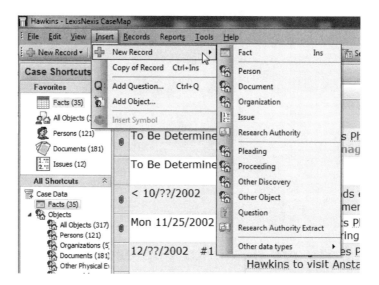

Figure 69

Once you have created the new row on your spreadsheet, you can begin to enter data. Although there is no "correct" way to enter data, some users begin by creating the cast of characters, i.e., the people, places, organizations, documents and other items upon which the fact chronology is based. Generally, in addition to using the Interview Intake Wizard, they enter this data on the fly, frequently on the All Objects spreadsheet. You can also import the data, or enter it "on the fly" as you enter your facts.

Each spreadsheet has a large number of potential fields into which you can enter data. However, each also has a "Favorite" view containing the most commonly used data fields. You will have to determine which fields, and which view, are best based upon the nature of your case. Of course, you can always go back and enter more data, as needed.

Entering Facts and Other Information—An Overview

Entering data is a simple process, regardless whether the information is a new fact or a new object. First, you open the spreadsheet into which you want to enter the new information, and select the view you want to use. Next, you fill in the fields, as explained below. Finally, you will link the new item to an object or other source.

Entering a Simple Fact

Consider the following example. In the Hawkins case, you want to add a fact explaining that, on January 15, 2005, Philip Hawkins and Linda Collins had lunch and discussed their problems with Susan Sheridan. The source of this information is the deposition of Philip Hawkins.

If you were in Date, Fact & Source view (View>Current View>Date, Fact and Source), you would first enter a new record using one of the methods described above to create a blank row (see Figure 70):

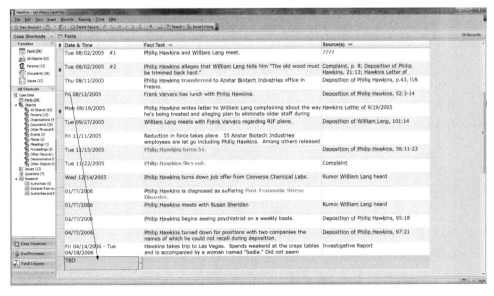

Figure 70

Next, you would enter in the date as 011505 (see Figure 71).

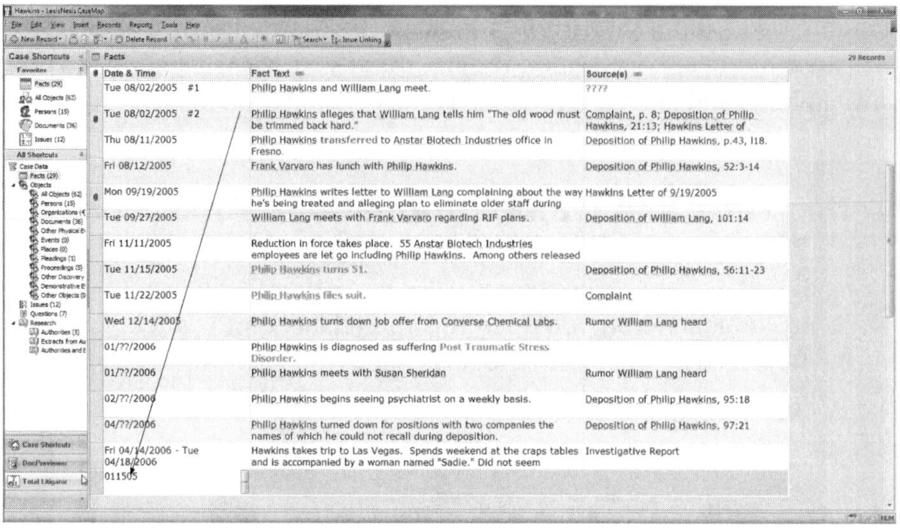

Figure 71

You would then type in the Fact Text: Haw (HawkinsP will display on the Link Assistant; you would hit Enter to accept the entry) has lunch with Col (CollinsL will display on the Link Assistant; you would hit Enter to accept the entry) to discuss problems with She (SheridanS will display on the Link Assistant; you would hit Enter to accept the entry). The Fact Text cell will display as follows while your cursor is still in it (see Figure 72).

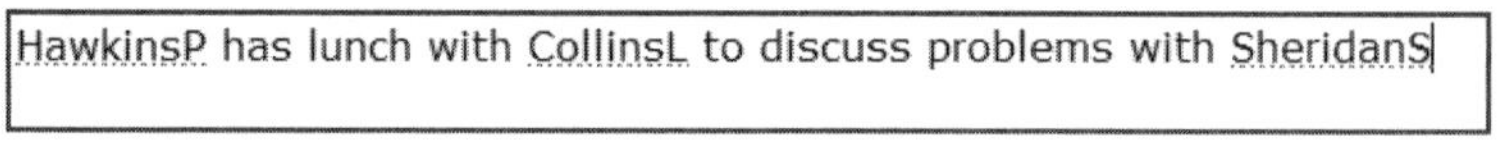

> HawkinsP has lunch with CollinsL to discuss problems with SheridanS

Figure 72

When you hit the Tab or move the cursor out of the cell, it will display as follows (see Figure 73):

> Philip Hawkins has lunch with Linda Collins to discuss problems with Susan Sheridan

Figure 73

You then go to the Source field and type "Dep" and you would see various options (see Figure 74):

> Dep
> DepoCollins
> DepoHawkins
> DepoLang
> DepoRandle
> DepoThomas

Figure 74

You would then select "DepoHawkins" and the cell would display as follows (see Figure 75):

DepoHawkins|

Figure 75

When you exit the cell, you are done. ***Remember, there is no "Save" button in CaseMap. As soon as you exit the cell, your work is saved.***

Entering a Fact and Creating Objects on the Fly

Consider the following example. In the Hawkins case, you want to add a fact explaining that, on January 15, 2005, Philip Hawkins has lunch with Mary Harrison. The source of this information is a January 15, 2005 memo from Hawkins.

If you were in Date, Fact & Source view (View>Current View>Date, Fact and Source), you would first enter a new record using one of the methods described above to create a blank row (see Figure 70). Next, you would enter in the date as 011505 (see figure 71).

You would then type in the Fact Text: Haw (HawkinsP will display on the Link Assistant; you would hit Enter to accept the entry) has lunch with Har, but no potential links will appear because Mary Harrison (and no one with a similar short name) is not in the database. Instead, continue to type HarrisonM. Your entry will appear as follows (see Figure 76):

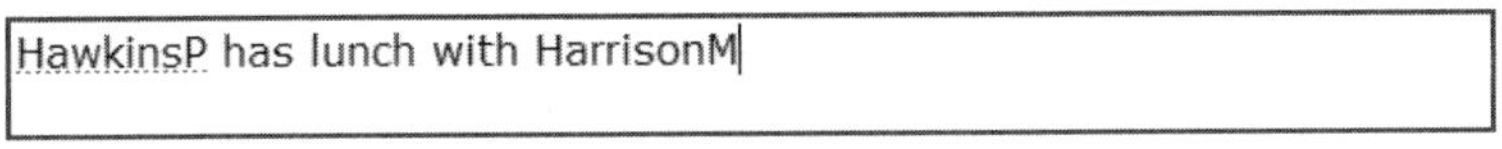

HawkinsP has lunch with HarrisonM|

Figure 76

When you hit the Tab or move the cursor out of the cell, it will display as follows (see Figure 77):

Philip Hawkins has lunch with HarrisonM

Figure 77

As you can see, HarrisonM remains and is not linked (linked items display with tiny dots under the item in the cell). To create Mary Harrison as an object, right-click on HarrisonM. The item will have a red line under it (if you have enabled spell checking on the fly) and a dialog will appear (see Figure 78):

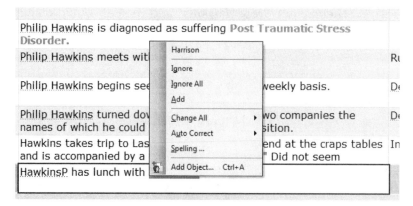

Figure 78

Click Add Object (or Ctrl+A) and the Add Object dialog will appear (see Figure 79):

Figure 79

Change the Full Name from HarrisonM to Mary Harrison and click OK (see Figure 80).

Figure 80

When you exit the cell, you will have created Mary Harrison as a Person and linked her to this fact "on the fly" (see Figure 81).

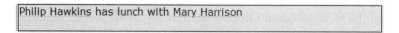

Figure 81

This procedure works to create any object type in any cell in CaseMap that accepts linked objects. You can also create an object on the fly by right-clicking in any blank spot in a linkable cell and selecting Add Object (or Ctrl+A).

Next, tab into the source field, and begin to type in 2005 to determine if the memo is included in the database. The Link Assistant will not display any items because none exists in the database. Therefore, you should type in the following: 2005-01-15HawkinsMemo (see Figure 82).

2005-01-15HawkinsMemo

Figure 82

You will then create the Memo as an object using the same procedure you used to create Mary Harrison as a person, i.e., right-clicking on the entry and selecting Add Object or using Ctrl+A to open the Add Object dialog (see Figure 83):

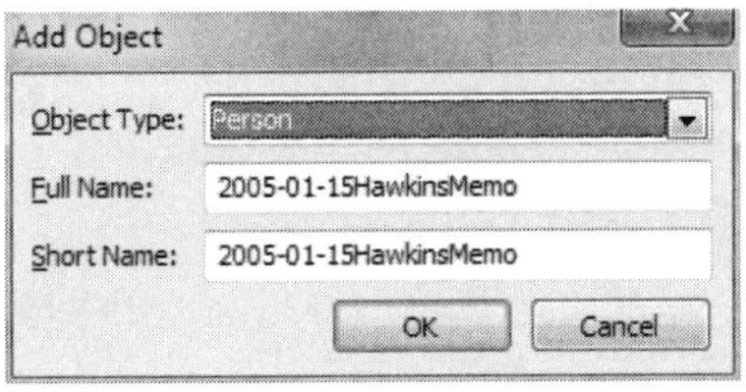

Figure 83

Change Object Type from "Person" to "Document" by either using the drop-down menu or entering the letter "D" (CaseMap uses logical entries such as this throughout the program in drop-down dialogs (see Figure 84).

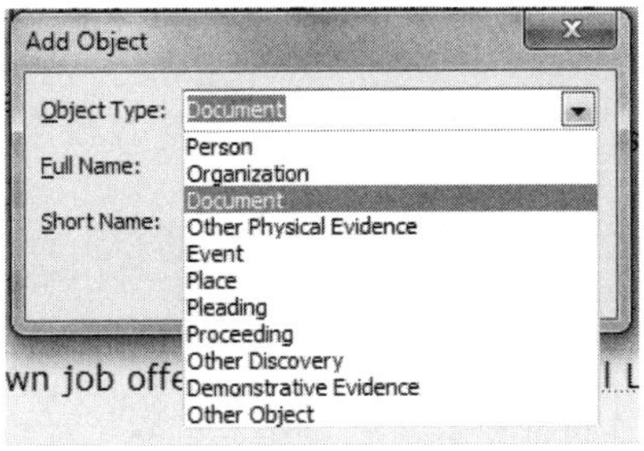

Figure 84

Rename the document's Full Name to "2005-01-15 Hawkins Memo" and click OK (see Figure 85).

Figure 85

When you exit the cell, you will have created the memo as an object, but you will not have linked the object file to the object, i.e., you cannot display the document directly from CaseMap. To create the memo as an object, you could do so from the Documents or All Objects spreadsheet, or you may do so from this cell "on the fly." To do so from this cell, right-click on the item and select Object Detail (or Ctrl+D) to open the Object Detail (see Figure 86).

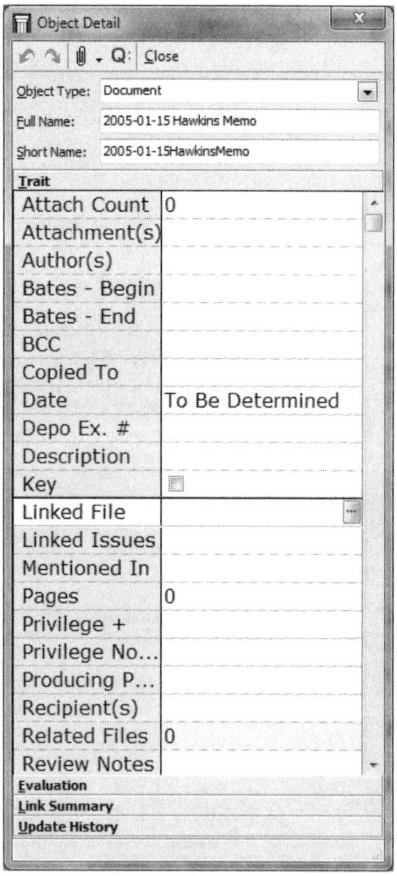

Figure 86

Go to the Linked File cell, click on the three ellipse link, and the Linked File Properties box will appear (see Figure 87).

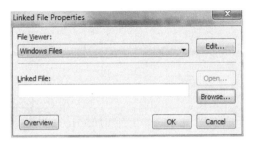

Figure 87

Click Browse, locate the file on your network, and click "Open" to include it in the File Properties box (see Figure 88).

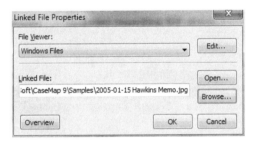

Figure 88

Click OK and then Close on the Object Detail box. After you exit the row with that file, the paper clip (link) icon will appear on the left, confirming that you have linked the file to the object and linked the object to the fact (see Figure 89).

Figure 89

Remember, you can link more than one object or source to any particular fact.

Linking an Object from the All Objects or Specific Spreadsheet

Suppose in the previous example that you had not linked the file with the object. You could instead go to the spreadsheet on which the object appeared, in this case either the All Objects or Documents spreadsheet. In that case, locate the item on the relevant spreadsheet and go to the Linked File cell (it will have the three ellipse dialog in it) (see Figure 90).

Figure 90

From this location, the procedure is identical to the manner in which you linked the document above. First, click on the three ellipse link, the Linked File Properties box will appear (see Figure 87). Next, click Browse, locate the file on your network, and click "Open" to include it in the File Properties box (see Figure 88). Click OK and then Close on the Object Detail box. After you exit the row with that file, the paper clip (link) icon will appear on the left, confirming that you have linked the file to the object and linked the object to the fact (see Figure 91).

Figure 91

Remember, there is no "Save" button in CaseMap. As soon as you exit the cell, your work is saved.

Using All Objects View

One of the ways in which many users create their "cast of characters" (all of the different persons, objects, documents, events, proceedings, etc.) is through the All Objects spreadsheet. The All Objects spreadsheet, which only contains columns for information that is common to all object types, is an excellent place to begin entering case data. By selecting Insert or New Record or Insert>New Record, you can create the information quickly, and link records as shown above.

By default, a new object in CaseMap begins with the designation of the object type and creation of the full and short names; all other information is optional. You can specify the object's role in the case and whether it is "key." To enter more data about any object from the All Objects spreadsheets, all you need to do is to select the Object Detail icon. Using this method, rather than going to specific spreadsheets, you can move more quickly through the process of creating objects without the need to switch back and forth between spreadsheets. If you are starting your case and want to input information quickly, the All Objects spreadsheet is generally the best way to create your cast of characters.

Don't Fill in Every Column

CaseMap offers users a wide range of fields to encode and describe facts, objects, issues, questions, etc. Just because CaseMap has lots of options to fill in information does not mean you have to enter information into all of them. Your goal should be to enter key information that you want to use later, not to fill in every possible cell just because it appears or may appear on a spreadsheet.

Entering New Facts

Whether you have entered large amounts of data through the All Objects spreadsheet, or are entering most of your information on the fly, you will almost certainly spend the majority of your time focused on the Facts spreadsheet. You will generally enter new facts by simply typing information into a new row on the Facts spreadsheet. When you enter a new fact, the first piece of information you will generally enter is the date on which that fact occurred.

After entering in the date, you will begin to craft your facts. There are two keys to writing facts: tell a story, and use short names. When you tell a story, your facts become more useful, more user-friendly, and readily adaptable for use in motions, memoranda, and when preparing opening and closing arguments for trial. When you use short names, you are maximizing CaseMap's ability to help you analyze your case, and saving time (it's much quicker to enter data using short names).

When writing facts, and linking them to sources and other data, you will use short names. Thus, in the Hawkins case, whenever you wrote a fact involving Philip Hawkins, you would type Haw and the Enter key when his name appeared in the Link Assistant. You would follow the same pattern, as outlined in greater detail below, for each person or other object with a short name.

Creating a Fact Chronology

Cases are about facts. The best trial lawyers, regardless of whether they represent plaintiffs or defendants, tell stories that judges and juries can understand. CaseMap can play a vital role in developing the facts of your case, allowing you to present information in a way that allows the judge or jury to understand the evidence. Thus, creating fact outlines is a critical factor in framing your case.

Just as lawyers practice their opening and closing statements, the outline you prepare in CaseMap is in many ways an outline of the evidence frequently included in an opening or closing statement. The fact outline, which links with other objects (the evidence in the case), should be written in a short and conversational way, as though the facts were being told to another person. Lawyers often make the mistake when entering data into CaseMap of describing facts based on the source of the fact rather than the fact itself. That is why the Fact Text field is perhaps the most important field in CaseMap. When all of the Fact Text fields are read together, and in order, they should tell the short story in narrative form about what happened at each date and time in the case.

One way to test your facts and to be certain that they are written in an appropriate and compelling way is to read them out loud to someone to see if they read like a story. A story would tell what happened, not where the information came from.

A well-written fact chronology, one that uses other important fields for data, can also be of vital importance when analyzing the strengths of your case. In particular, your Source field should include every source from which the information supporting every fact is derived, regardless of whether the source is a document, person, or other object. Because you can have multiple sources for information, they can serve as a way to buttress the evidence you intend to present or highlight areas where you have limited support for the evidence.

Writing Facts Well

Writing facts means telling the story of the fact or other information you are creating. Consider a medical report in which a doctor summarizes his examination, treatment, and recommendations for a patient. It would be easy to simply describe this report as a fact as follows: "Dr. Jones's report diagnoses Mary Smith with a herniated disc and outlines that her prognosis is poor." Although this fact describes what was in the report, the report is not the fact; *the fact is the information and the diagnosis*. On the other hand, the report is the source of the information contained in the fact.

A more effective way to write this fact is to state, "Dr. Jones diagnosed Mary Smith with a herniated disc." Then, either within the same fact or in an additional fact, you would indicate that the doctor concluded that Mary Smith's prognosis was poor.

These descriptions say the same thing, but one is describing the information based on the source of the information, whereas the other is describing the information and later links to the source, so that a user can verify the source of the information.

Conjecture, Guesses, and Speculation

Writing a thorough and accurate fact chronology is one of the keys to getting the most benefit from CaseMap. When you begin developing your CaseMap outline, there will often be "facts" that are more properly characterized as conjecture or supposition. This is normal, and outlines created early in a case should include every possible conjecture and speculation, so that you can see what information you need to prove and can see whether you can prove each of these "facts." As your case develops, you will learn whether some, all, or none of the information was accurate or complete, and your Facts spreadsheet can evolve. As you develop your fact chronology, you can delete those "facts" that were speculative or conjecture because you will not be able to prove them at trial.

Consider an intersectional accident in which the plaintiff claims that the defendant disregarded a red light, entered an intersection, and caused a collision. A well-developed fact outline could include numerous sources that establish/confirm that fact. There may be three witnesses who gave statements, your clients may have also seen the light turn red, etc. Regardless of the number of sources, the facts could read:

1. The light facing Alan Smith was red.

   OR

1. Mary Williams and Harry Lang told the police officer that the light at the intersection facing Alan Smith was red.

2. Alan Smith disregarded the red light and entered the intersection.

   OR

2. Mary Williams and Harry Lang watched Alan Smith drive into the intersection even though the light was red.

3. When Alan Smith entered the intersection, he collided with John Jenkins, striking the rear driver's-side door.

   OR

3. According to the police report, Mary Williams and Harry Lang saw Alan Smith's car hit John Jenkins's car.

In each example, the first fact tells what happened, while the second explains the source of the information—data that should be in the Source cell, not the Facts cell.

Writing facts is also an opportunity to take various elements of your case and place them together. With the use of filters, it is easy to view facts relating to discrete aspects of your case. In personal injury cases, for example, in which facts may address both liability and damages, you may want to create links for events such as office visits, hospitalizations, and physical therapy, as well as for various diagnoses, etc. By using filters to winnow the facts to only show one or more of these events or diagnoses, you can quickly create complete treatment outlines or discover treatment gaps that may be ripe for cross-examination.

Creating a strong fact chronology and creating effective issue outlines do not come automatically and cannot be taught in black and white. As a result, the best way to learn how to create fact outlines is to create them, to critically analyze them to see how effective they are, and to determine how they can be improved.

In conjunction with writing facts, many users also link issues to the facts. You can do so using the Link Assistant or the Issue Linking Toolbar, available from the Issue Linking icon on the CaseMap toolbar. With this toolbar, you can quickly link issues by checking the boxes next to the relevant issues and can use the up and down arrows to navigate from one fact to another. Plus, you can even add or rearrange issues from this toolbar.

Links

You link information in CaseMap using the short names for the particular person, document or other objects. Thus, links are critical to an effective use of CaseMap. Establishing links among case elements is a key step in organizing case information. Defining links makes it possible to explore your cases in new ways. For example, once you link facts to issues, you can filter the Fact spreadsheet so that it displays only those facts related to a specific issue.

At their most basic, links are connections between two elements in your case. For example, a link could be a connection between your client and a witness or between a document and the person who signed it. Links reduce the time it takes to enter information. Creating links among the elements of your case also helps you organize your case data and analyze it in many ways, including some you had never contemplated. Creating links also makes it easier to prepare for trial and to prepare or defend against motions for summary judgment.

While it is not practical to link every word in CaseMap, it is important to create links between every person, organization, and proceeding in CaseMap, along with every document, source, etc. While doing so may seem at first glance to be extra work in some cases, it actually saves time. Moreover, the ability to view the linked information quickly and efficiently is one of the most important aspects of CaseMap.

You can create numerous types of links, including:

- Links between a fact and an object
- Links between a fact and an issue
- Links between a document and its author(s) or recipient(s)
- Links between an object and the issue(s) to which it relates
- Links between a question and fact, issue or object relating to it.

To create a link, you can either type the short name of any person, issue, or objects in a linkable field—i.e., in a spreadsheet column that displays the chain-link icon at the top—or use the Link Assistant. To create a link between a question and the fact, issue, or objects to which it applies, click Insert>Add Question or enter Ctrl-Q.

Using Links Effectively

Establishing links among case elements is a key step in organizing case information. Defining links makes it possible to explore cases in new ways. As discussed elsewhere, when you link facts to issues, you can filter the Facts spreadsheet to display only those facts related to a specific issue.

Users can create numerous kinds of links. Among the most common are the links between a fact and an object or objects relevant to a fact. Links can be made in many of fields within CaseMap. It is easy to tell which fields allow links to be created because they contain the chain-link icon in the title of the field. For example, facts in the Fact Text and Source fields contain a link icon, demonstrating that the information within those fields may be linked. Similarly, any field including the word *linked*, such as Linked Issues, is by definition a linked field. Please note that the Linked File field, which associates a file from another program with an object, does not contain the chain-link icon.

Links also are established between links and # fields, which had been named "LS" fields in earlier versions of CaseMap.

Quick Linking of Facts to Sources

After you begin entering data into CaseMap, you will almost certainly want to be able to quickly link sources to specific facts in the Facts spreadsheet. The easiest and most effective way to accomplish this is by directly typing information into the Facts spreadsheet, generally in the Fact Text cell. When you do so, you will use the Link Assistant to link sources to facts based on their short names. Thus, if you are entering the first fact in the Hawkins case, which reads "William Lang meets Philip Hawkins while touring Converse Chemical Labs plant in Bakersfield," you would type the following (using the Link Assistant, you would not need to type all of this information):

Lan (LangW will display on the Link Assistant; you would hit Enter to accept the entry) meets Haw (HawkinsP will display on the Link Assistant; you would hit Enter to accept the entry) while touring CCL (CCL will display on the Link Assistant; you would hit Enter to accept the entry) plant in Bakersfield.

Similarly, for the Source field link to the Lang deposition (Deposition of William Lang, 25:14), your keystrokes would be:

Dep (DepoCollins, DepoHawkins, DepoLang, DepoRandle and DepThomas will display on the Link Assistant; you can either continue typing until you type "Depol" or you could highlight "DepoLang" and hit Enter to accept the entry)

In other words, you only need to enter the minimum data to use the short name of the object you want to link to the fact or other object to which you want to link it. You should not type in full names because they do not link to the objects and take far longer to enter. Remember, you can link any type of object to any cell that has the chain link displayed at the top of the column.

Thus, if all you know is that information about a particular event came from William Lang, but you do not have a more specific source other than "generally knowing," you would list LangW in the Source field as the source of the information in the Facts Text cell. As noted above, you can link a source to any object that has a short name.

Link Summary Fields

CaseMap Link Summary fields, which display information about a particular element in a case, are extremely helpful program-created fields that CaseMap updates automatically; users cannot enter or modify the information in this field. The titles of Link Summary fields begin with the # sign. For example, by default, the Objects-Persons spreadsheet displays four Link Summary fields: # Facts, # Docs Authored, # Docs Received, and # E-mails (see Figure 92). Each of these fields displays the number of facts, objects, or other items that include links to the particular object, etc.

If you look at the Phillip Hawkins entry on the Objects-Persons spreadsheet, the number 24 appears under # Facts. When you click on the box with the three ellipses, CaseMap displays a new summary spreadsheet that shows

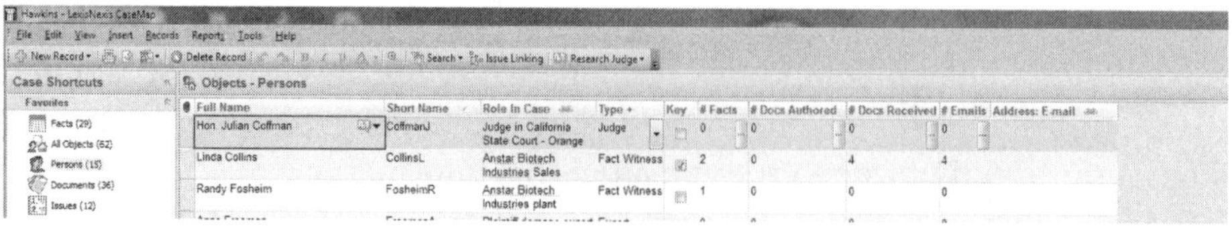

Figure 92

each of the twenty-four facts that have been linked to Phillip Hawkins. Similarly, if you look at the # Docs Authored column, you would see that Phillip Hawkins was listed as the author of twenty-four documents. From that cell, you can click on the three ellipses and see a new spreadsheet view showing all twenty-four linked documents (see Figure 93). From that spreadsheet, you could export the results or click on any of the rows with a dark paper clip and view the related objects.

Link Summary fields are an excellent way to analyze a particular aspect of your case. Thus, if Phillip Hawkins is being deposed, you would want to see all of the facts relating to him, all of the documents he authored and received, and any e-mails to or from him. These will almost certainly form the basis for any questions you will ask Phillip Hawkins at his deposition or would at least be the basis for questions at trial.

Link Assistant

The Link Assistant allows you to type in a short name in any column displaying the chain-link icon at the top and link that short name with the person, object, document or other object to which the short name applies. The Link Assistant is not only an enormous time-saver (it saves lots of typing), but it also prevents you from typing information incorrectly.

To use the Link Assistant, type the first few characters of a short name into a linkable field (see Figure 94). The Link Assistant will be displayed and will allow you to select or to scroll through a list of short names until you find the correct one. Once you have found the correct short name, just highlight it and press the Enter key, and the completed short name will appear in the cell. You can also use this tool to link multiple facts, persons, issues, etc. in virtu-

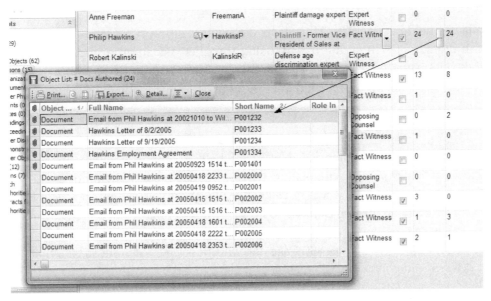

Figure 93

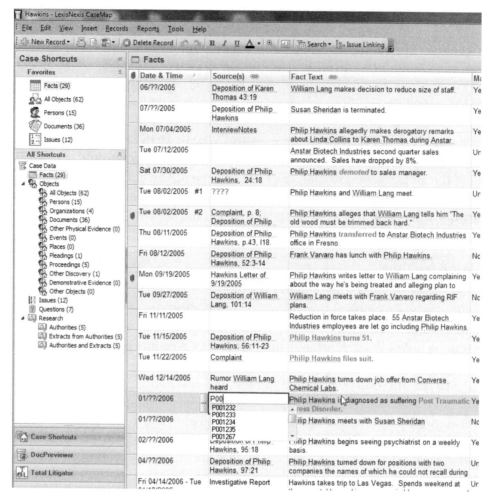

Figure 94

ally any field in CaseMap. Thus, if six documents support a particular fact, you can quickly link them all just by using the Link Assistant. You can separate linked items with a comma or a space. Last, when you hover your mouse over the short name, the program displays details about the object (see Figure 95).

Linking an Uncoded Object

Consider another possibility. For whatever reason, you did not code a particular person with a short name. You may have thought, for example, that the person was not relevant or that there was simply no need for a short name for that person. To correct this oversight, just highlight the object's name on the Facts or other spreadsheet, right click, and select Add Object (see Figure 96). CaseMap will know that you want to take that name and convert it into an object with both a full and short name.

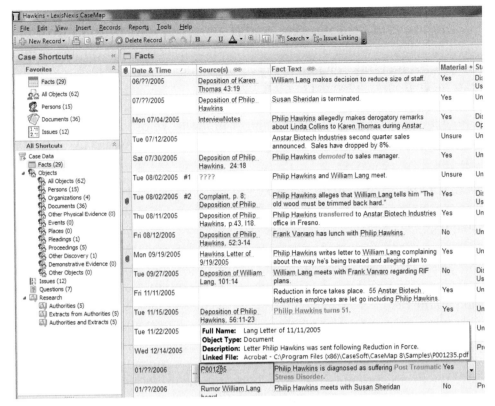

Figure 95

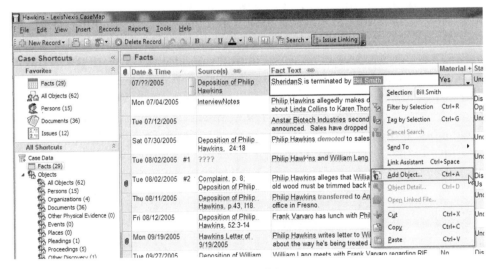

Figure 96

To control how the Link Assistant works, go to Tools>Option>General. The top section, Link Assistant, determines how the utility works (see Figure 84). The Link Assistant preferences determine whether you will use the utility and how sensitive it will be—i.e., how many characters you type before it appears. By default, CaseMap specifies three characters as the "sensitivity" for triggering the Link Assistant tool; in most cases, this setting will be sufficient. This means, for example, that the Link Assistant will display short names after you type the first three characters of its short name. You can set the sensitivity to range from two to six characters.

Although CaseMap allows users to turn the Link Assistant on and off, turning it off will almost certainly limit your ability to obtain the best results from CaseMap. As noted elsewhere, short name links are critical for analyzing data and preparing reports.

Record Detail/Detail Dialog Boxes

One of the methods many people use to enter information in CaseMap is the Detail Dialog box. At the top of every spreadsheet is an icon that shows a magnifying glass with a "+," which together stand for "record detail (see Figure 97)." You can access all of the details about a record by clicking on that icon, pressing Ctrl+F2, or going to Record>Record Detail. When you do so, you will bring up the record's Fact Detail box (see Figure 98), which contains all of the fields into which data may be entered for that record. While most users initially enter data on the fly, they will often return to the object to add more information, and, in that case, the Fact Detail dialog is the most effective way because the user is prompted by simply looking at the object to enter as much or as little information as possible.

Fact Detail boxes include the Trait information for each object, Evaluation information for most objects, Link Summaries, and the Update History area, which contains CaseMap-created fields that cannot be modified by the user that display the creation author for the particular item, the update or the last update author, as well as who entered the information and when the information was entered. The Fact Detail box also allows you, by using the blue arrows at the top, to go from one object to the next. It also allows you, by using the green plus sign, to insert a new object or, using the white X in a red circle icon, to delete the object. There are also options to undo any changes you have made. If there are linked files, you can see those linked files using the paper clip at the top of the Fact Detail box, and if there are questions links

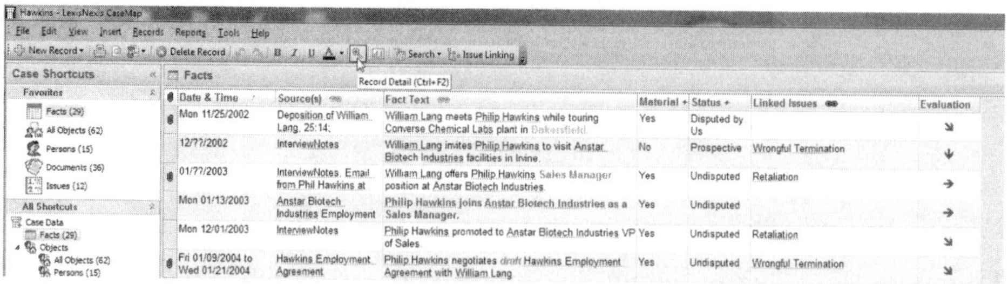

Figure 97

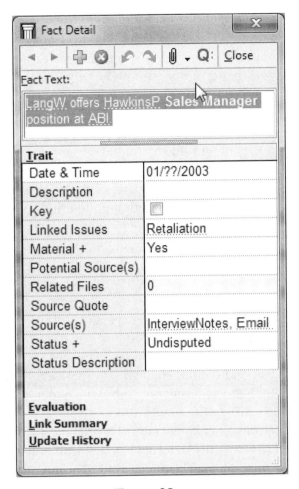

Figure 98

to the file, you can view them directly from or you can add them directly from the Fact Detail box.

Note that it is neither necessary nor productive to enter every piece of information about every object in CaseMap. If you do so you will likely never complete your case because there is a point where too much information leads to a lack of productivity.

Creating an Issues Outline

Another important aspect of CaseMap is the issues outline. In some cases, the issues are obvious and may be relatively narrow, such as in a routine automobile accident in which the issues are liability, duty, damages, and any mitigating factors. As cases become more complex, and additional theories of liability and additional defenses arise, the number of issues will increase.

Creating issues (and the resulting outline) is not always an easy or automatic process, and new CaseMap users tend to either create too few or too many issues, although there is no perfect number of issues for any given case. That said, creating an issue outline is very similar to analyzing your case and creating a hierarchy of your theories of liability, damages, and other items.

As discussed elsewhere, you can easily rearrange issues on the Issues spreadsheet using the up and down and indent and decrease indent arrows adjacent to the different issues. One strategy that tends to work for many firms is to have a conference at the outset of the case with the key persons who will be analyzing the data to determine the critical issues in your case. From there, you can analyze your case and determine what the key issues are. Once those issues are developed, they can be placed into CaseMap.

For example, in the Hawkins case, the default issues (and sub-issues) relate to the different claims of the plaintiff: wrongful termination, age discrimination, retaliation, and the defense of deserved termination. There is also a separate issue for damages. The sub-issues allow other case users to break down the matter into more specific composite parts. Thus, in the Hawkins case, damages include the failure to mitigate damages (actually an affirmative defense), lost wages, and mental anguish. Alternatively, you could have designated failure to mitigate as a separate sub-issue under affirmative defenses, as some firms do.

The key to creating an issues outline is preparing a logical hierarchy of issues so that users can easily determine which issues are of most relevance in a case. Issues, which also will link directly with TextMap issues, should be crafted so that they are clear and concise. Of course, issues have short names and can and should be linked to various objects on other spreadsheets by either using the Link Assistant or by using the Issue Linking Toolbar.

The Bulk Issue Linker

The Bulk Issue Linker, which is run from the Tools>Case Tools>Bulk Issue Linker menu, makes it easier to link *all of the records on display* in a Fact,

Be Careful Using the Bulk Issue Linker

Because the Bulk Issue Linker makes changes to numerous records at the same time, CaseMap will warn you to back up your database before making these changes. After you make changes with the Bulk Issue Linker, you will only be able to reverse those changes by restoring your database from a backup.

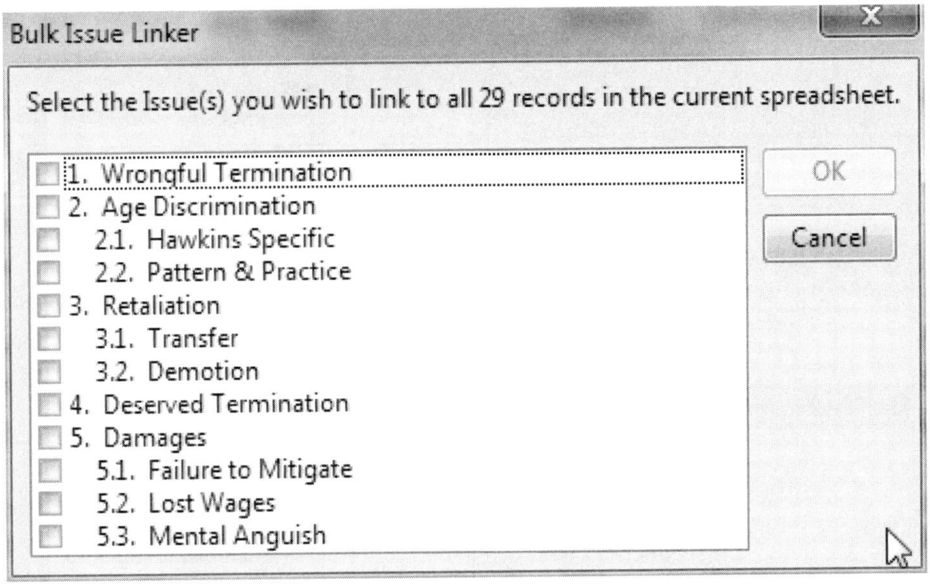

Figure 99

Object, Question, or Research spreadsheet to one or more issues and eliminates the need to make those links individually. For example, you can link one or more issues to all facts or to selected facts all at once (see Figure 99).

Generally, you will not link every entry on a spreadsheet to one or more issues. Thus, before running the Bulk Issue Linker, you will generally filter the spreadsheet so that it displays only those rows of data that you intend to link to a particular issue(s). When you run the Bulk Issue Linker, the selected rows will appear in the spreadsheet view along with a dialog box that allows you to select the issue(s) you wish to link and to link them globally.

Linking Facts, Objects, and Questions to Issues

Facts, objects, questions, and research may all be linked to issues in a case. To link these items to issues, while reviewing a particular fact, object, or research item, you can click on the Object Detail dialog and enter the issues in the Traits section using their short names in the Linked Issues field (see Figure 100). If the Issues column is not visible on the spreadsheet, you can also link the issues to the entry by inserting the Issues field on the spreadsheet by right-clicking on the title bar and selecting Insert Field and selecting the Linked Issues column.

You can also globally add Issues by selecting the Issue Linking icon (see Figure 101), which opens the Issue Linking toolbar, on which you can see all of the issues in your case and select/check or deselect the particular issues that apply to that question, object, or fact (see Figure 102). Finally, when using

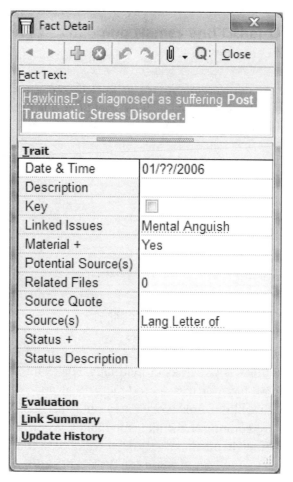

Figure 100

Figure 101

the Issue Linking toolbar, you can move from one item to another simply by clicking on the "Move to prior" or "Move to next" links at the top of the toolbar. You can also add an issue on the fly by typing in an issue's short name in the Linked Issues column and selecting the correct short name when it appears.

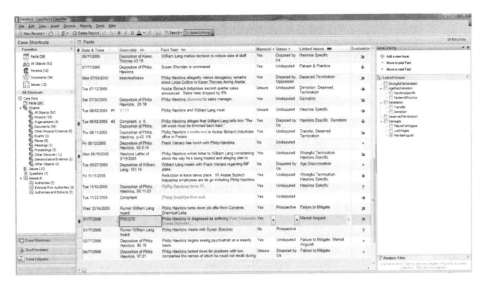

Figure 102

Viewing Information and Updating Information

Fields

CaseMap uses fields, which are displayed in spreadsheet views, in list windows and in detail windows to store and display information about each element of a case. Virtually every type of field associated with a fact, object, issue, or question is predefined, although users can add their own fields to their cases. Every field on a particular spreadsheet will have the same type of information associated with it for every entry on the spreadsheet. Thus, the Date & Time field on the Facts spreadsheet will contain information about the date and time when each case fact occurred.

CaseMap refers to the information contained in a field as its "value." The types of information that can be entered in a field vary based on how the field is defined. Some fields allow users to enter any value they want, while others

Renaming Fields: Be Careful About Doing So

Users may rename any field in CaseMap, including fields that CaseMap creates automatically. It is not recommended that users change/rename any fields created by default by the program because, unless all users are aware of the name change, changing the name of a default field could be confusing or could lead to data questions, etc.

limit the information to very specific types of data. In spreadsheet view and list windows, fields are displayed as columns, although the fields are fixed in list windows. Consequently, the Facts list window always displays the Date & Time, Fact Text, and the Source(s) fields. In detail windows, fields appear as rows and are listed alphabetically.

There are four types of fields: (1) Trait, (2) Evaluation, (3) Link Summary, and (4) Update History. Fields function identically regardless whether they appear as columns or rows and regardless of the type of information entered in the fields. You can only enter data into Trait and Evaluation fields; the program automatically enters and updates Link Summary and Update History fields. Users may enter or update data in spreadsheet views and in detail windows; list windows are read-only; read-only fields are displayed with a different background color than other fields. Fields have the following traits:

Check box (sortable)—A check box creates a check box within that field.

Date (sortable)—A date field contains date information.

Date & Time (sortable)—This field contains date and time information.

Description fields (non-sortable)—A description field can contain up to ten thousand characters and is used for lengthy analyses and other information.

Evaluation (sortable)—These fields allow users to create custom evaluations for case-specific purposes.

Fixed list (sortable)—This field contains a dropdown menu of specific information. The field may not exceed thirty-five characters, and users are not permitted to enter any information other than the information contained within the list. The information that users select may be changed, but information may be lost when making a change.

Number (integer) (sortable)—Users can enter non-financial numbers only.

Delete Fields with Care

While it is tempting to delete fields that are no longer necessary to your database, there is generally little or no reason to do so. First, you can hide any fields that are not necessary using the Define Views dialog, eliminating the need to view the fields or to enter data into them. Second, it can be time-consuming to delete the various fields that are not needed in your case, and there is little, if any, benefit to doing so. Third, if you later discover that you needed to use a deleted field, you will have to recreate the field from scratch. Finally, you cannot delete the basic CaseMap fields that the program creates for every case.

Number (currency)—Users can enter financial/currency data in this field; multiple types of currency may be entered.

Open-ended list (non-sortable)—This field, which contains a plus sign in its title, allows users to enter their own information.

Text (35) (sortable)—This field allows users to enter limited text information.

Detail Views

By default, whenever you add information such as a document or a fact to CaseMap, you will generally do so in the relevant spreadsheet, which will only contain some of the potential fields that could be used in the database or for which information may be entered. To view all of the field properties, you must click on the Record Detail icon on the toolbar or Ctrl+F2. This will bring up the Record Detail dialog box for any particular object, fact, or issue.

At the top of the Record Detail dialog, you can see all of the relevant information about the item; you can also navigate easily from record to record using the blue left and right arrows. You can also create a new record, delete a record, undo changes, link files to a record, add a question, or close the dialog. These options are standard on all of the Record Detail dialogs. Depending on the type of item being reviewed, you may also be able to change a short name in those fields that allow naming and renaming of short and full names, such as documents and persons.

Fact Detail Boxes

The Trait and Evaluation sections of the Fact Detail box permit you to view and code all of the information for a particular fact, including information entered or that could be entered in any custom fields. Even if the information is not displayed in the spreadsheet, it remains as part of the object detail. The Fact Detail box lists the Trait, Evaluation, Link Summary, and Update History fields for each entry (see Figure 100).

Traits include all of the coded data for the fact. The Evaluation section contains all of the evaluation fields for the fact. The Link Summary section contains details about the types of objects and other information to which the fact is linked and provides you with the opportunity to view that information directly. Similarly, the Update History section states the name of the creation author, creation scribe, and the date the fact was created. The last update author scribe and time fields will display that particular information.

Object Detail Boxes

The Trait and Evaluation sections of the Object Detail box permit you to view and code all information relevant to a particular object, including information entered or that could be entered in any custom fields (see Figure 103). Even if

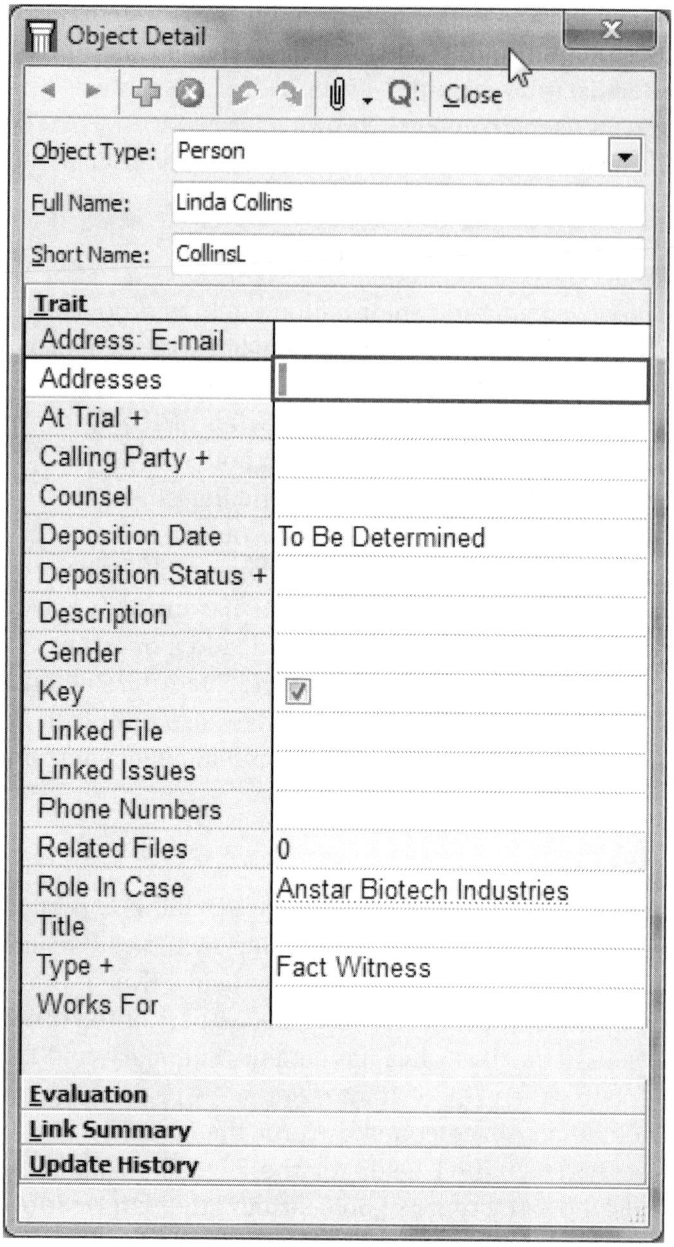

Figure 103

the information is not displayed in the spreadsheet, it remains as part of the object detail. You may change the object type from the All Objects row of the Object Detail box or from the dropdown menu on the particular row containing that object in the All Objects spreadsheet. You cannot change the object type, such as persons, organizations, and documents, from the specific object

Burden of Proof: An Important but Often Forgotten Trait

The Issues Detail screen has fields for Traits, Evaluations, Links Summary, and Update History for every issue. Although it is not generally necessary to code every field, one of the less commonly used fields, but one that can be particularly helpful, is the Burden of Proof trait, which specifies what the burden of proof is for that particular issue.

Thus, if the jurisdiction requires that you prove fraud by clear and convincing evidence, rather than by a preponderance of the evidence, you may wish to display that information. Similarly, with issue fields, users can include relevant information, including whether the issue requires a special jury instruction, whether the issue is the subject of a motion for summary judgment, or other information that allows a user to view highly relevant information concerning a given item.

spreadsheets. Changing the object type also changes the information displayed and could result in the loss of information.

The Object Detail box has fields for Trait, Evaluation, Link Summary, and Update History for each entry. Traits include all of the coded data for the object. The Evaluation section contains all of the evaluation fields for the object. The Link Summary section specifies the fields to which the object is linked and provides the user with the opportunity to view that information directly. Similarly, the Update History field lists the name of the creation author, creation scribe, and the date the object was created. The last update author, scribe and time fields will display that information.

Issue Detail Boxes

The Trait and Evaluation sections of the Issues Detail box permit you to view and code all information relevant to a particular issue, including information entered or that could be entered in any custom fields (see Figure 104). Even if the information is not displayed in the spreadsheet, it remains as part of the issue detail.

The Issue Detail box has fields for Trait, Evaluation, Link Summary, and Update History for each entry. Traits include all of the coded data for the issue. Evaluation lists all evaluation fields for the issue. The Link Summary contains details about the types of objects and other information to which the issue is linked and an opportunity to view that information directly. Similarly, the Update History section lists the name of the creation author, creation scribe, and the date the issue was created. The last update author, scribe and time fields will display that information.

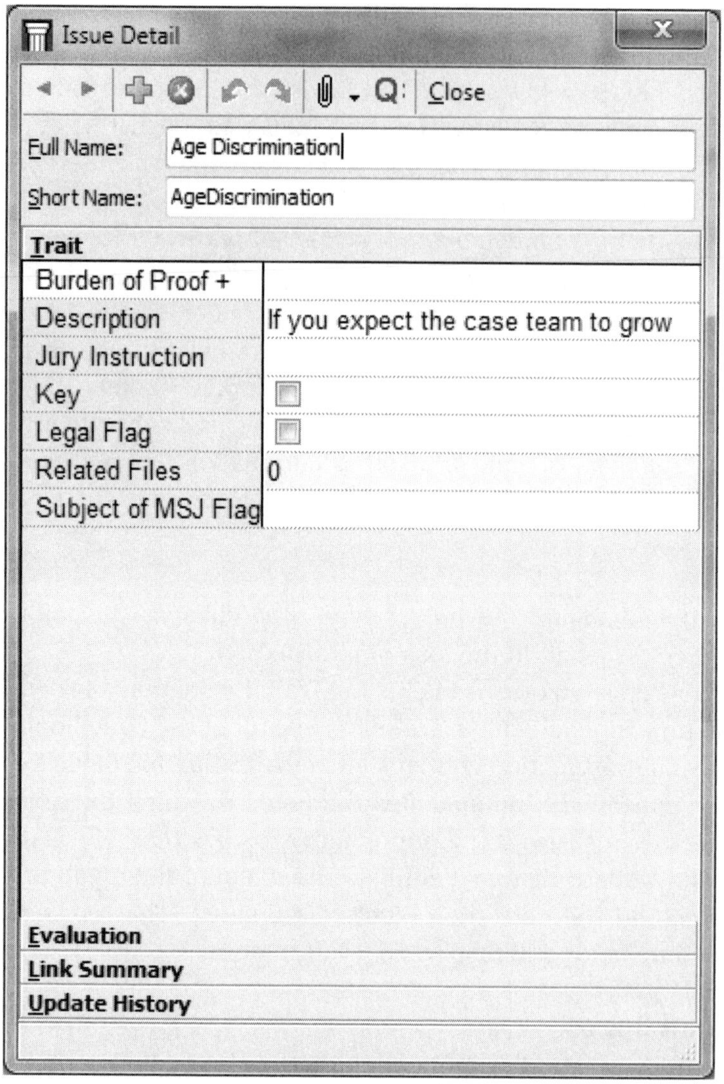

Figure 104

Question Detail Boxes

The Trait and Evaluation sections of the Question Detail box permit you to view and code all information relevant to a particular question, including information entered or that could be entered in any custom fields (see Figure 105). Even if the information is not displayed in the spreadsheet, it remains as part of the question detail.

The Question Detail box has fields for Trait, Evaluation, and Update History for each entry. Traits include all of the coded data for the question. The Evaluation section lists all of the evaluation fields for the question. The Up-

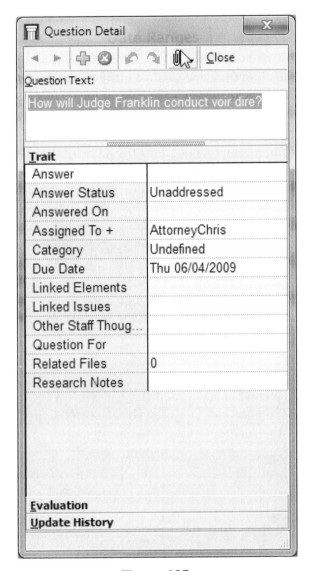

Figure 105

date History section contains the name of the creation author, creation scribe, and the date the question was created. The last update author scribe and time fields will display that information.

Research Detail Boxes

The Trait and Evaluation sections of the Research Detail box permit you to view and code all of the information for a particular research entry, including information entered or that could be entered in any custom fields on any of the Research spreadsheets. Even if the information is not displayed in the spreadsheet, it remains as part of the research detail (see Figure 106). The Research Detail box, which CaseMap labels as Authority Detail, has fields for Trait, Evaluation, Link Summary, and Update History for each entry.

Traits include all of the coded data for the research. The Evaluation section contains all of the evaluation fields for the research. The Link Summary section specifies the types of objects and other information to which the research is linked and provides an opportunity to view that information directly. Similarly, the Update History section lists the name of the creation author, creation scribe, and the date the research was created. The last update author scribe and time fields will display that information.

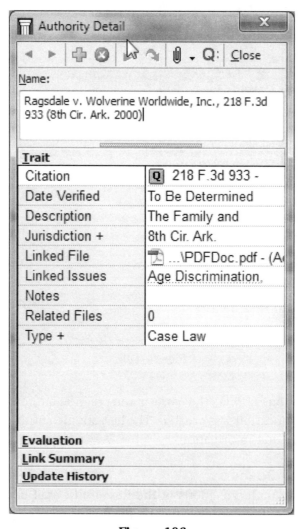

Figure 106

Custom Fields

By creating custom fields, you can include unique information in your CaseMap database that would not "fit" into other fields on a spreadsheet. Custom fields appear and function the same as CaseMap's default fields, can appear in spreadsheet views and detail windows, and can be used to filter and tag the data in a spreadsheet. Although CaseMap permits you to create an unlimited number of custom fields, the default fields created for every case will cover virtually every type of data your case may need. But in some cases, however, the data does not fit the mold. Thus, for example, if you have a case involving patients who had serious reactions to a particular medication, you could create a field that contained data directly related to the drug—e.g., blood counts, test results.

Custom fields are created using the Field Properties dialog. You can open this dialog by right-clicking on the Spreadsheet title bar or by going to View>Current View>Define View and clicking on the Field Properties button (see Figure 107). From this dialog, you can create a new field, edit the value of an existing field, rename a field, or delete a field that is no longer needed in your case. This dialog also displays which spreadsheets and searches are using a particular field and when the field was created and last updated.

If you click the plus (+) sign, the Add Field dialog appears, which asks for the name of the new field and the type of field—e.g., Check Box, Date, Evaluation. The program then walks you through the creation of the field, including any values specific to the field. You can specify the security settings for the field. By default, editing rights are granted to all staff members when a new field is added. When you have completed creating the custom field, click Close

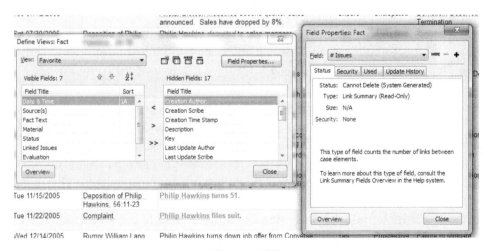

Figure 107

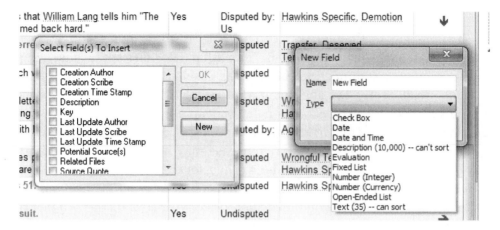

Figure 108

to confirm. Your custom field will not appear in your spreadsheet, however, until you insert it, as you would any other field.

Another way to create a custom field is to right-click on the title bar of the spreadsheet and select Insert Field>New. You will be presented with the same dialog and options (see Figure 108).

You would also use the Field Properties dialog to add or delete values for a field. Unless restricted by the field's security settings, users can modify any custom field's values. Users cannot modify or delete the values in predefined CaseMap fields. When you delete a field, you also delete any information stored in that field, as well as the related evaluation and Links Summary fields CaseMap has created.

Intake Interview Jumpstart

The Intake Interview Jumpstart (located at Tools>Intake Interview Jumpstart) makes it easy to collect important case background information from a client (see Figure 109). To use the Intake Interview Jumpstart, both the lawyer and the client must have Microsoft Word 2000 or later. In addition, no more than five intake interviews are permitted in any single case file. The Intake Interview Jumpstart allows the client or other person (such as a witness) to provide you with data to begin or to continue analyzing a case.

The first step on the Intake Interview Jumpstart is to e-mail an intake interview form to the client, who will fill in key information, such as the names of people involved, facts, and documents. The template for inserting this information is included with CaseMap along with complete instructions for the client. Although you may edit the instructions before sending a copy of the Intake Interview Jumpstart to the client, you cannot and should not edit the tables in the template because that would prevent the automatic import of the completed interview into CaseMap.

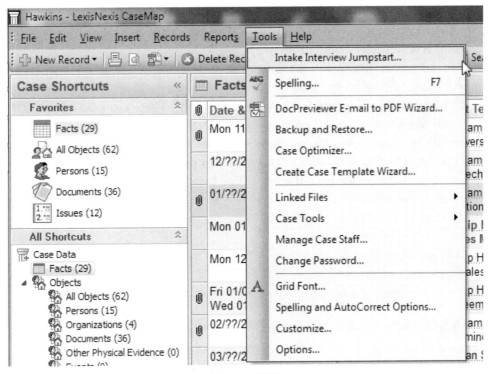

Figure 109

After reviewing the introductory screen for the Intake Interview Jump-start, you will be asked whether you wish to review an intake interview form, e-mail an intake interview form to a client, or import a completed intake interview form into CaseMap. If you are creating an intake interview, you will check that button and CaseMap will ask you to name the document that you are sending to your client. After that, the Wizard will create and display an e-mail in your default e-mail program containing the intake interview form template as an attachment. You will need to complete the "to" e-mail address for the client or other person to whom you are sending the template. When you press Finish, the e-mail dialogue will appear. You are welcome to change the information in the e-mail text but, as noted above, you should not change or modify the template.

If you are seeking to import an interview form, the Wizard will ask you to review the form you have received and to save any changes before continuing. The document should be open in Microsoft Word when you are performing the import. CaseMap offers you the option of simply reviewing the intake interview through this Wizard and importing it later or importing it when you review the document. Once you have completed the import, CaseMap creates facts and a cast of characters based on the information provided by the client. Although the information may not be "perfect," it provides a significant time-saver for your office and allows you the ability to modify any information by the client to be more consistent with CaseMap's own requirements and the manner in which you code your case.

In addition, when you use the Intake Interview Jumpstart feature to import a Word document with client data, CaseMap automatically creates a ReportBook of the imported information for you to send to your client. The program will prompt you to preview the ReportBook after you run the Wizard to import the data. This ReportBook contains additional fields, such as Key and Potential Sources, so that your client can provide additional information to assist with the analysis of the case. The Introduction page text, which can be edited like other ReportBook pages, provides instructions to the client about how to use the ReportBook. The only thing left to do is to e-mail the ReportBook to your client.

By using the Intake Interview Jumpstart, you will have saved a tremendous amount of time, will have likely compiled more data than by other methods, and will have impressed your client with your ability to do this.

Research Directly from Persons in Your CaseMap Database

CaseMap users who have purchased the appropriate research databases from LexisNexis may conduct research about persons listed in CaseMap directly from the Objects-Persons spreadsheet. If the person is a judge (using the Type field), as the Hon. Julian Coffman is in the Hawkins case, you can click on the book and magnifying glass icon and perform a variety of research, including a Judge Analyzer Report, a Judicial Litigation Profile Report, and a search of Dockets & Documents (see Figure 110). For other persons, there are a variety of searches functions available, including Background Check and Guided Public Records Search (see Figure 111).

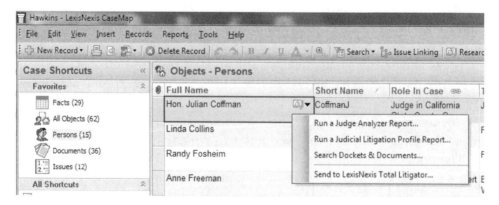

Figure 110

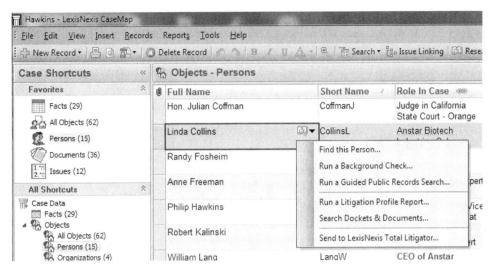

Figure 111

Importing Information

CaseMap can import four different types of information:

◆ PDF documents—using the Send PDFs to CaseMap utility (discussed in chapter 5)

◆ Text files—files created in .txt, .csv, .asc and .tab formats

◆ E-mails from Outlook—using the DocPreviewer E-mail to PDF tool or Outlook E-mail Linker tool

◆ Issues from NoteMap—issues copied onto the Clipboard from NoteMap.

CaseMap can also synchronize issues with TextMap.

Importing Text Files

Although most users input data directly into CaseMap, you can also import information saved in generic text formats created by programs such as Notepad, Microsoft Word, Corel WordPerfect, and Microsoft Excel. While it takes a bit of effort to ensure that the files to be imported are formatted correctly, importing data is an excellent way to convert information that you may have created in either Word or Excel into helpful CaseMap data.

To import a text file, which must be in a .txt, .csv, .asc, or .tab format, go to File>Import>Text File (see Figure 112). Because CaseMap must be opened exclusively to perform an import, the program will prompt you to open the case exclusively; you should allow it do so. CaseMap will also suggest that you back up your data before performing an import. Generally, you should back

Use Short Names When Importing Data

If you use short names when importing data, CaseMap will automatically link the short names when it completes the import, provided the short name is imported into a linked field. Thus, if you were importing records into the Hawkins case, you should make sure that your data fields say "LangW," "ABI," or "HawkinsP," for example, saving a lot of time and effort.

If CaseMap fails to automatically link all of the short names, that is not a problem. To correct this, just use the Short Name Assistant found at Tools>Case Tools>Short Name Assistant.

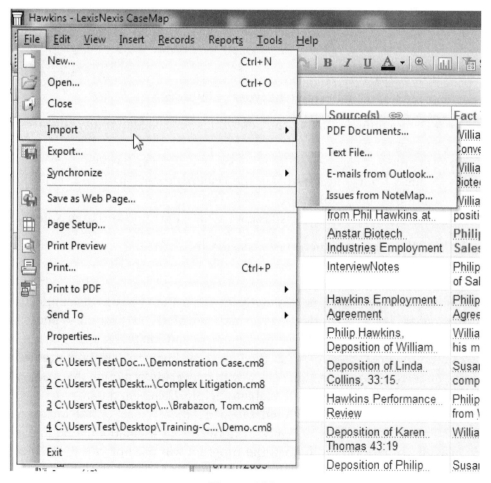

Figure 112

up your data in the event the data you import do not map properly or cause other problems with your database.

CaseMap then opens a Windows Explorer dialog, from which you navigate to the location on your computer where you have saved the file to be imported. Next, highlight the file to be imported and click Open. The CaseMap Import Wizard will open and confirm the name of the file to be imported in the dialog box. If the file name is correct, select Next. CaseMap will then attempt to determine what delimiter (separator between information) was used in your document; generally, it will be a comma, tab, or semicolon. Verify that CaseMap has selected the correct delimiter, or choose the correct one yourself.

This dialog will also inquire whether the first name of your document contains field names, and, if so, you will check that box as well. If you used a text qualifier—a symbol such as quotation marks (" ") at the beginning and end of each field—you would choose it in the Text Qualifier box. After verifying that all of the information is correct, click Next. CaseMap will preview the data being imported. You can review the data using the arrows at the top of the dialog box. When you are satisfied with the data, click Next. CaseMap will ask you to select the spreadsheet into which you are importing the data. Choose the correct spreadsheet and click Next.

CaseMap inquires whether you are importing every field in your file or whether you want to skip certain fields. Highlight each field you want to import, and, using the dropdown menu, select the appropriate spreadsheet field into which you want it imported. When you have completed mapping the fields, click Next. CaseMap will offer you another opportunity to review your choices. Select Finish, and CaseMap will display the number of records you are attempting to import and advise you that you cannot undo or cancel the procedure once it begins. When you are ready to proceed, click Yes.

When CaseMap completes the import, it will display a dialog listing the number of records imported as well as the number of records skipped because of errors. It will then display the location of the error report and ask you

Back Up Before Importing Data

Even the best planned data imports can go awry, leaving you with incorrectly mapped data and other errors. To avoid this problem, it is highly recommended that you back up your CaseMap database before performing an import. By doing so, you can restore your database should there be problems with the imported data. The procedure for backing up and restoring cases is found in Chapter 5.

Test Before Importing Files

Before attempting to import a file into CaseMap, you should practice on a "dummy," or "test" file. Creating one is easy. Open up your word processor and type the following information, inserting a tab where indicated by [tab]:

Date[tab]Fact
1/2/06[tab]LangW has dinner with CollinsL
2/4/05[tab]HawkinsP reviews documents from ABI
2/5/05LangW met CollinsL

Save the document as "Demo" and select Plain Text (.txt) as the file type. If asked by Windows, you should save the document with Windows (default) text encoding. Then close the document, making sure not to change the format.

When attempting to import this file, you should map the first column to the Date & Time field and the second column to the Fact Text field. When the process is completed, CaseMap should have imported two records, with one record skipped because of an error. If you used the sample data above, you will see that CaseMap determined that there was an invalid date in the third line of data:

"Record#","Error",DATE,FACT
"3","Invalid date in (Date & Time)","2/5/05LangW met CollinsL",

whether you want to open the error report. The report will display the record number for each error (the line in the text file containing the error) and the reason CaseMap was unable to import the record. You can then attempt to correct the error and enter (or reimport) that data, or you can disregard the information.

If you go to the spreadsheet into which the data were imported, you can view the information that was entered. If your import file contained appropriate short names, CaseMap will have linked them, provided the short names were in linked fields.

Importing E-mail from Outlook

CaseMap allows you to import e-mail files from Microsoft Outlook, thus offering an e-discovery tool that has generally only been available in more complex and more expensive e-discovery programs. When you select File>Import E-mails from Outlook, CaseMap offers you the option of using either DocPreviewer E-mail to PDF or Outlook E-mail Linker tools (see Figure 113).

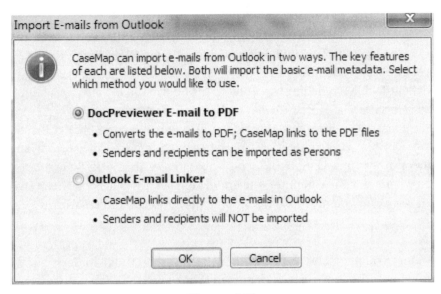

Figure 113

DocPreviewer: Convert & Import Outlook E-mail

The DocPreviewer E-mail to PDF dialog converts e-mail messages to PDF format and then links the individual e-mails as PDF files. Using this process, CaseMap imports the names of e-mail senders and recipients as "persons" in your database. Alternatively, you can use the Outlook E-mail Linker, which links individual e-mails directly with CaseMap. When you use the Outlook E-mail Linker, CaseMap does not import the names of senders and recipients; thus, you will have to enter the information manually if you would like the names included as persons in CaseMap.

When you chose the DocPreviewer E-mail to PDF Wizard, CaseMap provides some basic instructions and then asks where to locate the PST (Microsoft Outlook) file you are importing—i.e., are you using your copy of Outlook, is the file on a CD or DVD, or is it on your computer or your network? When you choose the first option, the DocPreviewer will locate the PST files on your computer and ask you to select the folder(s) you wish to convert. You will then choose the folder(s) you wish to convert using the options provided and specify where to store the converted PDFs that are being included in CaseMap (generally the same folder where you store your case documents).

CaseMap then asks you to specify how to display the time zone when an e-mail was sent, offering four options: (1) don't display the time zone, (2) show the Greenwich Mean Time (GMT) offset, (3) show the full time zone name, or (4) abbreviate the name of the time zone name, such as EDT for Eastern Daylight Time. After you click Next, CaseMap will confirm the number of

Clearing the Outlook E-mail Linker's User Selection

The Outlook E-mail Linker remembers a user's selection for future use. To clear your or another user's settings, hold the Shift key on the keyboard while launching the utility. This information is also provided in the Overview dialog that displays when you start the utility.

Please also note that this utility, also known as the Import E-mails from Outlook Wizard, does not permit you to import e-mails from anywhere other than Outlook folders. Thus, if you have a PST file located elsewhere on your computer, the Import Emails from Outlook Wizard will not work and you must use the DocPreviewer E-mail to PDF Wizard.

PST folders you have chosen, how many items are in those folders, and the location where the converted items will be saved. When you click Next, CaseMap will convert the e-mails to PDF. CaseMap will also show how many items it can convert to PDF format and provide the elapsed time and the estimated time to complete the data conversion.

When CaseMap finishes converting the e-mail, it will display a dialog summarizing the number of e-mails converted and the number of non–e-mail items that were skipped. It will also allow you to decide whether to (1) import the e-mails, senders, and recipients into CaseMap, (2) Bates stamp the PDFs, and/or (3) do nothing. Although not displayed in that order, if you plan to Bates stamp the PDF versions of the e-mails created by CaseMap, you should do so before importing the e-mails, although you can do so at a later time. *Note: At this stage, the e-mails have been converted to PDFs but have not been imported into CaseMap; you must complete the process to import them into CaseMap.*

If you choose to Bates stamp the PDFs, the DocPreviewer E-mail to PDF Wizard will launch Adobe Acrobat and the CaseMap Bates Stamp Utility, which is described in Chapter 5. When the Bates Stamp Utility is complete—or if you choose not to use this utility—CaseMap opens the Send PDFs to CaseMap Utility. As you proceed through the utility, you will specify the files to include (generally every PDF when importing e-mails) and the spreadsheet to which to import them (generally documents when importing e-mails). You will then select the appropriate Document field mappings. On the next screen, CaseMap displays the number of PDFs it is importing and the number of senders/recipients it will add to the Persons spreadsheet. At this point, you can review and/or customize the field mappings by clicking Yes at the PDF E-mail Preview dialog, although this is almost always unnecessary. When you click Next, CaseMap confirms the number of PDFs to be sent to the Document spreadsheet, the name of the case to which they will be added, and the number of Bates-numbered PDFs. When you click Finish, the Bulk Send to CaseMap progress screen appears, and, when it is completed, a message appears telling you that the process is complete, along with the total number of records that were added to CaseMap (on all spreadsheets). Click OK, and you are done.

You can then switch to the CaseMap Documents spreadsheet to see each of the newly imported items along with the Bates numbers (if added), the document type (e-mail), the author, the sender, the recipient, and any other information CaseMap obtained. Please note that the senders (the authors and the recipients) have also been added to the CaseMap Persons spreadsheet. At this point, you can edit the full names and short names of the newly added documents and persons.

Outlook E-mail Linker

If you use the Outlook E-mail Linker, CaseMap will import the items directly into CaseMap but will not convert them to PDF format. When you use this utility, it will import all of the e-mails from a selected folder in Outlook, create a Document Object record in CaseMap for each e-mail, and link each e-mail back to Outlook. The utility also monitors the e-mails that have already been imported so that a user can run it repeatedly on the same folder and only import e-mails that have been added since the last time it was run. *Note: The Outlook E-mail Linker does not import e-mails into CaseMap (as it does when CaseMap converts e-mails to PDF format) and cannot import e-mails from Outlook Express.*

When you run this utility, the Import E-mails from Outlook Wizard, CaseMap provides an overview of the process. When you click Next, CaseMap displays the Outlook folders from which it can link e-mails. You can then select the folder(s) to link with CaseMap (Step 1).

You will then be prompted to select the Outlook fields you want to import (Step 2) and the corresponding fields in CaseMap to which the fields will be mapped. You can skip fields during this step but cannot map more than one Outlook field to a CaseMap field. CaseMap will then confirm the field mapping (Step 3). When you click Finish, CaseMap begins to create links with Outlook and displays the progress of the import.

When the import is completed, the files will be linked in their native format to CaseMap. Although the authors and recipients are listed on the Documents spreadsheet, they have not been added to the Persons spreadsheet, which you must do separately.

CaseMap Can Only Convert E-mails to PDF

CaseMap can only convert e-mail files to PDF format. If you select files that do not contain e-mail but instead contain other items, such as contacts, CaseMap will not be able to convert those items to PDF format.

Importing Issues from NoteMap

CaseMap makes it easy to import issues that have been created in NoteMap. In fact, it may be easier to create an issues outline in NoteMap because of how easy it is to arrange and rearrange information in the program. Once you have created the issues outline, including subissues, select the issue(s) you want to import into CaseMap and select Edit>Copy, the copy icon on the toolbar, or Ctrl+C.

Switch from NoteMap to CaseMap. Open the utility by clicking on File>Import>Issues from NoteMap. The Import NoteMap Issues Outline dialog appears and should contain all of the issues you selected in NoteMap. CaseMap then explains that (1) CaseMap will create a new issue with the same issue full name used in the NoteMap outline, (2) the text will be trimmed if it exceeds 255 characters, (3) although you can deselect issues that you do not want to import, you must select at least one issue to import, and (4) the imported issues will be added to the existing issues in the case and can be reordered after they are imported into CaseMap.

At this point, you would select the issues to import and click OK. A dialog appears, outlining the number of issues to be imported, and advises you that you cannot undo this operation. When you click Yes, CaseMap imports the issues into your case's Issues spreadsheet below the already existing issues. You can then reorder the issues or make any other necessary changes.

Analyzing, Searching and Preparing Reports of Case Data

4

Searching, also called "filtering" in CaseMap, is one of the most important case-analysis tools in the program, allowing you to locate specific types of information quickly. While the goal of CaseMap is to maintain a comprehensive database of all of the people, documents, and information involved in your case, that information is only as helpful as your ability to search and analyze the data. CaseMap makes searching for specific data and analyzing individual or large amounts of data very easy. In this chapter, we will discuss some of the ways to search and analyze your data as effectively as possible.

Searching and filtering are virtually identical in CaseMap, and you will use the same methods regardless of whether you perform a search or run a filter. Not only are the methods the same, but so are the results—you will be able to quickly view the records that meet your search criteria, perform additional analyses on the data, save your search options, and create reports containing the relevant information.

There are many ways to search your spreadsheets. You can simply right-click and perform an "instant search" on any data in your spreadsheet (see Figure 114). Or you can perform a guided search using the Search menu on the toolbar (see Figure 115). You can also use the Advanced Search pane, which is

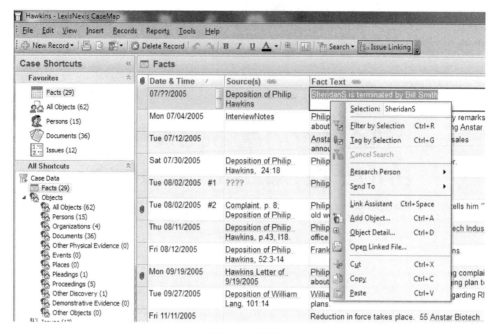

Figure 114

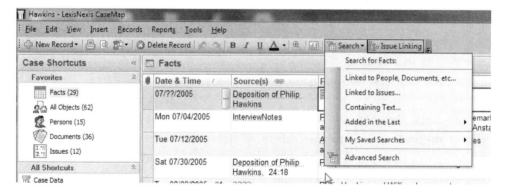

Figure 115

Saved Searches

When you save a search, you are saving the search criteria and not the results. Thus, if records are added to or deleted from your database, when you run the search again, you will see different results.

also available on the Search menu, to construct and save your searches and filters (see Figure 116).

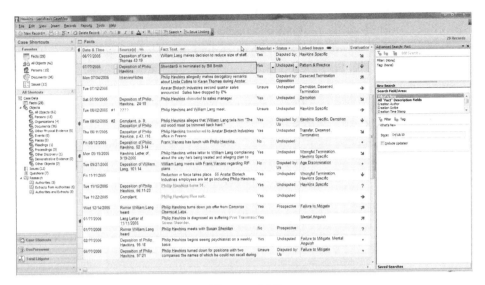

Figure 116

Basic Searches

There are two ways to perform a basic search in CaseMap. You can simply right-click in a cell on a spreadsheet in which you want to search, or you can use the Search feature on the main toolbar. When you right-click, CaseMap opens a menu, with four search-related options at the top of the menu. The first, Selection, allows you select any word, phrase, short name, or other entry and locate all of those records on the spreadsheet (see Figure 96). By default, the menu will enter the first short name or phrase in the cell in which you clicked as the search term. You can change this entry by typing in a new entry or by highlighting the word, short name, or phrase in the cell and right-clicking. After you have entered the correct search criteria, click on Filter by Selection, and CaseMap will perform the search. CaseMap instantly displays the results as a filtered spreadsheet. The navigation bar will display the number of records (Filtered: X of Y) at the top right of the spreadsheet, and a blue bar will appear telling you what the results display—e.g., Filter: Linked to Fact Text: "William Lang." You can then print your results (using the Print function), save the Search (using the Save button on the toolbar), or cancel the search by clicking on the Cancel Search button on the toolbar.

The other way to search is from the main toolbar, which includes a search feature. When you click on the Search button, you have a variety of options for how to search for information. The first, and most common, way to search is via Search for Facts. This basic search function also allows you to search for information linked to people, documents, issues, and any text, or information added within certain times; you can also perform advanced searches or re-run saved searches. If you select Search for Facts, you will have the option of searching for facts linked to people, documents, etc.; facts linked to issues; or facts containing certain text.

Thus, if you are on the Facts spreadsheet and search for facts linked to people, documents, etc., you will be shown a menu listing all of the persons, documents, or other items in your database (yet another reason to create an object for every person, etc. in your case) (see Figure 117). Then, all you have to do is select a name, such as Philip Hawkins, and click OK. The Search menu disappears, your results are displayed, and the navigation bar displays the current filter and the number of records found, as well as the total number of facts or records in the spreadsheet you search. For example, if you perform a

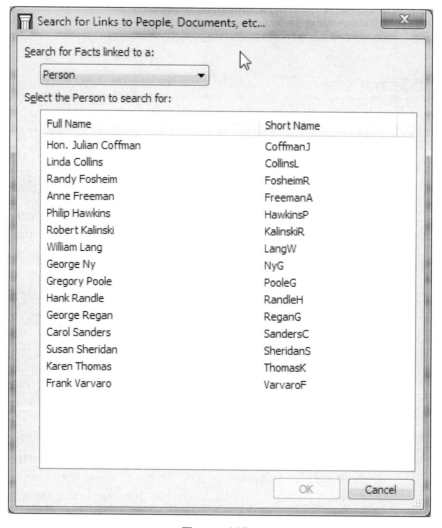

Figure 117

search for Philip Hawkins in the Hawkins case, the toolbar will indicate Filter: Linked to All Description Fields: "Philip Hawkins." To the right, the toolbar will show that twenty-four of the twenty-nine facts are linked to Philip Hawkins and will provide you with options to cancel or save the search so that you can perform it again at another time and view it along with any updated records.

Similarly, if you perform a search linked to issues, you will be asked to specify the particular issue that you are searching for. If you search for facts linked to a text, you are given the option of searching all of the description fields for the particular text or a particular field through the dropdown menu (see Figure 118). If, for example, you search for "outstanding" in all description fields in the Hawkins case, your results will show the one fact that contains that information.

When you use the "Added in the Last" search, you can quickly discover what information has been added to your database in the last day, week, month, or three months (see Figure 119). Because CaseMap tracks every record attached to every spreadsheet and timestamps each record, you can use the "Added in the Last" search to see what has been added most recently.

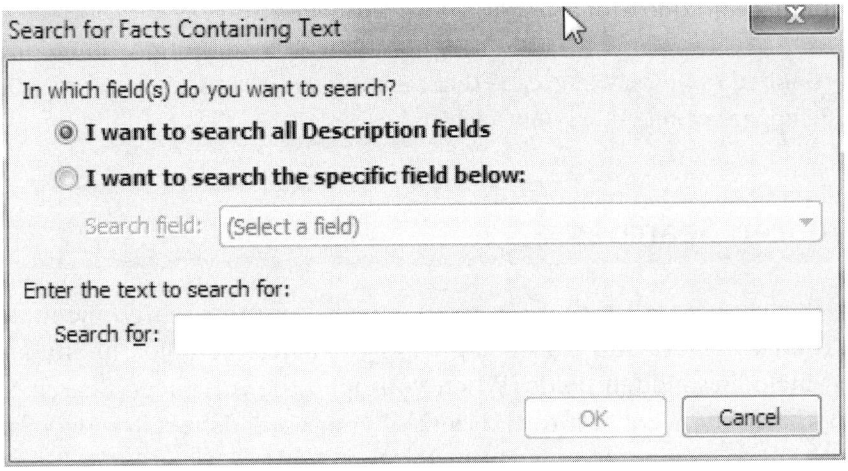

Figure 118

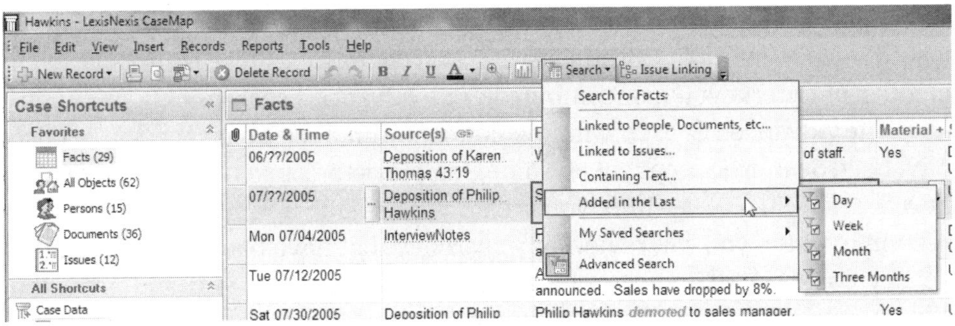

Figure 119

Performing an Advanced Search

When you perform an advanced search, CaseMap will search for information in the currently open spreadsheet. Thus, you must begin your advanced search while in the spreadsheet that you desire to search.

Let's begin an advanced search on the Facts spreadsheet for the Hawkins case. First, open the Advanced Search menu from the Search icon on the toolbar. Next, go to the New Search box, click on All Fact Descriptions, and type "sales" in the box, and then click on the Filter icon. Your results will appear in the spreadsheet, showing five facts containing the word *sales*. Next, go back to the text box and replace "sales" with "ABI" and click on the Filter icon. A dialog box appears, asking whether you want to add the results together (an "or" search), show only the common results (an "and" search), or discard the prior search and only display the results of the current search. Click on the middle option, the "and" search, and you should now have four results. If you hover your mouse over the toolbar that displays the Filter criteria, CaseMap displays the detailed criteria it used to perform this search.

To save this search, just click on the Save icon and tell CaseMap to save the filter. Name the search and you are done. If additional records are added to the Hawkins case that meet the criteria for this search, they will appear when you rerun the search.

Advanced Searches

The Advanced Search tool, which you access from the Search menu, allows you to create filters and tags using all of the available fields in any spreadsheet, including hidden fields. When you open the Advanced Search tool, a panel appears in a column to the right of your spreadsheet (see Figure 120). As with other columns, you can change the width of the column by placing your cursor between the spreadsheet and the Advanced Search panel and, when the icon appears, left-click to resize the panel. Although you can perform most searches from the Search menu, the Advanced Search panel allows you to include multiple criteria in your search; in fact, there is no limit to the number of criteria you can combine in one advanced search.

The Advanced Search window contains three sections: the top section, Advanced Search: [Spreadsheet Name], displays the current filter and tag; the New Search window is where you create your searches; and the Saved Search section is where you can review any searches that have been saved, including default CaseMap searches and any searches created by you and any other staff members. You can also rename and delete searches. Although CaseMap does not permit users to delete the What's New searches, you can delete

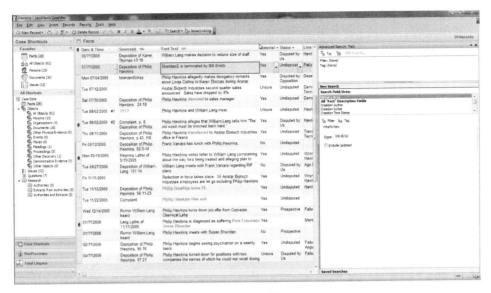

Figure 120

other default searches, although that is not recommended. In addition, if you wanted to perform an advanced search and tag records from a previously saved search, you can right-click on the current search and click Add to Tag and CaseMap will tag the records from your current search that also match the criteria from the saved search.

To perform an advanced search, click on Search>Advanced Search to open the Advanced Search panel. If your data are currently filtered from an existing search, the criteria will display in upper section of the panel. You may continue using those criteria or cancel the filter and start a new search. If no data are filtered, the upper panel will not display any criteria. Next, go to the New Search section and select the basis for your search under Search Field/Area. Select the criteria for your search, and the appropriate dialog will appear below. If, for example, you are searching facts or descriptions, you will be able to enter the relevant text and any limiting factors, such as "containing," "not containing," "equal," "not equal," "greater than," "less than," "greater than or equal to," or "less than or equal to." If your search involves other criteria, the appropriate data and filters, if relevant, will appear. Next,

"Containing" Searches

When using the "containing" option in a search, CaseMap searches whatever field you select for that particular pattern of letters or numbers. If you search the fact text for the word *leg*, the results will include the words *alleges*, *allegedly*, and *alleging*. Thus, analyze your search terms to obtain the best results.

click Filter, and the spreadsheet will display the filtered results. If your search produced no results, a message will appear advising you that you can click to cancel the search. You can also save, print, or cancel your search results, or you can add additional criteria.

When you add additional criteria, you follow the same procedure as above. When you tell CaseMap to perform the search, the Combining Two Searches dialog will appear. This dialog allows you to determine how CaseMap will display the results. The first option allows you to see any fields on the spreadsheet that contain one of the criteria (the "or" option). The second option displays fields that contain both elements (the "and" option). The third option ignores the prior search and displays only the results for the new search. After you perform these searches, the title bar on the spreadsheet will display the total number of entries on the spreadsheet and the number of filtered results. You can then send this information to Excel, TimeMap, or other programs by choosing the File> "Send to" option, or you can print the results or save the search for future reference.

To clear/cancel your search, click on the funnel with the red X (Cancel Filter) just below the Advanced Search title on the Advanced Search pane. If you wish to tag the records, you merely do so by clicking the Tag button. You have the ability to cancel tagging or filtering separately. If you cancel the filtering, the records that you tagged remain tagged.

Find vs. Filter

In CaseMap, the Find function, found at Edit>Find or Ctrl+F, is really what most programs call the Search function. In CaseMap, however, searching for all records that meet your "find" criteria is called "filtering," which is when the program displays only those spreadsheet rows that contain the data you are searching for. In essence, when you "find," you move from one record to another on a spreadsheet.

Filters and Tags: CaseWide

Filters and tags applied to the Facts spreadsheet affect the CaseWide graph. There is a one-to-one relationship between the facts displayed in the Fact spreadsheet and the facts displayed in CaseWide. Filters reduce the number of facts that are displayed in CaseWide. Tags do not reduce the number of facts displayed, but they transform CaseWide into a stacked bar chart in which each bar is divided into two sections—tagged and untagged.

When you filter data, you are actually telling the program to display only those records that match your search criteria—i.e., CaseMap hides the records that do not meet your search parameters. In most cases, you will use the Filter function, which is also more accessible because you can access it using the right-click Instant Search menu (see Figure 121). When you perform a right-click search, all you have to do is enter the information you are searching for in the Selection box and click Filter by Selection or Tag by Selection. In addition, you can also use the Search functions on the toolbar. Remember that when you run a filter it will also change the information shown in CaseWide, reducing the facts on display.

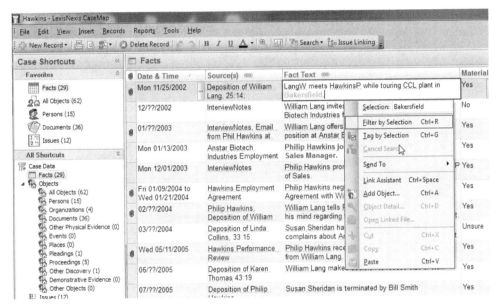

Figure 121

Tagging

Tagging is the process by which CaseMap marks records with an icon that confirms that those records meet whatever criteria you specify. Tags are run in the same manner as filters and can be run by right-clicking to access

Tagging

Tagging does not remove records from view. Rather, it marks the records that meet the tagging criteria with a horizontal red icon. The Tag icon makes items that meet your criteria easy to spot as you scroll through your spreadsheet or work with printed reports.

CaseMap's Instant Search feature, through the Search feature, or via the Advanced Search panel.

The tag icon—a horizontal red bar—marks those items that meet the criteria so that they are viewable as you scroll through a spreadsheet or work with printed reports (see Figure 122). When you tag selections, a second column appears on your spreadsheet (to the right of the column containing the linked item paperclip), and CaseMap will continue to display the entire spreadsheet. If you combine a tag with a filter, however, CaseMap will display only the results that meet the filter criteria along with any tagged results from the tag search.

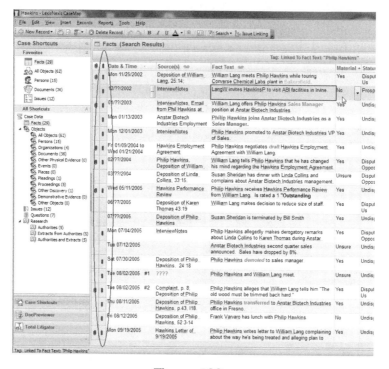

Figure 122

AND versus OR

When analyzing case data, one of the issues that frequently arises is the need to include more than one criterion in a search/filter. The key to narrowing your filters is to determine whether to use AND or OR when specifying the criteria for the filter.

If you perform a search/filter for Philip Hawkins, for example, and decide that you also want to perform a search/filter for William Lang, you would first filter for Philip Hawkins. When you add William Lang as a criterion, CaseMap will give you the option of combining the two searches or using only the latter criteria (William Lang AND Philip Hawkins OR Philip Hawkins) (see Figure 123).

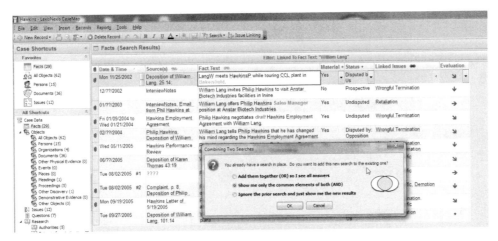

Figure 123

If you use the AND option (the middle of the three options provided in CaseMap), the report will only display the common elements of both queries—in other words, items that contain both items for which you have searched (or more if you have searched for more than two criteria). If you select the OR option, you will see results showing entries that contain either one of the items in your criteria.

You can continue to perform searches and determine which criteria should be added (AND) and which should be in the alternative (OR). If you display the Advanced Search bar (on the right side of your screen), CaseMap will display the criteria you have chosen and provide you with the opportunity to save the searches.

The Bates Analyzer

The Bates Analyzer, which performs various analyses on the Documents spreadsheet, examines the numbers in the Bates-Begin and Bates-End fields to discover any inconsistencies, duplications, or anomalies. The tabs on the Bates Analyzer dialogue box show a summary along with detailed information for the following categories: Invalid Documents (ones without a beginning or ending Bates numbers), Duplicate Documents, Duplicate Pages, Gaps, and Invalid Ranges. CaseMap will generate a report from this dialog box if you click Save Report on the bottom right of the box. If the Bates Analyzer discovers problems, you must manually correct those problems because the Bates Analyzer does not correct problems automatically.

You can access the Bates Analyzer by clicking on the DocPreviewer panel on the sidebar and selecting Analyze Bates Numbers (see Figure 124) or by going to Tools>Case Tools>Bates Analyzer (see Figure 125). The Bates Analyzer then examines the numbers in the Bates-Begin and Bates-End fields

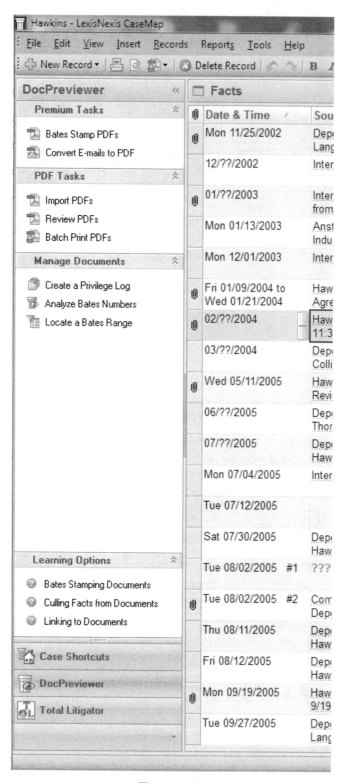

Figure 124

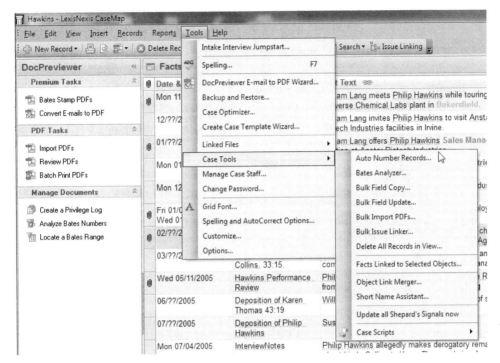

Figure 125

and performs several analyses to discover whether there are any inconsistencies or duplications. The results box displays a summary of the analysis, and the additional tabs (Summary, Invalid Documents, Duplicate Documents, Duplicate Pages, Gaps, and Valid Ranges) allow you to view the results in greater detail. You may also generate an HTML report displaying the results by clicking the Save Report button on the bottom right corner of the dialog box next to the Close button.

Reports

CaseMap's spreadsheets, which it calls "reports in waiting," and the ease and versatility with which you create them are at the core of the program. Because every spreadsheet is a "report in waiting," every view becomes a new report, without the need for any programming or advanced skills. In fact, all you have to do is click on the Print icon, or select File>Print, and your report is ready. Of course, you can also create PDF or HTML reports or customize your reports as much as necessary. In addition, CaseMap's ReportBooks feature allows you to create highly customized compilations of spreadsheets—replete with introductions, disclaimers, and other information—with just a few clicks of the mouse.

Create New (but Don't Delete) Standard ReportBooks

CaseMap includes eight default ReportBooks. Although users can modify or delete these ReportBooks, it is a better practice to create new ReportBooks, even if they are based on the defaults, rather than changing or deleting the originals. By creating additional ReportBooks, all users can continue to access the defaults, and other users who may prefer the defaults will still have access to them.

Simply put, CaseMap reports are printouts of some or all of the information in a case. All CaseMap reports are available on the Reports menu. Whenever you click the Print or Print Preview button on any spreadsheet (or from the File menu), you will immediately have a basic spreadsheet report for that spreadsheet, displaying all of the data from all of the columns and records on display in the current spreadsheet view. Every time you customize a spreadsheet (by inserting, removing, resizing, or rearranging fields), you have created a new custom report. Similarly, when you switch to a different spreadsheet, for all practical intents and purposes you are looking at a new report. To make your life even easier, CaseMap automatically creates and prints title pages for every spreadsheet report; you can, of course, modify or delete these features with ease.

Reports Menu

Found on the toolbar (see Figure 126), the Reports menu provides numerous ways to analyze data and determine the strengths and weaknesses of your case. The Reports menu has eight sections, plus a Help feature, to provide extensive versatility. Each subsection of the Reports menu also has various options. As with most other CaseMap printing features, you have many ways to modify reports, all done in a consistent manner throughout the program—i.e., when you learn how to customize one report, you have learned how to customize all of the reports.

Page Setup

Innocuously titled Page Setup, this CaseMap menu is one of the most important options to know when printing virtually everything in CaseMap. By using the Page Setup menu, you can customize every aspect of every report CaseMap generates. You can access the Page Setup menu from a variety of places in CaseMap, including from the Reports>Print or PDF Current View>Page Setup menus. Because many of the setup options are global—i.e., they apply casewide—it is easy to make casewide changes with just a few clicks of the mouse.

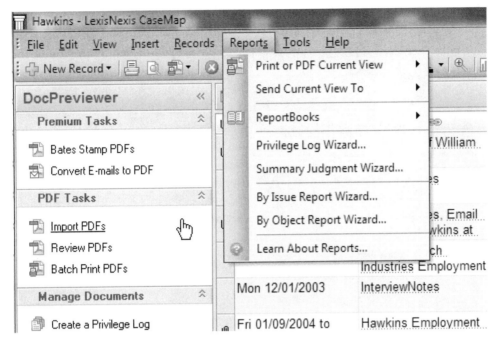

Figure 126

The Page Setup menu is separated into five separate tabs—Page, Report Options, Title Page, Title Page Into, and Case Options—each with numerous ways to customize your reports further (see Figure 109).

Limit Who Makes Changes to Report Title and Other Firmwide Pages

It is easy for users to make changes to the title page and other information on a report without fully realizing the impact of those changes. Because many report settings are case specific, it is recommended that only one or two users be permitted to or assigned the role of modifying report print settings; doing so will ensure consistency in your case and avoid unnecessary work revising changes made by other users.

Page Tab

The first Page Setup tab, Page (see Figure 127), allows you to specify the basic print setting for your report. These settings are spreadsheet specific— i.e., you must change them on each spreadsheet from which you are printing a report.

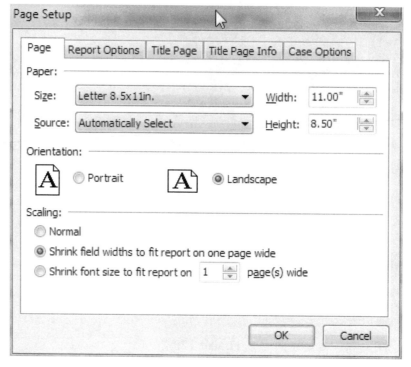

Figure 127

Paper

Size: Select the size of the paper on which you will print your report.

Source: Select the paper tray from which the paper will come.

Width and height: These settings display the size of the paper on which your report will print. If you change these settings, the entry on the Size menu will also change.

Orientation

By selecting the Portrait (vertical) or Landscape (horizontal) button, you specify in which direction your report will print. Because reports in CaseMap are "What you see is what you get" (WYSIWYG), it is generally the best practice to print reports with Landscape view so that all (or more) material will fit on one page.

Scaling

"Scaling" allows you to specify how text will appear when printed. CaseMap offers three scaling options. Generally, when possible, most users prefer to use the Normal scaling option.

Normal: When you select Normal, CaseMap will print your report with the same font that appears on the spreadsheet.

"Shrink field width to fit report on one page wide": With this option, CaseMap reduces the width of some or all of the fields in your spreadsheet so that all of the contents appear on one page; often, because of how CaseMap shrinks the fields, only a limited amount of information will appear on any particular page. Thus, because the printed cells may be very long and narrow, this report may be difficult to review and is not particularly user-friendly.

"Shrink font size to fit report on XXX page(s) wide": This setting will result in your report being printed on one (or more) pages based on the number you enter in the dialog box: CaseMap will reduce the report's font size so that all of the contents fits into the number of pages specified. While this setting may seem desirable, many users who try to shrink reports to one page learn that the resulting report prints with such a small font that it is difficult to read.

Report Options Tab

While the Page tab addresses more of the mechanical functions of printing a report, the second tab, Report Options, allows you to customize how a particular report will appear when printed (see Figure 128). Divided into three

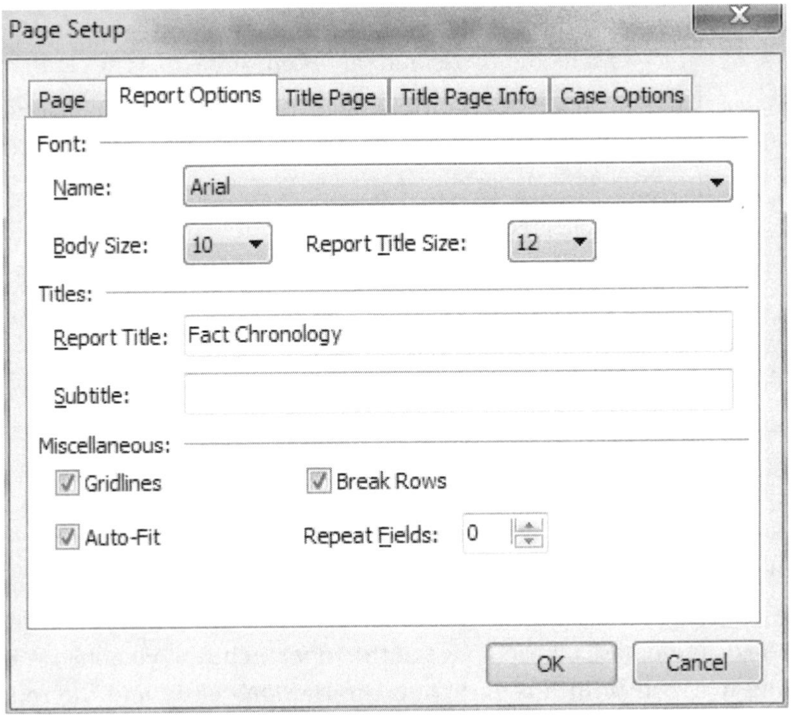

Figure 128

sections—Font, Titles, Miscellaneous—this tab allows you to customize reports so that they do not necessarily appear in the default WYSIWYG style.

Font

In this section, you select the font to be used in the printed report (Name), as well as the font size in the body (Body Size) and title areas (Report Title Size) of the report. These settings are spreadsheet specific—i.e., you must change them on each spreadsheet from which you are printing a report.

Titles

Report title: In this dialog, you specify the title that will appear on the printed report. By default, CaseMap will insert a default name into this field.

Subtitle: Although this section is blank by default, you may add information that will appear as a subtitle on the printed report. Thus, for example, you may wish to include information such as the person or company for whom you prepared the report, the date of the report, or any other information that would be helpful to the person viewing the report.

Miscellaneous

This section allows users to determine how certain aspects of the report will either appear or print. Each of the three settings—Gridlines, Break Rows, Auto-Fit—is selected by default, and Repeat Fields is set at 0.

Gridlines: When selected, the gridlines—i.e., the lines between the various fields on a spreadsheet—appear on your reports. Generally, it is easier to read reports with the gridlines present.

Break Rows: When selected, CaseMap will split the contents of any field that is too large to fit on one printed page—e.g., fields that start toward the bottom of a page and are continued onto the next page. If you uncheck this box, CaseMap will not split any cells, and you may see large amounts of blank space on your reports.

Auto-Fit: When you select Auto-Fit, CaseMap adjusts the contents of each cell so that it appears on the printed report. When you uncheck this option, CaseMap reports will only print the information that can fit in the display area—i.e., data will generally be truncated. In most cases, you should not change this setting.

Repeat Fields: When selected, CaseMap will reprint the number of specified fields (columns) on each page of the report. Thus, if you change this setting to 1 and print a report from the Hawkins case, and the report does not fit on one page, the first column—i.e., the date column—will be printed on every page. The setting specifies the number of columns (counting from the left) that will be printed, not the "number" of the column on the spreadsheet.

Title Page Tab

The Title Page tab allows you to specify whether your report will include a title page and, if so, the information that will appear on the page and how it will appear (see Figure 129). This tab includes a Preview button, which you can click and instantly preview your report's title page, and is divided into two sections: Report Settings and Case Settings. The Case Settings you select will apply to all reports in your case.

Report Settings

In the Report Settings, the only non–case-specific settings on this tab, you specify whether your report will include a title page. In other words, if you do not want a title page and only want to display the content, you should uncheck this box.

Case Settings (apply to all reports in this case)

Using these dialogs, you determine what information will appear in your case reports and how they will appear.

Orientation: In this dialog, you specify whether the title page will be displayed (oriented) in the same direction as the content of the reports.

Vertical Alignment: This is where you determine where the title information for a report will appear on the cover page in relation to any logos and other graphics at the top and bottom of the pages.

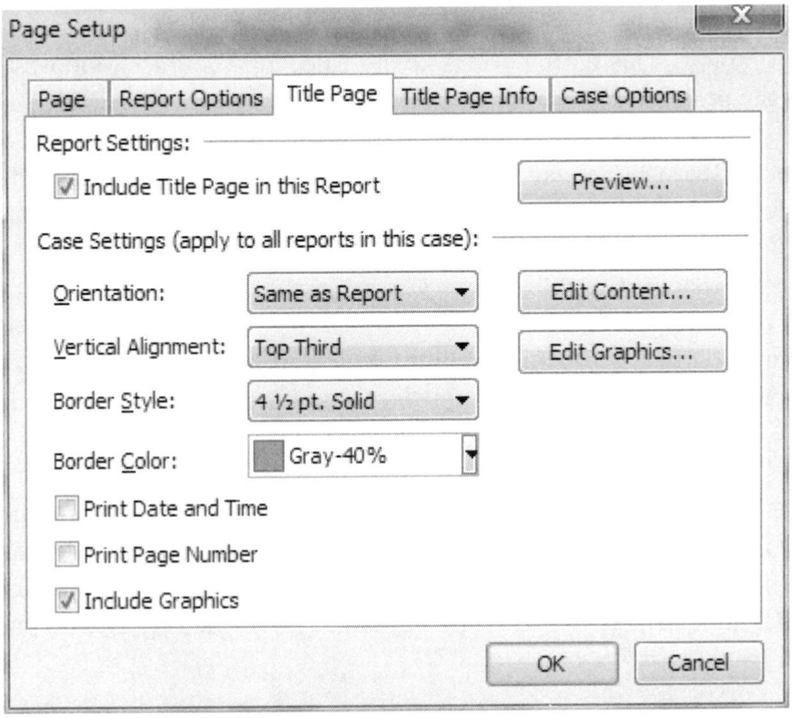

Figure 129

Border Style: In this dialog, you specify the type of border (or none, if you so choose) that appears on the border of the report's cover page (or none, if you so select).

Border Color: This is where you choose the color of the border you selected in the Border Style dialog.

Print Date and Time: Check this box if you want the date and time you created the report to appear in the upper right-hand corner of the title page. If you do not want the date and time to appear in the main section of the title page, you must change this setting after selecting the Edit Content button.

Print Page Number: Check this box if you want the page number to appear in the lower right-hand corner of the title page. If you do not want the page number to appear throughout the report, you must change this setting on the Case Options tab of the Page Setup dialog.

Include Graphics: By unchecking this box, CaseMap will not print any graphics that have been added to the title page through the edit graphics dialog on the title page; rather, CaseMap will only include text on the page.

Edit Content: When you select this dialog, you will see the Reports Title Page Content window, which allows you to customize the design, such as the fonts and other appearance-related aspects, and contents of the title page. This dialog also has an Insert Field menu that permits you to insert certain case-related information onto the title page.

Edit Graphics: This button brings up the Title Page Graphics window. The first tab provides a preview of how graphics will appear on the title page. The second tab, Header Graphic, allows you to remove or load (add) graphics that will appear above the text on the title page; this is where you would include a firm logo, for example. This is where you can specify the position (location on the page) and size of the graphic. Finally, the third tab, Footer Graphic, allows you to remove or load (add) graphics that appear at the bottom of the title page below the text on the page; this is also where you would include a firm logo, for example. You can set the position (location on the page) and size of the graphic at this setting.

Title Page Info Tab

The Title Page Info tab allows you to specify the case and staff information that appears on the title page of your reports (see Figure 130). This tab is divided into Staff Member Information and Case Information sections. Changes made in these dialogs may appear in all of the report title pages for the case.

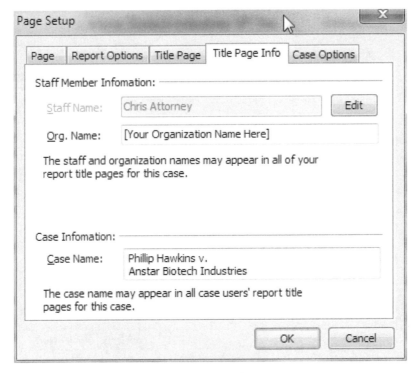

Figure 130

Staff Member Information

Staff Name: By default, the logged-in user's name is included in the Staff Name box on this tab. The dialog is "grayed out," however, because when you select Edit, CaseMap warns you that when you change the staff member's name in this dialog, you are changing it in the staff list. As a result, you should almost never change the staff member's name through this screen. If you want to change the name of the person whose name appears on the title page, or remove that information, you would do so by selecting Edit Content on the Title Page tab adjacent to the Title Page Info tab.

Org. Name: This is where you can change the name of the organization or law firm that appears on the title page of each report for the case.

Case Information

Case Name: This is where you can change the name of the case that appears in all report title pages for your case.

Case Options Tab

This section of the Page Setup menu determines whether the report title, subtitle, date and time, confidentiality statement, author names, and page numbers will appear in your printed report (see Figure 131).

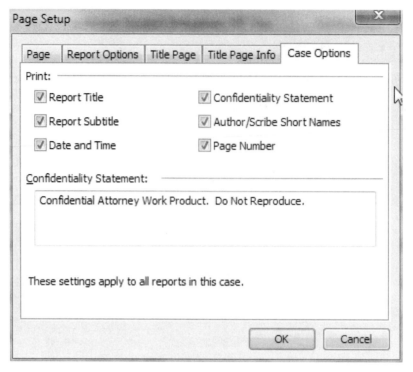

Figure 131

The Print section of this tab is where you specify which information will appear on printed reports for your case. Merely check or uncheck the various options:

Report Title
Report Subtitle
Date and Time
Confidentiality Statement
Author/Scribe Short Names
Page Number

In addition, you can modify the "confidentiality statement" that appears on all reports by entering your firm's information in the Confidentiality Statement section of this tab.

Print or PDF Current View

The first/top item on the Reports menu is the Print or PDF Current View menu (see Figure 132). This report—which is one users frequently print—allows you to print (or save in PDF format) whichever spreadsheet is on display at the time you select the report. As with all other reports for spreadsheets on

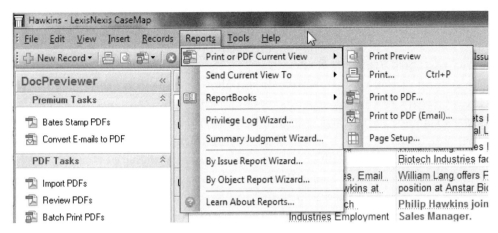

Figure 132

display, it is WYSIWYG. From the Print or PDF Current View menu, you have four print options and a Page Setup menu:

1. <u>Print Preview:</u> This option allows you to preview how the report will look, including the cover pages.
2. <u>Print:</u> This option brings up the Print dialog box (Ctrl+P), from which you can print the report, preview the report, convert the report into PDF format, or convert the report into HTML format.
3. <u>Print to PDF:</u> This option allows you to convert the report into PDF format using CaseMap's PDF conversion tool (you do not need a separate program to use this option).
4. <u>Print to PDF (E-mail):</u> This option allows you to convert your report into PDF format using CaseMap's PDF conversion tool and insert the report as an attachment to an e-mail created in your default e-mail program. The name of the spreadsheet (which is also the name of the report) is listed as the subject; CaseMap also includes instructions in the body of the e-mail (which you can change or delete) to assist the recipient in opening the report.

Always Use Print Preview

Regardless of which page format you choose with the Page Setup menu, you should always use Print Preview to see and confirm how your report will appear before printing it. By doing so, you can have greater comfort when printing your report, and can avoid wasting paper and toner on reports that you discard.

Finally, the Print or PDF Current View menu offers a link to the Page Setup menu, which you can also access from the Print Preview screen.

Send Current View to Reports

The second option on the Reports menu allows you to send the current view (the currently displayed spreadsheet, including any searches or filters) to LexisNexis TimeMap, LexisNexis NoteMap, Microsoft Word, Corel WordPerfect, Microsoft Excel, or a Web browser (in HTML format) (see Figure 133). These quick reports can be helpful in a variety of circumstances. For example, you could be writing a brief or a settlement memo and would like to include certain facts in your Word document, or you could be creating a timeline for a pretrial conference and would like to display the information in a TimeMap graphic. Because of CaseMap's WYSIWYG functionality, you can send any view easily and without concern about how the resulting information will be formatted.

In addition, reports created in Word, WordPerfect, HTML, or Excel can be utilized by anyone, even someone who does not own CaseMap. Thus, if you need to send information to an expert, consultant, client, etc., generally the best option is to send those reports in one of these formats. Another advantage of sending reports in Excel is that users can easily review and rearrange data, which they cannot do in HTML format.

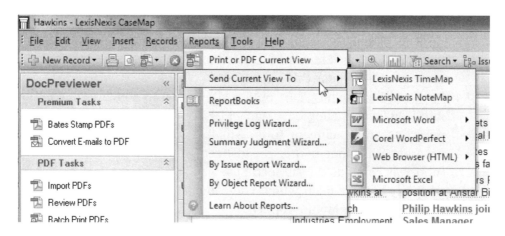

Figure 133

Send to TimeMap

To run this report, select Reports>Send Current View to>LexisNexis TimeMap. When you use the Send to TimeMap reports, CaseMap instantly sends the current spreadsheet view to TimeMap, provided it is installed on your computer. CaseMap also preserves the links to files in TimeMap, allowing you to click on the paper clip on the TimeMap fact to view the linked document.

Send to NoteMap (or Your Word Processor)

To run this report, select Reports>Send Current View to>LexisNexis NoteMap. The Send to NoteMap report is not well-named, because this utility allows you to copy information you specify and create an outline in NoteMap (if it is installed on your computer) or your word processor. These outlines can then be used in a variety of ways, including creating opening or closing statements and drafting chronologies for briefs or other documents.

When you use the Send to NoteMap report, CaseMap displays a list of all of the available fields on the spreadsheet so that you can select the field(s) to include in the parent field NoteMap. You will then see the Send to NoteMap Options dialog, which allows you to change the order of the "parent" note fields. Next, you will be asked to select the child fields to include in NoteMap; you can also reorder these fields. Finally, CaseMap displays another Send to NoteMap Options dialog, in which you select whether to include the field names for parent and child notes. By default, CaseMap includes the field names for child notes but not for the parents. When you click OK, CaseMap displays a dialog specifying the number of records that have been copied to the clipboard in outline format. Click OK and then open either NoteMap or a word processor and paste the results into the program. In NoteMap, the results will display in an outline form that you can easily change or rearrange; you can also revise the outline in your word processor, depending on the features of that program.

Send Current View to Word, Word Perfect, or Web Browser

To run this report, select Reports>Send Current View to> and select the desired program—i.e., Microsoft Word, Corel WordPerfect, or a Web browser (in HTML format). You must also decide whether to send the report in either grid view or record view. Although the resulting reports are identical in their content, they appear quite different when displayed or printed.

Grid view takes the information on the spreadsheet and turns it into a similarly appearing grid or spreadsheet in whichever program you choose. Thus, if you take the Facts spreadsheets and send it to grid view in HTML, it will look virtually identical to the spreadsheet in CaseMap. On the other hand, if you send it in "record view," it looks quite different because it creates a separate item for each entry within CaseMap.

Grid view is preferable when you need to perform a more detailed analysis of the information on a particular spreadsheet, whereas record review is better for conducting a record-by-record analysis. Thus, record view is a highly effective way of reviewing issue linking, status determinations (e.g., whether a fact is key or material), etc.

Send Current View to Excel

To run this report, select Reports>Send Current View to>Excel. When you use the Send to Excel report, CaseMap instantly sends the current spreadsheet view to a new Excel spreadsheet, from which you can easily manipulate the fields and review the data.

Other Report Wizards

CaseMap users have a variety of reports at their fingertips. While every spreadsheet is an instant report, the various Report Wizards offer users tremendous versatility when analyzing case data. Among the most popular features are the By Issue Report Wizard and the By Object Report Wizard.

By Issue Report Wizard

The By Issue Report Wizard allows users to create a report of case information organized by issues. Among the reports available are Facts Grouped By Issue, Documents Grouped By Issue, Witnesses Grouped By Issue, and Research Grouped By Issue. As with other CaseMap reports, these reports can be generated as Microsoft Word, Corel WordPerfect, or HTML documents.

When you open the By Issue Report Wizard and click Next, you can select the spreadsheet to use in a report. In essence, you will be able to choose any spreadsheet in the report but may only choose one spreadsheet at a time for the By Issue Report. If you choose CaseMap's default options, it will list every issue in the case along with a list of every object of the type specified linked to the issue. If no objects are linked to the issue, CaseMap's report will specify this.

On the other hand, if you elect to customize the By Issue Report, you can select which issues will be included in the report. You may also choose only to include the Issue field in the report or to include additional fields in the report. By default, when you choose the "Yes Include The Additional Fields And Customize" option, you will be able to add or remove visible fields in the report. As with other reports, the customize dialog allows you to move various fields up or down and to show or hide various fields in the report.

Similarly, when displaying linked fact fields, you can choose to show the fields in the current spreadsheet or to customize and select the fields that will display in the By Issue Report. Finally, you can specify whether the report should be sent to Microsoft Word or Corel WordPerfect or be presented in HTML format in a browser.

By Object Report Wizard

The By Object Report Wizard allows you to create a report of case information organized by links to people, documents, organizations, etc. The By Object Report can be generated in Microsoft Word, Corel WordPerfect, or HTML format. When you open the By Object Report Wizard, you can select one of four prebuilt reports or design a custom report. The four prebuilt reports are Facts Grouped by Document, Facts Grouped by Persons, Facts Grouped by Proceeding, or Documents Grouped by Person. By default, each of these reports will list the particular document and all facts linked to that document.

Remember, although documents and other objects can be linked to multiple facts, this report allows you to specifically analyze each object in a manner similar to clicking on the ellipses on the document spreadsheet. The reports, by default, are all similar in appearance and information. You also have the ability to customize that report to include only the name of the object in field in the report or to include additional fields. The types of fields to be included will vary based on the type of object. Thus, in a By Object Report field for documents, the fields will differ from a custom report by person.

The By Object Report Wizard also allows you to create a completely custom report. First, the Wizard will ask you on which type of objects spreadsheet it should base the report. The user then has the option of choosing all objects on a spreadsheet or only the objects with links. Thus, for example, you could create a report in which the proceedings spreadsheet is grouped by persons, etc.

Report of Facts Spreadsheet Report

The most popular report most users create is the Report of Facts Spreadsheet. This report is really just a printout of the Facts spreadsheet. You can generate the report from the Facts spreadsheet by clicking on the Print Preview icon, which will display report, which contains a cover page and your facts chronology. You can change the setup of the page, remove the cover page, and determine whether the report is being printed to PDF, HTML, or to a printer in your office. You can also verify whether all of the information can fit in an easy-to-read manner or whether it will extend beyond one page. To permit the report to fit onto one page, you can either hide columns or resize columns by narrowing certain columns, thereby lengthening the height of the rows of data.

The Page Setup option allows you to determine whether you want a title page in the report and to add information to the title page because, in essence, you are merely printing another report. In fact, you can print the Report of Facts Spreadsheet by going to Reports>Print or PDF Current View, and selecting one of the options. The other way to work with the Report of Facts Spreadsheet, as with any other spreadsheet report, is to use the "Reports>Send Current View to" command to have CaseMap send the current view to TimeMap, NoteMap, Microsoft Word, Corel WordPerfect, a Web browser view (HTML), or Microsoft Excel. When sending these reports or views, you will again have the option to select a grid view for the report (as it appears on the screen) or a record view, which will place one fact in after the other. For ease of viewing, grid view is generally preferred.

Use the By Issue Report to Prepare for Summary Judgment

To establish a claim, or to defend against a claim, lawyers need to know what facts exist to support or dispute a particular claim. As with the Summary Judgment Report, the Facts By Issue Report can be particularly helpful in analyzing your case. By running the By Issue Report Wizard, a lawyer can quickly analyze the state of the case, including whether additional discovery is necessary, etc. If the report demonstrates that no facts exist in the Hawkins case, for example, to support a claim for age discrimination, then the plaintiff's lawyer will know that he or she must determine whether any such facts exist. On the other hand, if defense counsel reviews the facts in a case and sees that there are numerous facts mustered by the plaintiffs to support a claim for age discrimination, then defense counsel should be mindful and prepare her defense or settlement strategy based on this knowledge. Of course, all of these reports are generated in a matter of seconds and provide tremendous insight into how a case has developed or is developing.

Summary Judgment Wizard

Summary judgment has become an extremely common tool in litigation both as an offensive tool (to seek dismissal or to preclude certain defenses) and as a defensive tool (to fight the dismissal of a case or the preclusion of evidence or issues in a case). When analyzing cases, lawyers have historically noted those facts that are important for purposes of summary judgment. Traditionally, they would do so by either writing them out or, in response to a motion for summary judgment, reviewing depositions, documents, etc., to ascertain which facts were material and either in dispute or undisputed, depending on which side of the summary judgment motion the lawyer was on.

By coding facts within CaseMap—and using the Summary Judgment Report Wizard—you can save tremendous amounts of time and create reports that make preparation of either the motion or the response to the motion easier and far more thorough. It is very difficult and time-consuming to review transcripts and other documents to locate the facts needed for purposes of a motion for summary judgment. On the other hand, by coding those facts appropriately in CaseMap, your ability to use those facts is literally instant. The time saved, the efficiency gained, and the benefits to clients are enormous. In fact, preparing one case and responding to one motion for summary judgment, or preparing just one motion for summary judgment on behalf of a client, can easily save more time and provide a far better result, thereby paying for the entire CaseMap suite in one case.

The Summary Judgment Report creates a report that organizes your facts by issues to prepare or defend against a motion for summary judgment. Summary judgment reports can be generated as Microsoft Word, Corel Word-Perfect, or HTML documents. To create a summary judgment report, a user must, when analyzing facts, determine which facts are material, whether each fact is disputed by the opposition or disputed by "us," or whether the fact is "prospective," "undisputed," or "unsure."

The Summary Judgment Wizard generates a report that shows all of the facts that are disputed or undisputed—doing so in a format that can be instantly used as either a reference or as a table within the motion or response. To create this report by any other means would take many extra hours and would not necessarily provide as comprehensive a result. While, admittedly, the Summary Judgment Wizard requires information to be coded, so does the preparation of any motion or response to a motion. By coding the facts in CaseMap when entered—rather than returning to do so later in a case (when dispositive motions are filed)—lawyers save significant time and effort.

The Summary Judgment Wizard is easy to use. First, click on Reports>Summary Judgment Wizard, and the Wizard opens. After viewing the introductory screen, click Next to view the Customize Report options. You may use CaseMap's default options or customize the report in any way you choose. By default, the Summary Judgment Wizard includes all issues. Similarly, the default setting for selecting facts is "undisputed," and the default fact layout is a table. If you desire to change any of those aspects of the report when using the Summary Judgment Wizard, you would choose "Yes, I Want To Customize The Report." If you choose the option of customizing the report, you will be able to check which issue or issues are included in the report. The

Summary Judgment Report: Facts Must Be Linked to Issues

The Summary Judgment Report is an extremely valuable tool for analyzing the strengths and weaknesses of a case. For this tool to be valuable, however, users *must* properly analyze the facts in a case, or relevant facts may not appear in the final report. To be included in the final report, each relevant fact must be linked to one or more issues. Facts that are not linked to issues will not appear in a Summary Judgment Report.

Similarly, facts that have not been analyzed and those not categorized as material (by checking the Material box) will not appear in the Summary Judgment Report. While it is not necessary to include or code every field for every fact, because so many cases involve motions for summary judgment, it is extremely important to consistently code those fields to ensure that all relevant facts appear in the final report.

Use the Summary Judgment Report for Case Analysis

Many users only utilize the Summary Judgment Report when preparing or responding to a motion for summary judgment. The Summary Judgment Report is far more versatile, however. In particular, the Summary Judgment Report allows lawyers to analyze a case at any stage to determine whether there are sufficient facts to warrant proceeding on a particular issue or to defend against a particular claim.

Thus, if a case is progressing and the lawyer wants to determine, as in the Hawkins case, whether there is any evidence of wrongful termination, the lawyer could simply create a Summary Judgment Report on the issue of wrongful termination. If the lawyer represented the plaintiff, the lawyer would run that report seeking all undisputed material facts as to the issue of wrongful termination. If, in fact, none or very few facts appear on the report, then the lawyer knows that there are either minimal facts necessary to support the claim or that the lawyer must conduct further discovery to verify whether there is a sufficient factual basis to proceed on that claim. Conversely, counsel for the defendants could look at the same issue and analyze whether there are any or sufficient facts to dispute the plaintiff's claim for wrongful termination.

Consequently, it can be good practice to run the Summary Judgment Report periodically—and well before motions are filed—to gain yet another perspective on the strengths and weaknesses of a case. In essence, the Summary Judgment Wizard provides the opportunity to analyze a case at any step for the issues and facts critical to either the prosecution or defense of a claim.

Summary Judgment Wizard also allows you to select all issues or limit the report to specific issues. After you click Next, the Wizard will produce a list of the facts that are either disputed, disputed by opposition, disputed by us, prospective, undisputed, unsure, or none of the above. By choosing "none" as the filter for either status or material, you essentially display a list of all facts, regardless of the categorization of that particular filter.

Thus, to create a Summary Judgment Report of disputed facts, regardless whether they have been deemed "material," you would code the status as "disputed," etc., while leaving the material filter set to "none." On the other hand, by selecting only those facts that are material and either disputed, undisputed, etc., you can dramatically narrow the information produced in a Summary Judgment Report. By using the default options for the Summary Judgment Report, all you see are undisputed facts for each issue in a case, without regard to whether the facts are deemed "material."

In the final report, if the facts are listed in a table format, you can insert the resulting table directly. By arranging the facts in a list format, you can more easily convert those facts into a narrative form. Either style can be effective and thorough depending on the type of motion and the judge before whom the motion is being presented. Also, if an issue is listed on the report and there are no facts coded appropriately for that issue, the report will advise you. This becomes very important when analyzing a case because it is extremely helpful to know when you have little or no evidentiary support for an issue.

Printing a Spreadsheet

Every spreadsheet can be transformed into a report by simply printing it. In fact, as you customize the format of your spreadsheets you are also customizing the way the spreadsheets will appear when you print them, because printing in CaseMap is WYSIWYG. Thus, when you change from one spreadsheet to another, or customize the appearance of a spreadsheet, you are in actuality creating a new "instant" report.

To print a spreadsheet, simply arrange the spreadsheet the way you want it to look when printed—e.g., add or remove fields, change the width of various fields, rearrange columns, change fonts. Then, either click the Print icon on the toolbar, go to File>Print, or enter Ctrl+P to bring up the Print dialog box. This dialog box, the same one you will see when you print a report, offers numerous options for further customizing your print job. You can select a specific printer, preview your print job, or convert the report to a PDF or HTML format. In addition, if you select Page Setup, you will be presented with the same options you are given when printing a ReportBook. For example, you can specify which pages of the report will print, whether there will be a title page and its contents, and various other aspects of the report. (For more details, go to the Reports section).

Printing

Printing in CaseMap is "What you see is what you get." As you explore the program, you may wish to print certain screens to review the information. When you print (by clicking on the Print button), you will print exactly what information is displayed on your screen. As a result, if you display many columns on your screen, you will print information that may run onto more than one page. On the other hand, you may wish to hide information so that when you print you will be able to include all of the information as it appears on the spreadsheet in a format that is easier to read.

PDF Printing

CaseMap includes its own PDF printer. Thus, although you will need Adobe Acrobat Standard or Professional to use the DocPreviewer, you do not need those programs to convert any report to PDF format.

To print a spreadsheet or report as a PDF, click on the Print to PDF icon on the toolbar, which allows you to Print to PDF or Print to PDF (E-mail); these features are also available from the File menu on the Menu bar. When you use the Print to PDF option, CaseMap saves a copy of the report as a PDF file on your computer at whatever location you specify. If you select Print to PDF (E-mail), CaseMap will convert your spreadsheet report to a PDF and attach it to an e-mail from your default e-mail program. Then all you need to do is add the recipient's e-mail address and any message, click Send, and your report is on its way.

The CaseMap PDF printer works identically with ReportBooks.

HTML (Web Page) Printing

CaseMap also includes its own HTML (Web page) printer, which allows you to convert any report into a generic format that can be read with any Web browser. The Print to Web Pages option creates a series of HTML pages and also includes a First Page, Prior Page, Next Page, and Last Page navigation bar that makes it easy to browse through the report.

To print a spreadsheet or report as a Web site, click on the Print to Web Pages icon that you can add to your toolbar, which allows you to Print to Web Pages, Print to Web Pages (Zip), or Print to Web Pages (Zip and E-mail); these features are also available from the File menu on the Menu bar. When you use the Print to Web Pages option, CaseMap converts the report to an HTML format at whatever location on your computer you specify. If you select Print to Web Pages (Zip), CaseMap will condense the HTML report into one file that can be unzipped (expanded) using one of the many available zip/file compression programs. Finally, if you select Print to Web Pages (Zip and E-mail), CaseMap will convert your spreadsheet report to HTML format, zip the pages, and attach the zip file to an e-mail from your default e-mail program. Then all you need to do is add the recipient's e-mail address and any message, click Send, and your report is on its way.

The CaseMap Print to Web Pages printer works identically with ReportBooks. Plus, when you create HTML output from the ReportBooks, you will have the option of creating Web page reports in Grid View (horizontal) or Record View (vertical). You will also have the option to create Web page By-Issue reports and Summary Judgment reports.

Send to Features and Formats

CaseMap offers a variety of ways of sending information to other programs. Whether you are in the File>Send To menu (see Figure 134) or Reports>Send Current View To menu (see Figure 135), CaseMap offers you the opportunity

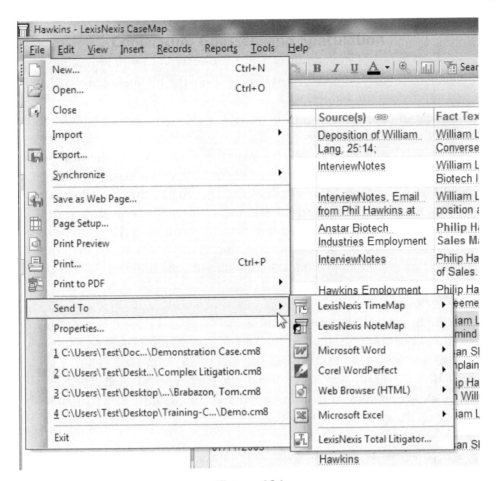

Figure 134

to take the information on your screen and use it in other programs. The Send To menu allows you to send a current spreadsheet or current highlighted record to various programs.

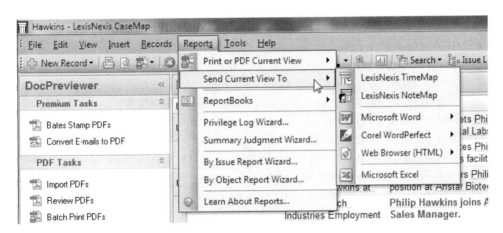

Figure 135

When you select the spreadsheet option, CaseMap will send the spreadsheet as displayed on the screen to the other program. Thus, if you have filtered facts, only the filtered facts will be sent when you choose to send a spreadsheet. If you choose Current Record, only the highlighted record will be sent.

CaseMap can send records to its sister products, TimeMap and NoteMap, as well as to Microsoft Word, Corel WordPerfect, a Web browser (HTML format), and Microsoft Excel. When sending records, you will have the opportunity to send them in a current Record View or a Grid View or another Record View. The Grid View displays the records in the same format as in CaseMap, whereas the Record View displays the items one after another. In addition, when you send items to NoteMap, you will have the option to select the fields to display in the parent note, and in any child notes, including the option to include the field names for the parent note and the child notes.

CaseWide

CaseWide is a graph/visual timeline of the facts in a case that provides you with the opportunity to explore the various ebbs and flows of case activity. CaseWide, which is accessed from the CaseWide icon (see Figure 136), displays a timeline/graph across the top of the Facts spreadsheet. The CaseWide graph can be adjusted so that its height takes up as little as a half an inch or as much as the entire Facts spreadsheet.

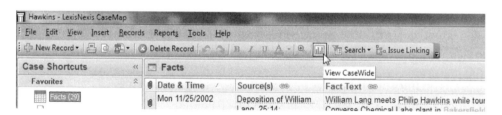

Figure 136

CaseWide fact graphs are displayed based on the current spreadsheet, including any filters. The earliest date of a fact in a spreadsheet would be the earliest date displayed in CaseWide, and the latest date of a fact would be the latest date displayed. If you right-click on a blank area on CaseWide, you can change the way you view the timeline from Year View to Month View to Day View (see Figure 137). You can also go to any specific date by selecting the Date navigator. If you want to display gridlines, click Gridlines on the right-click menu; to view averages, click Averages on the right-click menu.

CaseWide also allows you to "drill down to the facts" that any bar on the graph represents. If you place your cursor over a bar on the CaseWide bar, it will display the number of facts for that particular date, etc. If you right-click

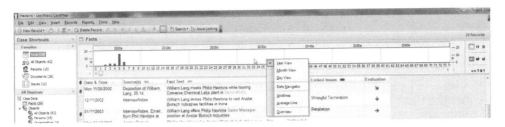

Figure 137

on any bar on the graph, you can view a new spreadsheet with only the facts for that bar by selecting Fact List. You can then print or export the results. If you select Scroll Facts from the menu, CaseMap will highlight the first fact on the spreadsheet that meets the bar's criteria.

The Y, M, and D icons on the right side of the CaseWide bar allow you to change their view of the facts by year, month, or date. In Year View, you can see over three decades of history without the need for scrolling. The CaseWide graph is recalculated as the fact sheet is refreshed. In Month View, the CaseWide graph displays a thirteenth month—represented by a "?"—known as a "fuzzy month," for facts with unusual date values. Similarly, in Day View, each month has an additional day, a "fuzzy day" for that value.

At the right of the main CaseWide graph is a separate chart with bars for facts with date values "to be determined," "not applicable," and "fully fuzzy" (i.e., ??/??/????). These bars, labeled "T," "N" and "?," respectively, scale independently from the bars in the principal CaseWide graph but do work in relation with each other. You can double-click or right-click on those bars, as you can with the CaseWide bar, to display the facts relevant to them.

Simple Filter Report

CaseMap's versatility is demonstrated by its ability to "instantly" create reports containing information. As outlined in Chapter 4, there are many ways to search for or to filter data. The easiest way to locate data is to create an "on the fly" report by going to the Facts spreadsheet and selecting a word, phrase, name (short name), or other item and right-clicking on that item.

When you right-click on an item, a dialog box will appear showing the selection (the item you have chosen to filter) and a wide range of choices. The dialog, for example, will allow you to send that information to another program, link the item, etc. within CaseMap or perform other functions. Most important, you can filter your chosen selection by highlighting the item, right-clicking, and selecting Filter by Selection, or Ctrl+R on your keyboard. CaseMap will immediately display the results of your search/filter. The top of the Facts spreadsheet will display the number of facts containing that filtered item and the number of total facts on the spreadsheet.

For example, if you filtered for Philip Hawkins on the original CaseMap training database, it would tell you that twenty-four out of twenty-nine facts related to him (see Figure 138). You could then simply click the Print Preview button to see a report containing just those facts. You could also customize the report and either print it, create a PDF, create an HTML file, or otherwise export the data or place them in a format to be reviewed either by your office or by another office. Within an individual filtered report, you could add additional filters.

Figure 138

ReportBooks

ReportBooks, the third item on the Reports menu, are the heart of CaseMap's reports. A ReportBook, which displays the most current data in your case, is a predefined but highly customizable compilation of various CaseMap reports, supplemented with optional features such as a cover page, a table of contents, and report-specific title pages. When you use the prebuilt ReportBooks that are included by default with every new case file, or build your own, or modify a prebuilt ReportBook, you can see a wide range of information in very simple form. In addition, you can create customized ReportBooks based on your own ReportBook Definitions.

To access the ReportBooks menu, select Reports>ReportBooks and then select from three ReportBooks options or the list of prebuilt ReportBooks CaseMap includes with every new case (see Figure 139). Every case can contain an unlimited number of definitions, and ReportBooks can be printed or converted into PDFs. Despite their flexibility, ReportBooks can be created quickly and will always be based on your selected ReportBook definitions and the most current data in your file.

It is easy to create a ReportBook, and you can create predefined ReportBooks in only three mouse clicks. In addition, you can print ReportBooks, convert them to PDF format, or convert them to HTML format. Every CaseMap case can contain an unlimited number of ReportBooks, which are automatically updated to include your most current case information every time you print one.

ReportBooks can be modified, renamed, deleted, copied, etc., although it is not recommended that you delete default reports. Managing ReportBooks

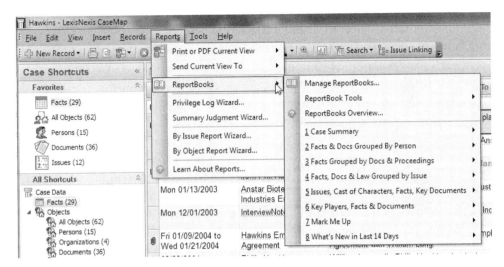

Figure 139

(in essence customizing them) is also simple. First, go to Reports>Report-Books>Manage ReportBooks (see Figure 140). From the Manage ReportBooks tab, you are offered a variety of options, which are essentially the same for every report. This dialog also provides you with the ability to review

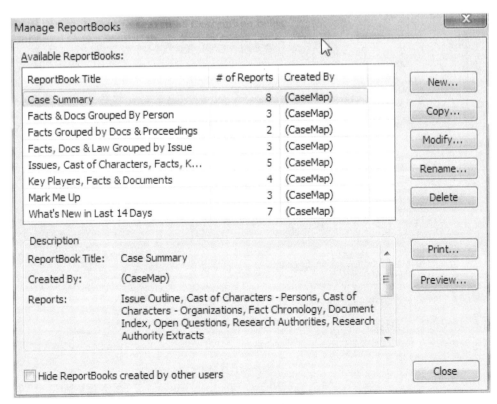

Figure 140

Eliminating CaseMap's "Folksy" Language

The dialogs and content provided with CaseMap are often somewhat folksy, using contractions, which many firms do not like. You can easily revise the ReportBook introduction content to change or eliminate those types of materials. Similarly, you can make other changes to include or exclude any other information you so desire.

ReportsBooks created by a particular user or to review the ReportBooks created by all users. At the bottom of the Manage ReportBooks screen is a check box that allows you to hide ReportBooks created by other users.

When you click on any ReportBook title, you will see the Customize ReportBook tab (see Figure 141). This tab is the same for each ReportBook, regardless of whether the ReportBook was created by CaseMap or by a particular user. The Customize ReportBooks dialog lists the name of the ReportBook being customized at the top of the box. From there, you select the options that will apply to the specific ReportBook, including the title page, confidentiality statement, the table of contents, introduction, reports (the specific items to be included in the ReportBook), and other options. You can also print a report directly from the Customize ReportBook dialog or preview the report before printing it.

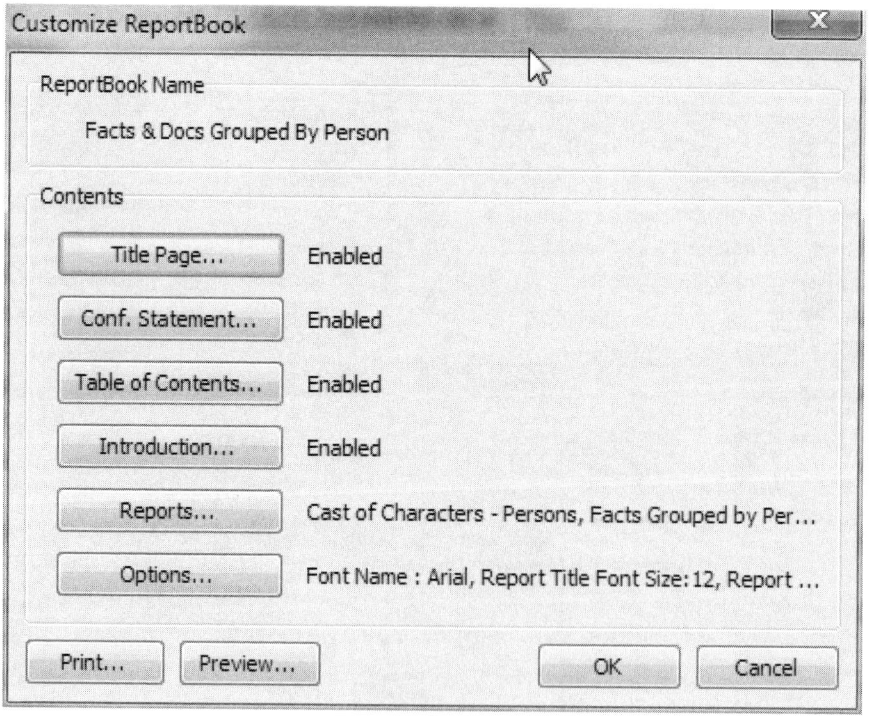

Figure 141

In addition to being completely customizable, the title page, confidentiality statement, table of contents, and introduction may also be enabled or disabled for any particular report (see Figure 142). As with other reports, when you click on the Title Page dialog box, for example, you have the option to "enable" it. If you uncheck that box, the title page, or the confidentiality statement, or the table of contents, or the introduction, will not be included in the final version of the ReportBook.

Similar to other report dialogs, the Edit ReportBook dialog allows you to specify the orientation, vertical alignment, borders style, and border color of ReportBooks, just as you can do from the Page Setup tabs. In fact, the Manage ReportBook customization options function virtually identically to the Print>Page Setup commands for reports. The difference, however, is that the Edit ReportBook dialogs also permit you to select options. There are two options for these various pages. If you check Save as Default, then a particular modification will be the default for all reports in a particular case. The Load Defaults option on the Options tab allows you to simply load a default title page or other page for the particular case.

The Edit ReportBook Confidentiality Statement permits users to edit the contents of the confidentiality statement included by default with CaseMap (see Figure 143). While this statement may be sufficient, users may enable or disable it and may also modify the contents and appearance of the confidentiality statement in any way they desire. This is particularly helpful because most law firms will develop their own confidentiality statements, which allows for a consistent confidentiality statement to be used throughout a firm.

The Table of Contents dialog determines whether contents of the ReportBook will be listed in the contents (see Figure 144). Generally speaking, it is helpful for users to retain the table of contents. The Introduction dialog for customizing the contents of a ReportBook permits your firm to edit not

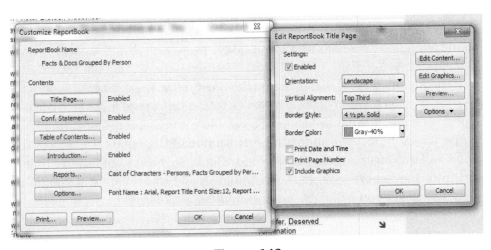

Figure 142

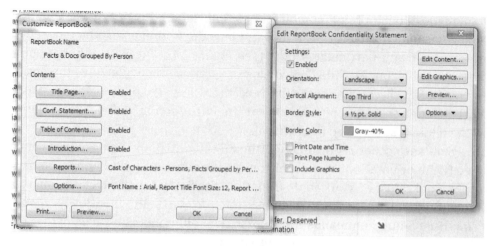

Figure 143

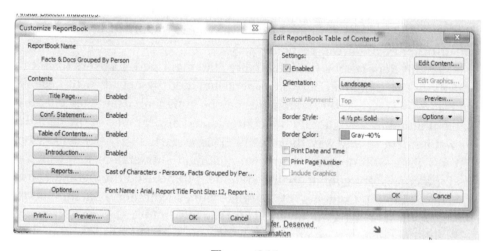

Figure 144

only the appearance of the introduction, but also the content (see Figure 145). As a result, it is generally a good practice to review and to consider modifying this introduction to reflect the information that your firm wants to include with your report.

The Reports tab or dialog within this Customize ReportBooks window allows you to select which of the various CaseMap reports to include in the final ReportBook and in what order (see Figure 146). When you deselect (uncheck) any particular report within the Reports section of the Customize dialog, that report will no longer appear in that ReportBook. This does not remove that report from the ReportBook, but merely allows you to exclude it if you so desired. Whenever you highlight a report in the available report sections for the Customize dialog, at the bottom you can view a description of the report along with any filters, sorts, or groupings that have been made. You can also double-click on any of the particular reports and edit the contents of those reports.

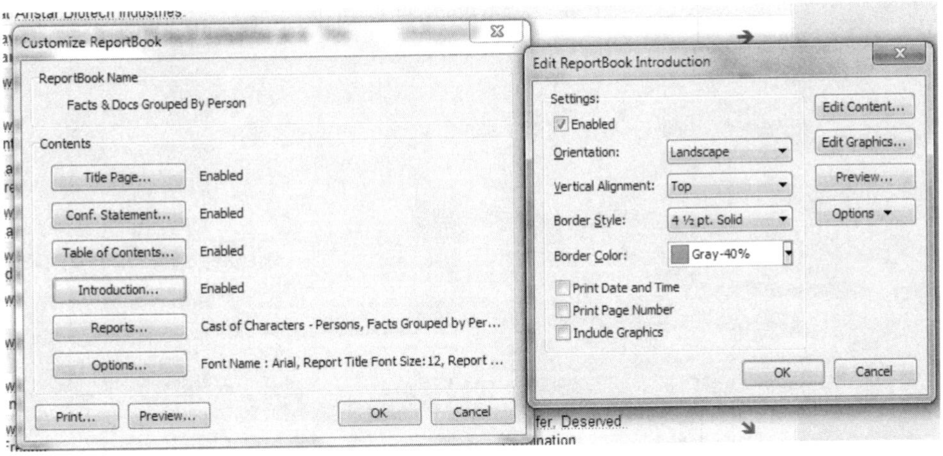

Figure 145

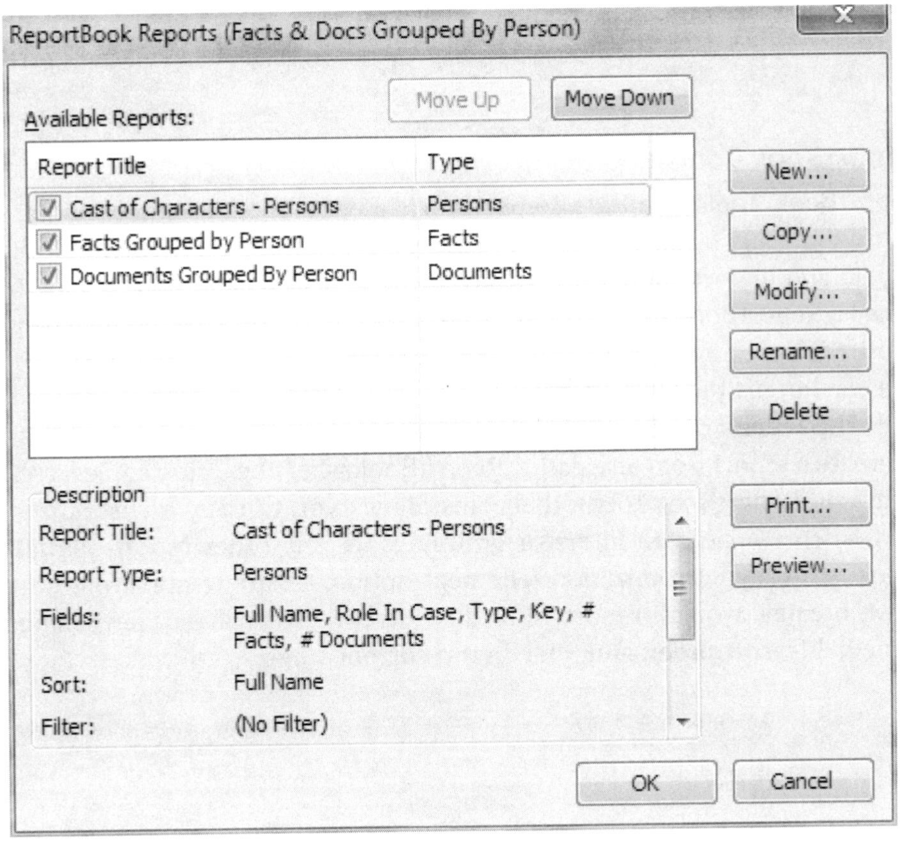

Figure 146

The Report>Options tab also permits you to customize the fonts for the reports (see Figure 147), as well as the types of paper, and other information to be included with ReportBooks for a particular case.

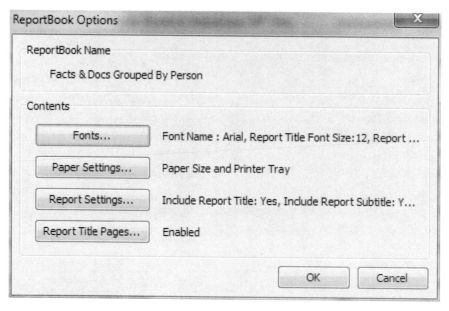

Figure 147

ReportBook Tools

ReportBook Tools (Reports>ReportBooks>ReportBook Tools) provide very quick shortcuts for managing ReportBooks (see Figure 148). The first option, Export and Import, allows you to save a ReportBook definition to a file or to e-mail a ReportBook definition to another CaseMap user so that it can be used in other cases. Similarly, by using the Import feature of the ReportBook Tool, you can import ReportBook definitions created in other cases.

The second option, Create Report from Existing ReportBook, allows you to create a report from an existing ReportBook—i.e., the utility copies a report from one ReportBook to another. This allows you to copy a customized report, such as one with filters or groupings, to any other report, permitting quick and easy customization. The next option, Create Report from Current View, creates a quick report from the current spreadsheet view, using the same fields, sort order, and filter as the current view.

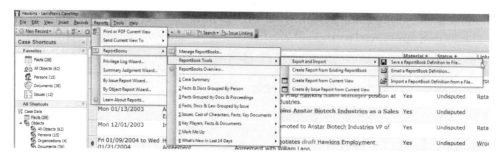

Figure 148

Finally, the Create By Issue Report from Current View creates a quick report from the current spreadsheet view, using the same fields, sort order, and filter as the current view. The report will be grouped by issue with default grouping options. In either case, the dialog will ask you to specify the ReportBook to which you want to add the report, along with a title for the new report. You will then specify in which location in the ReportBook where the report will appear.

ReportBooks Overview Report

The third option within the ReportBooks option of the Reports>ReportBooks menu is the ReportBooks Overview. This is merely a shortcut to the Help function for ReportBooks and does not create or modify any existing reports or ReportBooks.

The Various ReportBooks
Introduction

By default, CaseMap includes eight predetermined reports: Case Summary; Facts & Docs Grouped Like Persons; Facts Grouped By Docs & Proceedings; Facts, Docs & Law Grouped By Issue; Issues, Cast of Characters, Facts, Key Documents; Key Players, Facts & Documents; Mark Me Up; and What's New in Last 14 Days (see Figure 149). Each of these reports serves a particular function and, as with all other reports within CaseMap, can be completely customized for every case.

Each of the eight prebuilt ReportBooks (and any others that you create) offers you the ability to print the reports, preview the printed reports, save the printed reports in PDF format, or save and e-mail the reports in PDF format. Similarly, each of the prebuilt ReportBooks has a customize option that brings up the customize ReportBook dialog. From this dialog, you can quickly customize each aspect of any report, such as the title page, confidentiality statement, table of contents, and introduction.

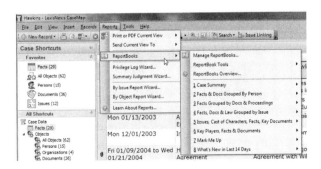

Figure 149

The Specific ReportBooks

The Case Summary ReportBook contains a report for every primary spreadsheet in CaseMap. By default, the reports appear in the following order: Issues; Cast of Characters—Persons; Cast of Characters—Organizations; Fact Chronology; Document Index; Open Questions; Research Authorities; and Research Authority Extracts. You may customize the appearance of the case summary, including the order in which the reports appear. As with every other ReportBook, by default, this ReportBook contains a statement of confidentiality, table of contents, and introduction.

The Facts & Docs Grouped By Person ReportBook lists all of the facts associated with every person listed in the cast of characters for whom there are linked facts. The Documents By Person ReportBook lists every document in the case in which each person is linked as an author, recipient, etc.

The Facts Grouped By Docs & Proceedings ReportBook contains a report for each fact to which documents or proceedings are linked. Similarly, the Facts, Docs & Law Grouped By Issue ReportBook contains reports for each fact, document, or authority that is linked to an issue in the case.

The Issues, Cast of Characters, Facts, Key Documents ReportBook creates a ReportBook containing each of these four reports. Key documents are those documents coded as "key" on the Objects–Documents spreadsheet. The Key Players, Facts & Documents ReportBook contains reports listing the key persons and organizations, the key facts, and key documents; each spreadsheet is based on those items coded as key on their respective spreadsheets.

The Mark Me Up ReportBook is one of the more versatile ReportBooks because you can send it to clients and others, and it can be of enormous assistance when analyzing a case. Whether used initially, after the Jumpstart Wizard, or later on in the case, the Mark Me Up ReportBook permits clients and other persons associated with the case to review the information contained in CaseMap and to provide comments, corrections etc. You can use Mark Me Up after meeting with your client and creating a cast of characters, document index, and fact chronology. Or you can use Mark Me Up after your case has been progressing for some time. Either way, the Mark Me Up ReportBook explains how a client can review the reports and assists you in understanding and preparing the case.

When you use Mark Me Up at the outset of a case, clients can review basic information. If you use it later in a case, clients can review the facts and issues you have developed (both positive and negative). Doing so also allows a client to fully appreciate a lawyer's analysis and recommendations because it provides a context that may be harder to understand or explain otherwise.

The final prebuilt ReportBook is What's New in the Last 14 Days, which lists all new records entered into a case during the fourteen days prior to the date on which the ReportBook is run. This report only includes new records and does not include modified or updated records.

Printing ReportBooks

Printing ReportBooks in CaseMap uses the same steps as printing other reports and spreadsheets. From the ReportBooks menu, you can select Print, Print Preview, Print to PDF, or Print and E-mail a PDF. The Print menu again allows you to print the ReportBook, preview it, convert it to a PDF, or convert it to HTML format, along with whatever other options your printer permits.

If you choose Print Preview, you will be given yet another opportunity to print the ReportBook or convert it to a PDF or HTML format. Print Preview also permits you to change the orientation of the report and make other minor changes.

If you choose to convert the ReportBook to PDF format, CaseMap will prompt you to name the PDF and to specify where it should be saved. Regardless, printing is easy and is WYSIWYG.

Customizing ReportBooks

Like CaseMap reports, ReportBooks are extremely easy to customize. First, select the ReportBook you want to customize. CaseMap will then display the Customize Report dialog, which allows you to customize every aspect of the ReportBooks. Although the dialog looks different from the Reports customization options, the dialog works the same.

The top section of the Customize ReportBook dialog displays the name of the ReportBook you are customizing. The Contents section is where you will customize every aspect of the ReportBook. Initially, you will note that you can enable or disable the use/insertion of the title page, confidentiality statement, table of contents, and introduction for every ReportBook. To do so, just click on the section's button and check or deselect the Enable box.

Assuming you intend to include one or more of these sections in your ReportBook, the customization dialog boxes are identical, although you cannot include graphics on the table of contents. Each of the dialogs on the left column allows you to specify the orientation (landscape or portrait) for that portion of the ReportBook, how it is aligned on the page, what border will accompany the section, and the color of the border. You can also specify whether CaseMap prints the date and time and/or page number and whether it should include a graphic on the page.

From the right column, you can edit the content of the pages, edit the graphics that appear, preview that section of the ReportBook, and (under Options) specify whether the current version of the ReportBook is the default for your firm, or whether you want to load the firm's default into your current case.

In the Reports section of the dialog, you can specify which reports will appear in the ReportBook and the order in which they will appear. From this dialog, you can also modify the features of any report (as you would with any report) and make various other changes to the ReportBook.

The Options menu allows you to modify the fonts, paper, and report settings and determine whether to display the title pages for the reports. In short, as with reports themselves, you can modify every aspect of the ReportBook so that it contains only the information you desire and in the format you desire.

Exporting and Importing ReportBooks

Because ReportBooks are so versatile, and you can devote significant effort to customizing them to appear exactly how your firm wishes, CaseMap makes exporting and importing ReportBook definitions very easy. To import or export ReportBook definitions, go to Reports>ReportBooks>ReportBook Tools>Export and Import and select whether you want to import ReportBook definitions or want to export ReportBook definitions (or export and e-mail the definitions) (see Figure 150).

If you choose to export ReportBook definitions, CaseMap will ask you to specify which ReportBook you want to export and where you want to save the file (in a proprietary format). That is all you have to do.

To import a ReportBook, use the same menu and choose "Import a ReportBook Definition from a File." A window will open and you can navigate to the folder in which the definitions file is saved. Select the file and click OK, and the file will be imported into CaseMap and named. It is ready to use.

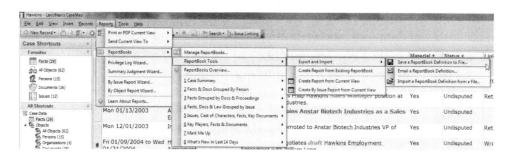

Figure 150

Privilege Log Wizard

The Privilege Log Wizard permits you to create a Privilege Log from the documents in CaseMap and to send the log to Microsoft Word. To create a privilege log, users go to Reports>Privilege Log Wizard. This will bring up the Welcome To The Privilege Log Wizard, which guides you through three steps: selecting the privilege types to include, selecting the document fields to in-

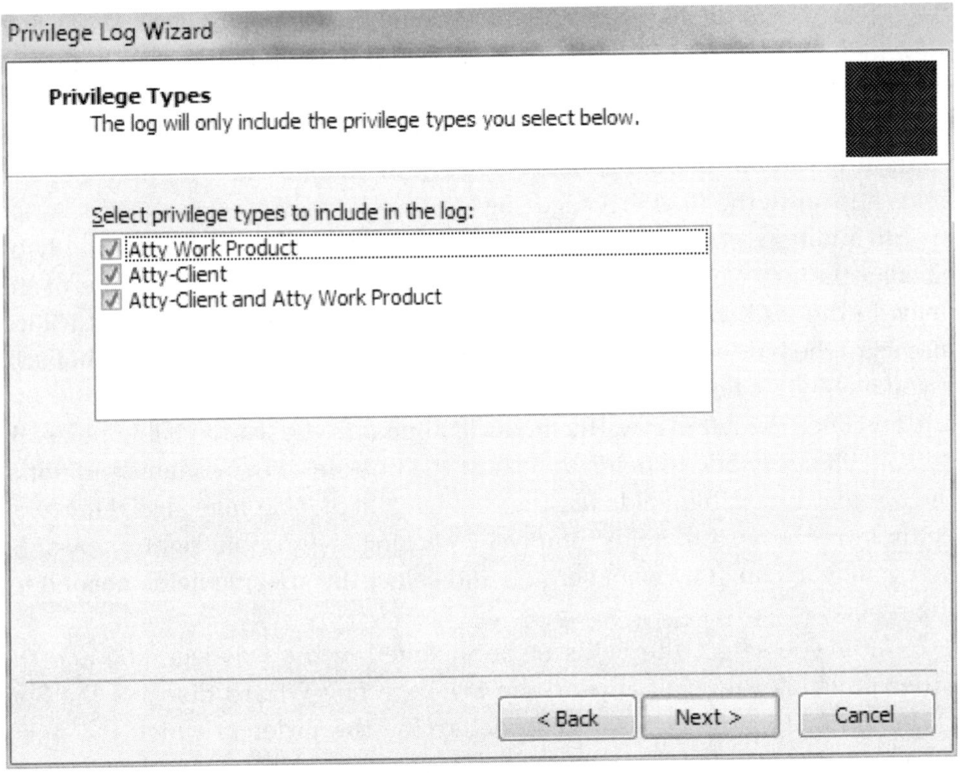

Figure 151

clude, and selecting the order in which the documents will appear in the log. After opening the Wizard, you will click Next to determine which types of privileged items will be included in the Privilege Log. These can include attorney work product, items protected by the attorney-client privilege, or items that are categorized as protected as both attorney-client work product and subject to the attorney-client privilege (see Figure 151).

After selecting which or all of the privilege types to include in the Privilege Log, you will select Next to bring up a list of document fields for each of the documents to be included in the Privilege Log (see Figure 152). You may

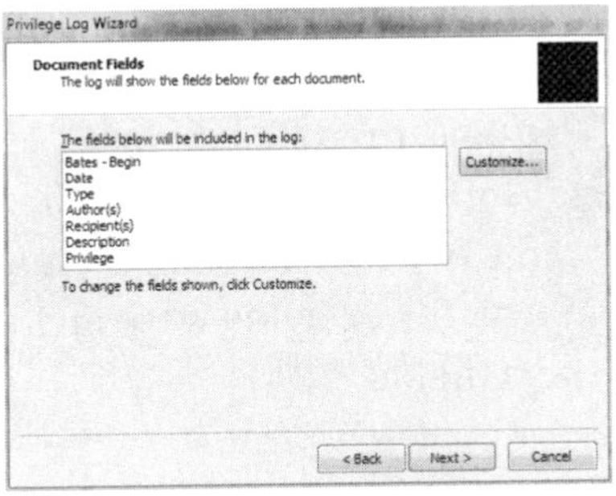

Figure 152

change the fields displayed simply by clicking Customize, and the Customize View menu will display. The left column lists the fields that will be visible in the report, and the right column lists the fields that will be hidden/not displayed in the final report. By highlighting any particular field and clicking the up or down arrow for visible fields, a user can change the order in which the fields appear in the final Privilege Log.

In addition, you can remove or add fields to the Privilege Log simply by clicking the left carat or right carat arrows. When you highlight one of the fields in the visible fields column, and click the right carat, the field will be moved to the hidden fields column and will not appear in the report. Similarly, if you highlight a field on the hidden fields column of the Customize View dialog, and click the left arrow, the field will appear in the list of visible fields. By default, all newly added fields appear at the bottom of the column and not at the spot in the visible fields list that is highlighted. You may also remove all fields from the visible fields simply by clicking the double right arrows. By doing so, you can start from scratch and select the specific fields needed for the report.

After you select the fields to be included in the Privilege Log and the order in which they will appear, the Privilege Log Wizard displays the Sort Order dialog, which allows you to determine the order in which the documents will be displayed. Documents appearing on a Privilege Log may be sorted by up to three criteria, which will be sorted in the order specified. By default, CaseMap sorts documents by the beginning Bates number of the document. By clicking on the Modify dialog box on the Sort Order portion of the Privilege Log Wizard, you can specify whether documents will be sorted by Bates number or by various other criteria, such as creation author, creation time stamp, exhibit number, etc. There are numerous possible initial sort functions, and the Privilege Log can generate the sort order in either ascending (A–Z) or descending (Z–A) order.

Of note, only fields that are displayed in the spreadsheet view may be used as a basis for sorting. If you want to use a field that is not in the view to sort it, you must add that field by right-clicking a field header and selecting Insert Fields. You cannot use the following special fields to sort views: Fact Text; Source(s), Description Fields, Question Text, Linked Issues For Facts, Linked Elements For Questions, and Link Summary. After you determine the sort order, you simply click Next and then Finish, and CaseMap will generate the Privilege Log and convert it into a Microsoft Word file. The final Privilege Log created in Word lists the name of the case, the date and time at which the Privilege Log was created, and whichever fields were included in the report by the user and the content of those fields.

Evaluation Fields

Evaluation Fields, denoted by the "+" sign, are used to (a) capture opinions concerning the information in a case, (b) analyze data and provide a better understanding of the strengths and weaknesses of a case, and (c) assist in determining which aspects of your case need bolstering or are particularly strong (see Figure 153). Evaluation fields can also be used to analyze how different members of your staff, or other people who are evaluating the case, view particular facts and information in comparison with others. Evaluation fields do not display text or provide specific information; rather, they display symbols that serve as shorthand for the text.

When CaseMap creates a new case, it only generates one evaluation field (criticality) on the Questions spreadsheet using the default set up. Prior versions of CaseMap created new evaluation fields (for us/against us) for every author added to the case staff. Although CaseMap no longer does so, it is highly recommended that you create evaluation fields for the Facts, Objects, and Issues spreadsheet for each case file. By creating multiple evaluation fields, you can compare evaluations by viewing the various staff evaluations in spreadsheet view or by using the Evaluation Comparison dialog box to more thoroughly analyze the similarities and differences among evaluations.

Another way to ensure that you have evaluation fields for all staff members is to create a template or to modify your office's default template to include evaluation fields for those staff members who regularly review cases. As with other custom fields, you may create as many evaluation fields as you need using the Field Properties dialog box (by either right-clicking any column title, selecting Insert Field and then New Field to access it, or by right-clicking any column title, selecting Field Properties and then the plus sign to add a new field). Evaluation fields can appear in spreadsheet views, in detail windows, and in the Evaluation Comparison dialog box. Evaluation fields are displayed as columns in spreadsheet views and as rows in detail windows.

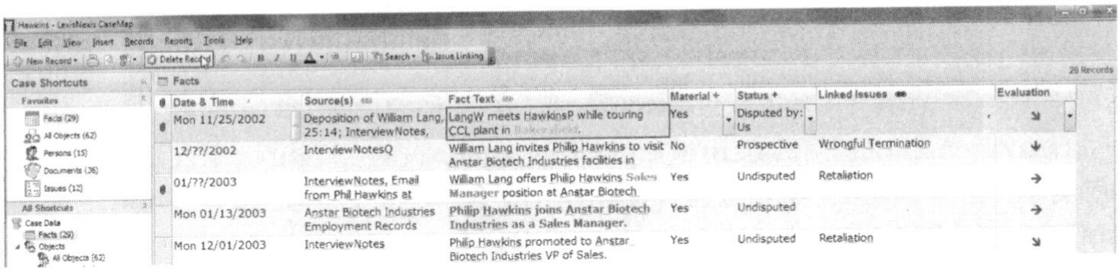

Figure 153

Issue Traits and Evaluation Field Features

Because issues are so central to analyzing your case, it is very important to understand the various issue-related fields and the objective information they contain. In addition, as with most spreadsheets, you can create other fields, although CaseMap's default options encompass most of the information you will need in virtually every case. CaseMap also sets up evaluation fields automatically for each author on a case. You can also create additional evaluation fields whenever necessary.

The following are some of the key issue, trait and evaluation fields:

Burden of Proof: Specifies the level of proof, such as beyond a reasonable doubt, associated with an issue.

Jury Instruction: The text of the jury instruction (proposed or as given to the jury) for the issue.

Legal Flag: This is used to denote whether the issue is a legal or nonlegal issue. For example, race in the O. J. Simpson murder case would be considered a nonlegal issue, whereas motive would be a legal issue.

Subject of MSJ Flag: Although not linked to Summary Judgment Wizard, this field is used to denote whether the issue is or may be the subject of a motion for summary judgment. By displaying this check box, your staff can be sure to focus on facts and other items relevant to the issue.

Key: This evaluation field allows a user to assess whether an issue is very important simply by placing a check in the box (you can check the box by double-clicking or by pressing the spacebar).

Evaluation Comparison Dialog

In the Evaluation Comparison dialog box, you simply choose two evaluation fields and compare their particular values. To evaluate any fact or other element of a case, click into the cell in the evaluation field. By clicking on the down arrow on the right side of the cell, you will see a list of possible values for that field. Then choose the value that represents your assessment for that field, and you are done.

In the Material field, for example, your choices are Yes, No, or Unsure (see Figure 154). In other fields, such as the Evaluation field, CaseMap uses a weight scale with the following values: Heavily for Us, For Us, Neutral, Against Us, Heavily Against Us, Unsure, and Unevaluated (see Figures 155 and 156). In fields such as Status, which is used for the Summary Judgment Report, your options are Disputed By: Us; Disputed By: Opposition; Prospective; Undisputed; and Unsure. You can also create your own evaluation fields and your own evaluation values.

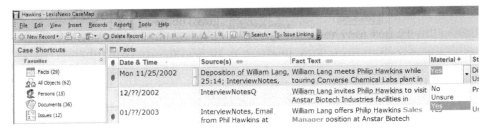

Figure 154

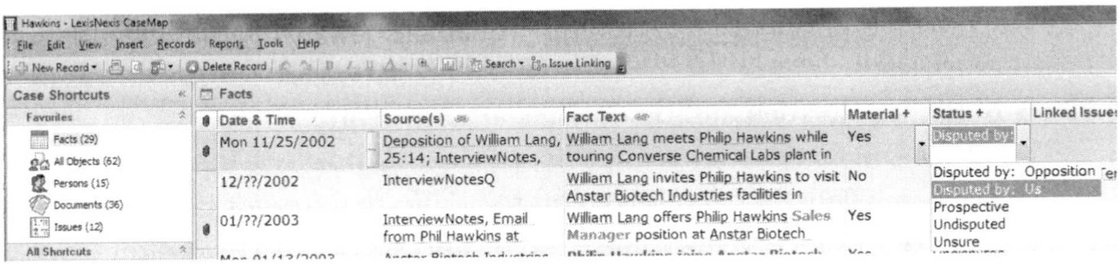

Figure 155

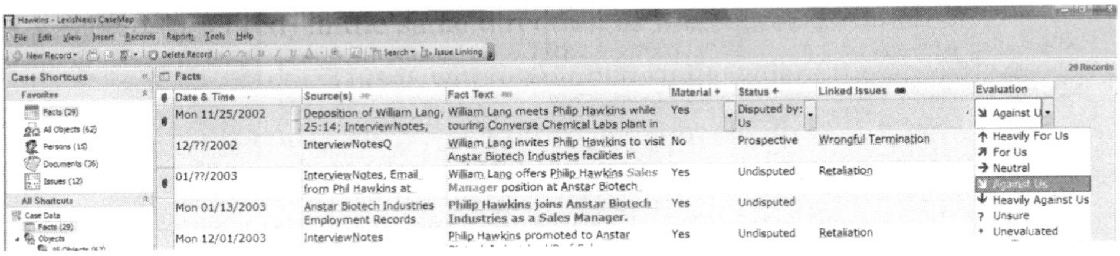

Figure 156

Although the meanings of the evaluation fields are fairly obvious, it is helpful to know how to use these fields for your cases and to discuss how your staff should evaluate the data to avoid misunderstandings and to ensure that evaluations are performed consistently.

Questions should be based on how important the question is to the overall assessment of a case and are evaluated using a criticality scale as follows: A–Extremely Critical, B–Very Critical, C–Critical, D–Not Very Critical, ?–Unsure, and ◆–Unevaluated.

Fact, Object, Issue, and Authority evaluations are based on a weight— i.e., Is it helpful? Can it help the case? Does it hurt the case?

Another advantage of evaluation fields is the ability to filter and tag spreadsheets based on the information in those fields. Doing so allows you to examine different fields and determine which data are most favorable or unfavorable or which data require additional examination. Filters based on evaluation fields can be combined with non-evaluation fields to allow you to refine your data further. To sort a spreadsheet based on an evaluation field, just right-click the title of the field and select either Sort Ascending or Sort Descending.

Evaluation Comparison

One of the advantages of creating evaluation fields for multiple users is the ability to compare individual evaluations. If you create a spreadsheet view that includes one or more of your evaluation fields, as well as those of other members of your staff, you will be able to see where evaluations agree and where they disagree. This same assessment can be performed using the Evaluation Comparison dialog box, which allows you to view a more detailed analysis of the similarities and disparities among evaluations.

To access the Evaluation Comparison dialog box, go to Records>Evaluation Comparison. This dialog allows you to evaluate different information relating to any fact, object, issue, question, or authority in a case. The process for using this dialogue box is identical for facts, objects, issues, and questions. Next, select the first evaluation field to be reviewed from the A list, and then select the evaluation field with which it will compared from the B list. Click Compare, and CaseMap will produce a comparison analysis displaying the results.

These results are displayed in a gridlike style, with the values of one evaluation in rows and the values of the second evaluation in columns. When the evaluations compared are identical, the cells appear in green (see Figure 157). Red cells denote those values that are most dissimilar. White fields do not have any values in them. From the results, you can click on any field containing a number to see the information on which that field is based. If you are running a filter, you can also base your evaluation on all of the evaluations or only on those elements that have been filtered.

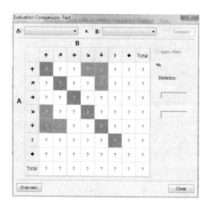

Figure 157

 # Fields

Throughout CaseMap, you will see numerous fields that contain the # (Links) icon. Links are connections between two elements in a case, such as the connection between a witness and a fact that mentions the witness. The # fields can appear as columns in your Facts, Objects, Issues, and Research Authorities spreadsheets, as well in Fact, Object, and Issue detail windows. As with all fields, you decide in which views to display the fields and the order in which they are placed. The # fields are not available on the Questions spreadsheet or in Question detail windows.

All # fields are read-only (users cannot change the information displayed) and typically begin with #, as in "# Facts." The # indicates the number of links (connections) between two elements (such as facts and persons) in a case. The # fields count the relationships between different types of elements in CaseMap and display the resulting count. For example, in the Hawkins case, there are eight facts and five undisputed facts linked to the issue of age discrimination.

The # fields allow you to analyze the connections between facts and issues, between facts and objects, and between objects and issues, as well as the connections between questions and facts, objects, and the issues that relate to the question. Each time you refresh a spreadsheet displaying a # field, CaseMap recounts the links and updates each cell.

There are two types of # fields: pure count fields (which CaseMap calls vanilla fields) and filtered count fields. A vanilla # field counts all the links between two elements in a case (e.g., five facts are linked to the issue of damages in the Hawkins case). On the other hand, a filtered # field counts only those links that meet certain criteria. For example, the # Undisputed Facts

The Difference Between # Facts and # Fact Text Fields

CaseMap has both a # Facts field and a # Fact Text field. Any object whose short name is mentioned in a Fact Text cell is included in the number listed in the # Fact Text field. The # Facts field includes all linkable description fields on the Facts spreadsheet. For example, if you add William Smith to the Hawkins case, and then add facts mentioning SmithW (his short name) to the Facts Text field, values would appear in both the # Facts and the # Facts Text columns on the Persons and All Objects spreadsheets. However, if you add SmithW to any field other than the Facts Text field on the Facts spreadsheet, the values would appear or increase only in the # Facts field.

Understanding a # Field with Zeros

In the Documents spreadsheet, individual document records have values for "Privileged and Reviewed," if you use those fields. If you insert the # Documents, # Privileged/Not Privileged, or # Documents Reviewed/Not Reviewed column into a spreadsheet in the Hawkins case, for example, the # Documents Reviewed/Not Reviewed field will display zeros. This is not an error. The only time that one of these fields will display a number is if you have referred to another document in a *description* field, such as Role in Case or Description—i.e., you have linked a document to a document. Thus, the values in # Documents, # Privileged/Not Privileged, and # Documents Reviewed/Not Reviewed provide values for linked documents and not the document record you have selected.

field, which counts the number of undisputed facts linked to an issue, is a filtered # field that is only displayed on the Issues spreadsheet.

By using the # fields, you can easily view the entries linked to that item. When you select a cell in a # field, the cell displays three ellipses at the right side. When you double-click the cell or click the ellipse symbol, CaseMap displays a spreadsheet listing the elements or sources that the # count represents. You can then print that spreadsheet or export it for further use. You can also filter the # fields using the filter tools built into CaseMap.

Case Tools

5

Case Tools, found on the Tools menu, are utilities that CaseMap performs that would otherwise have to be done individually/on a record-by-record basis. Previously known as "Case Scripts," Case Tools are essentially batch-processing utilities that perform many of the most popular CaseMap features. Many of these tools contain wizards to assist users with the particular tool.

Auto Number Records

The Auto Number Records (Tools>Case Tools>Auto Number Records) utility sequentially numbers the records in the current spreadsheet using a specified number and increment. You will need to have a number or text field in the spreadsheet before using this feature. You can use a text field and then use a prefix for the numbered records.

The Adobe Acrobat DocPreviewer

With the introduction of the DocPreviewer, CaseMap has dramatically improved its integration with the Standard or Professional versions of Adobe Acrobat; *the DocPreviewer does not work with the Adobe Reader or other PDF products.* Because so many litigation documents are now produced in PDF format, this feature is one of the most valuable in CaseMap. The DocPreviewer gives

> ### Limit the Information Sent to CaseMap
> ### from the DocPreviewer
> When sending facts to CaseMap, you should limit the amount of text
> you send to CaseMap. When you append text to your CaseMap fact, the
> entry can be lengthy. In other words, create proper CaseMap facts rather
> than relying on the text of the PDF that is the source of the information.

you the ability to Bates stamp individual PDFs or large groups of PDFs while
permitting you to select the format and style of the Bates numbers. CaseMap's
DocPreviewer also offers a wide range of other options, including the ability
to link and review documents quickly and easily without having to open and
close each document when going from one to the next.

Adobe users will notice that a toolbar (see Figure 158) and a menu bar
(see Figure 159) are added to Adobe Acrobat when CaseMap is installed (and
you have purchased the CaseMap DocPreviewer). From this menu item, you
have a variety of options, including Send PDF to CaseMap, Send Fact to
CaseMap, Edit CaseMap Document, Bates Stamping, Review PDFs, Send Multiple PDFs to CaseMap, and other features. In addition, CaseMap adds a toolbar to Adobe Acrobat (which can be hidden or displayed) that contains the
CaseMap DocPreviewer Tools, in addition to icons that allow you to perform
the same actions as those listed on the DocPreviewer menu.

Figure 158

Figure 159

Unlike other features in CaseMap, the Adobe Acrobat plug-in works directly from Adobe Acrobat rather than directly within CaseMap. Thus, if you use the Adobe features, you will use them while working in Adobe—*and your CaseMap database/case must be open.*

Initially, you will probably want to send and link PDFs to CaseMap. To do so, you will either select CaseMap DocPreviewer>Send Multiple PDFs to CaseMap on the DocPreviewer menu in Adobe Acrobat, or click on the CaseMap icon on the Adobe toolbar and select Send Multiple PDFs to CaseMap. When you select this feature, the Send PDFs to CaseMap utility appears. This utility adds a new record for each PDF that you send to CaseMap, but recognizes and excludes any PDFs that are already included in your CaseMap database. If the PDF has CaseMap or Adobe Acrobat Bates numbers, the utility will also update the linked records to include the Bates Number field. If there are multiple Bates numbers, the utility will not import them into CaseMap for that PDF. The utility will not work, however, with Adobe Acrobat packages or with secure PDFs.

After viewing the introductory dialog, you will be taken to a screen that allows you to either add individual files or folders. You click the appropriate button and select the appropriate files and or folders to include in your CaseMap database. When you select folders, CaseMap will process the folder and determine the number of PDFs to send to CaseMap. You can also highlight a particular file to have CaseMap remove it, or you can choose to remove all of the files from the utility if you have selected the wrong ones.

There is also a button that allows you to view a PDF in a PDF viewer or directly from the dialog box. After selecting the PDFs to send to CaseMap, you will be taken to a screen that lists any documents that cannot be processed. The screen explains why the documents cannot be processed; this dialog is helpful because it allows you to either correct the PDF, or prompts you to manually link the PDFs at another time. When you select Next, CaseMap brings up the name of the currently open case and asks which spreadsheet you want to import the PDFs into. Next, you will import your PDFs to the Documents spreadsheet. When you select Next, CaseMap will display mapping fields, from which you may select the appropriate information and map the fields. Generally, CaseMap can determine which fields are properly mapped to each other, including the number of pages, etc.

CaseMap also allows you to set the object short name to the PDF Bates-Begin number. If you deselect that feature, the object's short name will not be named based on the Bates number and will instead be named based on the document name. When you select Next from the Send PDF feature, CaseMap advises you if you are sending any e-mails to the Document spreadsheet, and advises you whether it has sufficient information to complete the import. You can choose either to customize the field mappings or to allow CaseMap to use

Splitting Documents with Adobe and the DocPreviewer

Generally, documents are produced in bulk, even electronically, and one file can contain numerous documents and subparts. While it is easy simply to link the one large document to CaseMap, this can make it difficult to find the specific page or record you need, especially when you are in a rush.

Instead, use Adobe's Extract Pages feature, found at Documents> Extract Pages, to simplify your efforts. First, make sure you are working in a *copy* of the originally produced document, not the original itself. Second, find the page or pages that constitute the specific discrete document that you want to link to CaseMap. Next, click on Document>Extract Pages and fill in the page range—e.g., pages 2 to 5—of the document you want to include in CaseMap. *Make sure Delete Pages After Extracting is selected/ checked*, and then click OK (see Figures 160 and 161).

Adobe will extract the pages as a separate document. Save the document with an appropriate name. You can then add it to your CaseMap database using the DocPreviewer or from the specific Fact or Object cell. After you have confirmed that the document is properly linked to CaseMap, save the original file without the extracted pages (by clicking Save). As you do this, you will reduce the number of pages in your original file until every relevant document is linked separately to CaseMap.

To get rid of unnecessary pages, just select Document>Delete Pages from the Adobe menu.

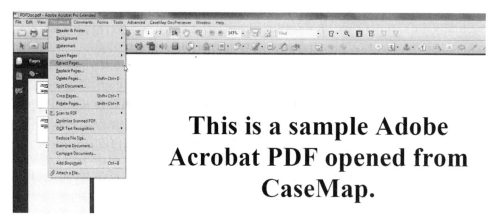

This is a sample Adobe Acrobat PDF opened from CaseMap.

Figure 160

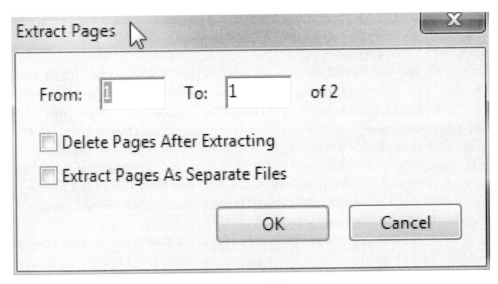

Figure 161

the defaults. In the next screen, CaseMap reminds you of how many PDFs you are sending to the spreadsheet and how many have Bates numbers. When you select Next, CaseMap sends the PDFs through Adobe to your CaseMap database. The final screen indicates the number of records processed, how many new records were processed, and whether any existing records were updated, after which you will click OK.

If you switch to the Documents (or other) spreadsheet, you will see the documents have been listed in CaseMap. If you elected not to use the Bates number feature for the short name, the DocPreviewer will create a short name consistent with the full name of a document.

Reviewing documents with the DocPreviewer is equally easy. You can perform your reviews in a number of ways. First, if you are reviewing PDFs that have not been loaded into your CaseMap database, the CaseMap DocPreviewer toolbar menu gives you the option to send the individual PDF to CaseMap or to send a fact to CaseMap. If you choose to send the PDF to CaseMap, the program first verifies that the document is not already linked to CaseMap. If it is linked to CaseMap, it provides the option to remove the link. If it is not included in your CaseMap database, a dialog box allowing you to add a new CaseMap object appears, asking for the document type and the full name and the short name. You can then either save the item or save and edit the item. If you choose to save an item, the Detail dialog box appears. When the PDF is saved in CaseMap, you can click on the CaseMap DocPreviewer menu and use the Edit CaseMap document command to edit the document.

You can also send a fact to CaseMap based on the document you are reviewing. If you choose this feature, CaseMap creates a new fact linked to that document. The top portion of the screen, Fact Text Selection, explains whether CaseMap should append the text in the PDF (provided it has been OCRed, i.e., the text of the document can be searched) to the fact text, to the Description field, or to other fields in CaseMap. You can also choose not to append by selecting Do Not Append within this box. Below this section is the Favorite Fields section of the dialog, in which you can add the date and time, fact text (using short names, where appropriate), source, whether the document is a key document, and any linked issues. You will have the added option to use the Issue Linker to select your issues quickly. When you click OK, CaseMap will create a new fact.

Another valuable feature of the CaseMap DocPreviewer is the ability to review PDFs in an efficient and orderly manner, thereby ensuring that every document is reviewed. To access this dialog, you would either choose Send Multiple PDFs to CaseMap from the CaseMap icon on your toolbar or select CaseMap DocPreviewer>Review PDFs from the menu, both of which are in Adobe Acrobat. If you have not selected a PDF to review, the only option you will be given is to start reviewing PDFs. This brings up the DocPreviewer PDF Review Wizard, which explains that you must select a spreadsheet to review and then select a PDF to start the review. You can turn off the Wizard's introductory screen if you so desire.

When you select Next, CaseMap asks which PDF you want to start your review with. If you choose to use a currently open PDF, you must have opened it directly from CaseMap rather than in Adobe. If you have been reviewing PDFs, you will have the option of continuing your review from the PDF at which you had stopped. You also have the option of selecting a CaseMap spreadsheet from which to begin your review. From that point, you will be able to choose from the Documents or other spreadsheets from which to review your PDFs. Note that you can only review PDFs and not other file types with the PDF Review Wizard.

When you select a spreadsheet for review, CaseMap will provide you with a list of all of the documents and the review order. You can change the first PDF to be opened by selecting that document and selecting Finish. CaseMap will then open the document for your review. The toolbar reflects that you can edit the record linked to the PDF, you can create a fact linked to the PDF, you can stop your review session, or you can open the previous or next PDF in CaseMap. These options are available from either the CaseMap DocPreviewer toolbar in Adobe or from the CaseMap DocPreviewer menu under Review PDFs.

This is a very handy tool because, by selecting the next record, you will be able to go from one record to the next without having to open and close the document in Adobe.

The DocPreviewer also has advanced functions that allow you to send a PDF to CaseMap, to update a PDF that has been sent to CaseMap, or to update a fact that has been linked to CaseMap. If you do not link a fact to a particular PDF, you will be prompted to go back to CaseMap to select the fact you wish to update.

If you ask to update a PDF, a Send to CaseMap dialog box opens and shows you the object type, full name, and short name and asks whether you want to keep the existing link. If you say Yes, then the dialog will end. If you say No, then you will be asked whether you want to remove the link to the existing record. If you say No, the dialog will end. If you say Yes, that you want to remove the existing link, you will be permitted to edit the link.

Integration With Other Applications

CaseMap easily integrates with many other litigation support applications. As a result, users can easily transfer information between a wide variety of products. Because the list of applications with which CaseMap integrates changes, users should search Integration With Other Applications, in CaseMap's Help menu. From the resulting page, you can click a link and go to the page on CaseMap's Web site that lists the latest products that link with the program.

In addition, certain products offer the ability to Bulk Send to CaseMap, which allows users to send multiple records to a CaseMap database rather than sending them one by one. Many of these products require a plug-in. Many are available at no charge.

Bulk Field Copy Tool

The Bulk Field Copy tool (Tools>Case Tools>Bulk Field Copy) copies data from one field to another for all of the visible records in a spreadsheet. Thus, if your documents spreadsheet lists various persons as the author of e-mails and you wish to list them as senders, you could use the Bulk Field Copy utility to copy the data from the Author column to the Sender column.

It is important to note that all data in the destination field are overwritten when you use the Bulk Field Copy utility. CaseMap will not be able to undo any of the changes made using this feature.

Bates Analyzer

The Bates Analyzer (Tools>Case Tools>Bates Analyzer), which works with the Objects-Documents spreadsheet, examines the numbers in the Bates-Begin

> ## About the Bates Stamping Tool
> The Bates Stamping Tool requires that you have Adobe Acrobat Professional or Standard (Version 6 or higher) installed on your computer. It does not work with Adobe Acrobat Reader.

and Bates-End fields and performs various analyses to discover any inconsistencies, duplications, or anomalies. The tabs on the Bates Analyzer dialog box show a summary along with detailed information for the following categories: Invalid Documents (ones without a beginning or ending Bates numbers), Duplicate Documents, Duplicate Pages, Gaps, and Invalid Ranges. CaseMap will generate a report from this dialog box if you click the Save Report button on the bottom right of the box. If the Bates Analyzer discovers problems, you must manually correct those problems, however, because the Bates Analyzer does not correct the problems automatically.

Bates Stamp Tools

Bates stamping, a premium feature of the DocPreviewer, automatically installs an Adobe Acrobat plug-in containing additional options and features that allow you to review, code, and analyze documents more easily than ever. Using the Bates Stamper, you may Bates stamp individual PDFs or large groups of PDFs from formats you create.

To use the DocPreviewer's Bates Stamp Wizard to Bates stamp PDFs from within CaseMap (see Figure 162), click the Bates Stamp PDFs option on the DocPreviewer pane of CaseMap's navigation bar; you can also access the Bates Stamp tools from the CaseMap DocPreviewer menu in Adobe (see Figure 163). Initially, CaseMap will advise you that you must have Adobe Acrobat Standard or Professional (Version 6.0 or higher) installed to use this feature. Next, the Bates Stamp Wizard dialog box appears and warns

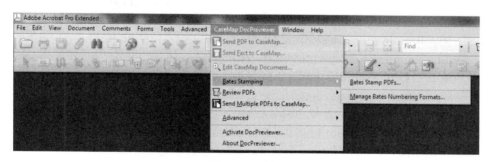

Figure 162

Figure 163

Make a Copy of Your Documents Before Bates Stamping

Before using the Bates Stamp Tool, or changing any documents, you should always make a backup copy to avoid making permanent irreversible changes to the originals. In addition, you should use optical character recognition (OCR) on your PDFs before Bates stamping, because Bates stamping may prevent Acrobat from being able to OCR documents.

that the Bates Stamp tool modifies your PDFs and does not create a backup copy of them.

When you proceed, the tool will recognize PDFs that contain CaseMap Bates stamps; the tool can only identify Bates stamps that it has created. By default, the tool ignores files containing CaseMap Bates stamps; you can, however, check the box that allows CaseMap to delete the original stamps and replace them with new stamps. After reading the information, click Next and select the PDF files you want to Bates stamp. Use the Options menu on the left side of the dialog box to add individual files or a folder containing a number of files to be stamped. You can also use the Options panel to remove a file from the list to be stamped or to clear all the files. The panel also has a View PDF button. Click Next.

You will be given the option to create a Bates numbering format or to use an existing format for your PDFs. Select the appropriate option. If you create a new format, you will be asked to select the maximum number of documents to be Bates stamped and to provide a starting Bates number—e.g., generally 1 for a new set; click Next to create a prefix for your number. This step is optional. Then enter a name for the new Bates format, and click Finish. You will be given an opportunity to review the Bates numbering format and can change the settings and beginning Bates number by clicking the Edit button. Review your settings and, if acceptable, click Next. CaseMap then offers you an opportunity to arrange the PDFs in the order you desire by highlighting a file and using the up and down buttons.

Installing the Adobe Acrobat Plug-In

If you purchased the Adobe Acrobat Plug-In for CaseMap, it will be installed when you install CaseMap. If you installed CaseMap before installing Adobe Acrobat, you can install the plug-in for Adobe Acrobat by going to the Help menu, selecting the Detect and Repair option, and selecting Modify and proceeding.

You will then be shown the Review and Begin Bates Stamping dialog, which will summarize the number of PDFs to be stamped, the total number of pages to be stamped, the starting and ending Bates page numbers, the font to be used, and the location of the Bates stamp. The CaseMap Bates Stamp utility also will again warn you that it modifies PDFs and does not create backup copies of the files. If you want to make a backup copy of your files, do so before proceeding. The dialog also explains that you will not be able to OCR your PDFs after the CaseMap Bates stamps are applied; thus, if you plan to OCR your PDFs, you must do so before adding the CaseMap Bates stamps.

You must check the box agreeing to the information contained in the dialog and click Finish. CaseMap will apply the Bates numbers, and a dialog will appear asking if you want to launch the Send PDFs to CaseMap utility. The box will be checked by default; uncheck the box if you do not want to import the Bates-stamped documents into CaseMap. CaseMap then launches the Send PDFs to CaseMap utility.

Case Optimizer

The Case Optimizer utility defragments your case database by reclaiming unused disk space and rebuilding the internal database structures. CaseMap recommends that you optimize your cases frequently to ensure maximum performance.

To run the Case Optimizer, which should only be run when no other users are accessing a case, go to Tools>Case Optimizer. You will be provided with an explanation of the Case Optimizer and will then be asked to click OK. CaseMap will open a browse window, and you will select the case to be optimized. CaseMap then optimizes the case and advises you that case optimization is complete. The process is generally very quick and very easy.

File Viewers

One of the remnants of earlier versions of CaseMap is the File Viewer tool, which is used when linking objects from outside of the program. Because CaseMap does not have its own internal software to display documents and other objects, CaseMap allows you to open documents and other objects using various other programs. By default, CaseMap will list Windows files and Acrobat as File Viewers; if you have purchased Text Map, it will also be listed.

You can access File Viewer information in two ways: First, by selecting Tools>Linked Files>Manage File Viewers, you can add a file viewer to the

CaseMap menu. While there may be limited circumstances when this may be required, in virtually all cases this is an unnecessary step. The other method of accessing File Viewers occurs when you link a file to a document or other object. In that circumstance, the Link Assistant will permit you to designate whether Windows files or Adobe (or some other program) should be associated with the object.

Although you may choose to select a specific program, by default, CaseMap sets Windows files as the default viewer for a case.

For PDF files, you may also use Acrobat as the File Viewer, which may be helpful if you use the Bulk Change File Viewer tool. When you select Windows files as the default viewer for viewing objects and other items, CaseMap will, when you try to open a particular item, look at the file extension, such as .pdf, .doc, and .wma and determine which program on your computer is the default program designated to open that type of file. CaseMap will then use that default program to open the particular file.

As long as your computer has a program capable of opening a particular type of file, CaseMap can open it without a problem. Thus, you can link virtually any type of file to a CaseMap database, with the only limitation that the program used to open the file must be installed or operable on that user's computer.

Bulk Change File Viewer

In limited circumstances, you may need to change the Viewer (program) associated with a particular file type, e.g., tifs, etc. CaseMap provides a Bulk Change File Viewer (Tools>Linked Files>Bulk Change File Viewer) to change all files associated with one viewer to another.

Spelling and AutoCorrect Options

The Spelling and AutoCorrect Options menu (Tools>Spelling and AutoCorrect Options) (see Figure 164) allows you to customize how CaseMap handles spelling and corrections in the program. The top portion of this dialog box offers you specific options that permit you to specify whether CaseMap will check spelling as you type, correct spelling errors as you type, and to control other features, including ignoring words in uppercase, ignoring words containing numbers, suggesting corrections from the main dictionary only, and automatically correcting "DUal" capitals.

In most cases it is advantageous to select the "Check spelling as you type" and "Correct spelling errors as you type" because CaseMap uses a standard English dictionary and will correct the types of common typos that many

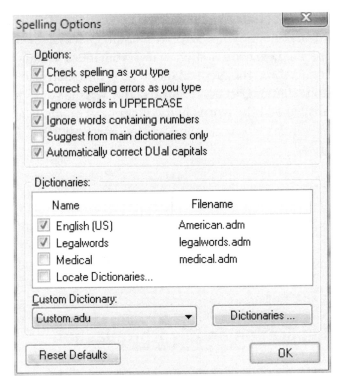

Figure 164

of us make. You should be careful before enabling the commands to "Ignore words in UPPERCASE" or "Ignore words containing numbers" because of the possibility that document names may include those characteristics. If you select/enable those features, CaseMap does not check items with those characteristics and you will have to manually review that information, which can be time-consuming.

Spell Check

You cannot spell-check more than one field at a time in CaseMap. In addition, you can only spell-check text and description fields. CaseMap ignores short names when spell-checking.

The American English and legal dictionaries that ship with CaseMap are turned on by default when you install the program. If you want to use the medical dictionary, you must enable the feature by going to Tools>Spelling and AutoCorrect Options and checking the box next to Medical in the Dictionaries section of the dialog box. To obtain new and/or updated dictionaries for the spell checker, you may visit the Web site located at **www.addictivesoftware.com/dicts-extern.htm**.

The bottom half of the spelling options screen lists the dictionaries that apply to or are enabled for your case. By default, CaseMap enables its English dictionary and its Legalwords dictionary; you must manually enable (by checking the dialog box) the medical dictionary. CaseMap also permits you to create a custom dictionary, which stores the words you add during spell check. You can also edit the words in the dictionary or add words to it so that CaseMap does not flag words that are written correctly but are not in the default dictionaries.

Spell-Checking

Every CaseMap field into which data is entered can be spell-checked. To check spelling, you can either press F7 or go to Tools>Spelling. A dialog box will come up asking which field you want to spell-check on the displayed spreadsheet. When you click OK, CaseMap displays the Spell Check dialog, which is virtually identical to the dialog found in Word and other programs.

Replicas: Replication and Synchronization

One of the CaseMap's most versatile features is its ability to create a replica—a complete working copy of any particular case. A replica is a copy of your case file that can merge back into the original ("master") copy. Synchronization is the process by which CaseMap merges the changes made to the information in a replica back into the master version of the file. Replicas are created through the Create Replica Wizard found at File>Synchronize>Create Replica.

When you or a member of your staff leaves the office, or if you collaborate with members of other law firms, each person can take a replica of the case file with them. Users can change or add information, etc., to the facts, ob-

Replicas: Make Sure the Computer You Use the Replica on Has All the Other Programs You Need

Many times users will take databases with them as replicas. It is important to make certain that, when taking a replica database with objects, the computer on which the replica will be used (if the documents and other objects are going to be replicated as well) has the software to open the various documents and objects. While virtually every computer has a PDF reader such as Adobe Acrobat, not all computers will be able to open all other types of files. Thus, it is important before placing a replica on another computer to be certain that that computer has software compatible with all of the file types linked to CaseMap.

jects, issues, and questions in the case in a replica. While you and the others are working with your replicas, the staff in your office can simultaneously make changes and additions to the master version of the case. When a replica is returned to the office, you can synchronize it with the master case file, thereby incorporating any changes made to the replica with any changes made to the master.

To create a replica, go to File>Synchronize>Create Replica, which opens the Create Replica Wizard (see Figure 165). The Wizard will ask whether you want to take the replica offline on your own computer (which allows you to copy documents for offline access). If you choose Yes, the program will copy all of the linked files to either the default location listed in the off-line folder box or you may select another location you choose. If you have a large database, for example, you may want your off-line location to be an external hard drive rather than a laptop computer. If you check No, you can save the replica to any location but cannot copy the linked documents. This screen also has a Comments section, where you can add information about the replica you are

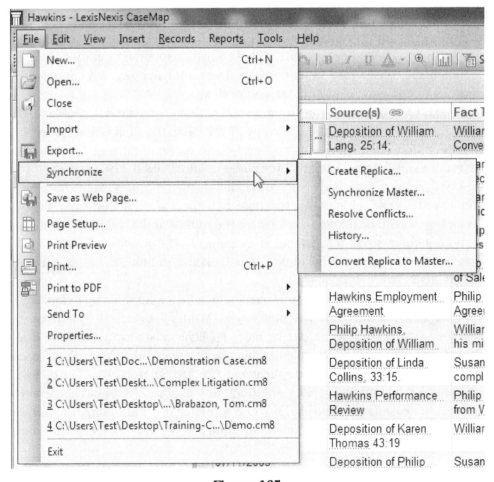

Figure 165

Never—*Never!*—Copy the Original Database and Work on It

You should never make a copy of the original database in CaseMap and take it with you. This is a recipe for disaster. If you take a copy of the original database and work on it, and someone else works on the original, you will not be able to merge the changes. Instead, you should always create a replica, which is an identical working copy of the database that can be easily merged with the original.

creating. Because CaseMap's default names for replicas are not particularly helpful, it may be helpful to include information in this box, such as the name of the person who is receiving the replica and any other relevant data. This can make it easier to identify the replica when you synchronize it or to perform other replica-related maintenance in CaseMap.

The next screen in the Create Replica Wizard asks for the name and location for the documents that will be copied and linked to the replica. If you do not change the location, the replica will be saved in the location specified in that dialog, and as noted in the Tools>Options>File Locations. If you have chosen to copy linked documents, CaseMap will display the number of linked documents, as well as the number of documents it can copy; if it cannot copy all of the documents, it will advise you of this.

Next, CaseMap asks you to name the replica. By default, CaseMap calls each replica "Replica of" and the name of the case, which is not very helpful. You should consider choosing a name for the replica that includes the date the replica was created and any other helpful information. For example, if you are involved in a case with eight other law firms, you may wish to name it "Replica of XXXX," along with the date and the name of the other firm to whom it was sent. CaseMap then creates the replica and, if selected, copies all of the documents to the designated location. In the process, CaseMap also changes the location of the files in the Linked File field in the Documents spreadsheet.

When you reopen the original case, which CaseMap does by default, you will note that the blue title bar now says "[Master]" before the name of the case (see Figure 166). When one or more replicas exists for a case, the original case will be renamed the master, and the title bar will reflect this information. If, on the other hand, no replicas exist or are outstanding, [Master] will not appear. If you open a replica, the title bar will state "[Replica]" before the name of the case (see Figure 167). When a replica is outstanding, the person with the replica can make additions and updates to facts, objects, issues, and

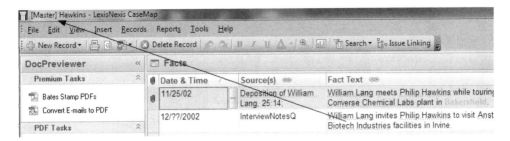

Figure 166

Replica Limitations

When a replica is outstanding, CaseMap places some minor restrictions on the databases. For example, users working in the master file cannot delete case issues. Similarly, users working with a replica cannot create new fields or add members to the case staff. The following table lists the database restrictions applicable when a replica is outstanding, as of Version 9.0. (Note: The term *preexisting* in the table below has the following meanings—master, preexisting: a record or value that exists in one or more replicas that have not been synchronized; replica, preexisting: a record or value that exists in the master copy of a case.)

Area	Master Case	Replica Case
Object Spreadsheet	Cannot change the object type of a preexisting object. Cannot delete a preexisting object.	Cannot change the object type of a preexisting object. Cannot delete a preexisting object.
Issue Spreadsheet	Cannot delete a preexisting issue.	Cannot delete a preexisting issue.
Staff Dialog	Cannot delete a preexisting staff member.	Cannot add, edit, or delete staff members.
Field Properties	Cannot delete a preexisting field. Cannot delete a preexisting value of a fixed or open-ended list.	Cannot add, rename, or delete fields. Cannot delete a preexisting value of a fixed or open-ended list.
File Viewers	Cannot delete a preexisting viewer.	Cannot delete a preexisting viewer. Changes to preexisting viewers are not synchronized.
Spreadsheet Views	No restrictions	Changes are not synchronized.
Case Properties	No restrictions	Changes are not synchronized.
Saved Searches	No restrictions	Changes are not synchronized.
Related Files	No restrictions	Changes are not synchronized.

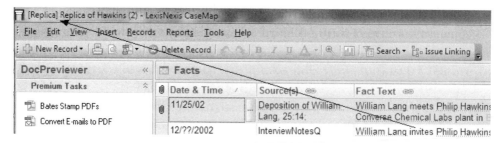

Figure 167

questions. At the same time, persons working on the master can also make changes to the database, but cannot delete issues.

You must carefully use the replication and synchronization process and follow all of the instructions provided. Synchronization is also limited to the specific copy of the file created during the replication process. ***Thus, you cannot synchronize a copy of your case file, and you cannot synchronize a replica more than one time.*** In other words, if a replica has been synchronized to the master case, it should be deleted so that it is never accidentally used again.

When synchronizing a replica with the master, you must do so from the master case. In addition, when synchronizing a replica with the master, the case must be opened exclusively, which means that no other users may be logged into the case other than the person who will be performing the synchronization. When a file is opened exclusively, only one user may be in it. By default, when you attempt to synchronize a replica, CaseMap will look for the replica in the default location specified under Tools>Options>File Locations. CaseMap then asks whether you are sure you want to continue with the synchronization and proceed from there. If there are no changes in the replica file, CaseMap will warn you that the file has no changes and that, unless you are certain that no changes were made to the replica, you should cancel the operation and find a copy of the replica to which modifications were made in the database. The program will also warn you that if you later find another copy of the replica file, you will not be able to synchronize it. Thereafter, CaseMap will complete the synchronization; it also advises you to delete the replica because it cannot be synchronized again. Rather, you should create a new replica. Generally, you should always delete the replica. When all replicas have been synchronized with the master file, [Master] will no longer appear in the title bar of the case.

Should there be any conflicts between a replica and the master, you will be prompted upon synchronization to resolve the conflict. CaseMap will display each conflict and the person performing the synchronization will decide which change to keep and which to discard.

Managing Case Staff

Every user who logs into CaseMap should be listed in the case staff listing. By managing your case staff, you can control who gains access to a case. Users should not, as a best practice, log on as anyone other than themselves. Even if security is not an issue, having a separate login for each user is important so that you can track, when necessary, the activities of any particular user. Thus, if you wanted to see all entries made by Chris Attorney in CaseMap, you could easily do that by using the Creation Author or Last Updated Author fields on a particular spreadsheet. If everyone in the office had logged in as Chris Attorney, however, that would not be possible.

Adding Staff Members

To manage staff, go to Tools>Manage Case Staff. There is no limit to the number of staff (whether designated as authors or scribes) who may be added to a case. Use of CaseMap is instead based on the number of licenses purchased, and you should consult the LexisNexis CaseMap Licensing Agreement to determine how many users may log in to CaseMap at a time. Click the plus sign to add a new staff member record (see Figure 168). Enter the new staff member's name in the Full Name field. When you exit the Full Name field, CaseMap will generate a short name and initials for the new staff member. You may change these settings. Next, enter the name of the organization for whom the staff member works in the Organization field. Select the staff type of the new staff member. Lawyers and paralegals are typically designated authors. Secretaries are typically designated as scribes. CaseMap then asks you whose views and searches to copy to set up the new staff member. You can choose a default set or a set defined by any other staff member.

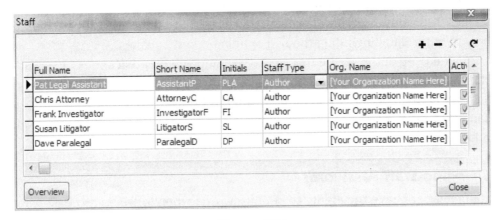

Figure 168

When staff members leave, they may be made inactive merely by unchecking the active box in the staff column. By designating a staff member as "inactive," all of the user's spreadsheet views and fields are preserved.

You may also delete a staff member when that person will no longer be involved in a case. If you delete a staff member, the times and stamps, such as Last Update Author and Creation Author, will reflect that the staff member created the information or updated it, but the staff member will be listed as "deleted."

Staff Types

CaseMap designates all staff who access the program as either an author or a scribe. An author has the authority to develop the information being entered into a case or to determine whether information is worth entering. Typically, partners, associates, paralegals and other counsel working on a case are designated as authors. By default, the person who creates a case is listed as the first author for the case.

When an author is added, CaseMap will create a series of custom spreadsheet views, searches, and evaluation fields for the new author. By doing so, the new author can be productive immediately. Thus, if you create a new author and look at the Evaluation column on the Facts spreadsheet, you will see that that author's name appears automatically.

On the other hand, you may designate individuals as a scribe. A scribe enters information on behalf of an author, but does not determine which information should be entered and does not typically make any determinations or generate reports, etc., on the scribe's own behalf. When a scribe opens a case, CaseMap will display the Scribe Entering For dialog so that the scribe can specify the name of the author on whose behalf the scribe is entering case information. Typically, legal secretaries and others may be designated as scribes. It is important, if not critical, however, that scribes be fully trained in how to enter data, including the use of full and short names.

When you add a scribe to a case, CaseMap will create a series of spreadsheet views and searches for the new scribe, but will not create evaluation fields because a scribe, by definition, will not be evaluating the data. Scribes can perform all other tasks that authors do and can update case information, print reports, and complete most other functions that authors would.

Changing Staff Passwords

Staff members have the ability to set passwords when logging in to CaseMap. To change a password, a staff member must go to Tools>Change Password.

Backup and Restoring

The Backup and Restore utility allows you to create and/or restore compressed backups of case databases. The backup files are completely compatible with the zip file format used by numerous file-compression software programs. To use this utility, CaseMap must be running.

Backups

To backup a case, go to Tools>Backup and Restore, select the Backup option, and click Next. Select the case to back up by entering the name of the case (including the path) or by clicking Browse and locating the file. By default, CaseMap will back up a case to the location listed for case files under Tools>Options>File Locations. If you want to change the location for storing the backup, go to Select Destination Directory, choose Browse, and select the desired path.

Click Next to select the name you want to assign to the compressed file and the case contained within it. Click [Case Name] if you want to use the existing case name; click Copy of [Case Name] [Date & Time] if you want to prefix the case name with "Copy of" and append to it the "[current date and time]"; or, click Custom if you want to choose the name of the case you want to use in the "Save backup file as" box. Click Next to review the backup and destination directory information you have entered. If this information is correct, click Finish. CaseMap will back up your case, and, when complete, the program will display a confirmation message.

If your database is large, the Backup and Restore utility will allow you to store your backup on multiple disks, and if you need more than one disk, the utility will prompt you. Because the backup utility compresses your data, your case will "shrink" during backup and return to normal size when you restore it.

Backups

It is important to know that when CaseMap backs up your database, it does not back up *any* of the linked documents or other files. *They must be backed up separately.*

It is highly recommended that you back up your CaseMap database and the linked documents regularly and that you do not rely on the CaseMap Backup and Restore utility. If you do not regularly back up your database and documents, and you suffer a crash, CaseMap will not be able to restore data entered since the last backup.

According to CaseMap, backup compression is typically about 75 percent—i.e., a database will be about 25 percent of its original size when compressed.

Restore

To restore a case, go to Tools>Backup and Restore, select the Restore option, and click Next. Then select the case you want to restore by entering its name (including the path) or by clicking Browse and locating the case file. By default, CaseMap will restore a case to the location listed for case files under Tools>Options>File Locations. If you want to change the location for restoring the backup, go to "Select destination directory," choose Browse, and select the desired path. Click Next to review information you have entered. If the information is correct, click Finish. CaseMap will restore the case and, when the process is complete, display a confirmation message. When you perform a restore, any information that was contained, added or modified in the database after the backup had been completed will be lost.

Case Scripts

Case Scripts are various programming options run by CaseMap. CaseMap supports creating scripts in VBScript, JavaScript, or JScript and allows the automation of tasks within a particular case.

To open the Case Scripts task pane, go to Tools>Case Tools>Case Scripts, and a Case Scripts submenu appears. Click on the Manage Scripting menu, and the Case Scripts task pane will open on the right side of the CaseMap's main application window. This menu will not be visible to users who do not have access to case scripts; to change user options, go to Tools>Options>Case Scripts.

Create a New Case Script

Open the utility, select New Script, and begin creating your script.

Copy a Case Script

Open the utility and select the script you want to copy. Then follow the instructions for editing a case script. Select the Save As menu item located on the File menu of the script editor. When the Save Script As dialog box appears, enter the new name for the copy of the script (each script name in a folder must be unique). Click OK.

Run a Case Script

(Option #1)
Open the Case Scripts menu, and the Case Scripts submenu will appear, listing the available scripts in the case. Click on the name of the case script to run.

(Option #2)

Open the Case Scripts task pane. Select a case script to edit in the tree view, and click on the Run Script item in the Manage Scripts commands list.

Users will receive an error message when they click the Edit Script item if they do not have user access rights to modify case scripts.

Creating a Case Template

CaseMap lets you create "case templates," which are predesigned case outlines containing information that you use as the starting point for a new case. Case templates are extremely versatile and allow you to jump into a case without dealing with a lot of the bureaucracy you might confront when starting from scratch. The advantage of using templates is that they allow you to introduce issues, objects, questions, staff, and other features into new cases without have to enter the information again. Thus, rather than using the default CaseMap template, if your office always adds the same users to every case, you could simply modify the default CaseMap template to include the names of all users so that they do not have to be typed again and again.

Templates can be helpful and save time when you handle many similar types of cases that may have a standard group of issues or a common set of questions, objects, or other fields. Case templates are created from existing cases, so you must first have created a case with the relevant fields before making a new template. When creating a template, you will use the Template Wizard to determine which facts, objects, issues, questions, and research records are maintained as part of the new template.

To create any case template, go to Tools>Create Case Template Wizard to open the dialog box. By default, CaseMap selects the case in which you were last working as the basis for the new template. If, however, there is another case you wish to use as the source of your template, you can navigate to it

Creating Staff-Based Case Templates

If the same staff members work on most cases, you should consider creating a case template that includes each staff member, along with an Evaluation field for each person. Remember, however, that only authors can have Evaluation fields, not scribes. A scribe can only change the values of an Evaluation field for the author for whom the scribe is logged in. Other authors (and the scribes entering data for them) can view your Evaluation fields but, cannot change the values in them.

using the Browse menu. On the next screen you will be asked to name your template. When you do so, CaseMap will require you to go to a directory and name the case template. Case templates are named with an extension of .ct8, while cases are named with the .cm8 extension in CaseMap 8. When you click Next, CaseMap will ask which of the existing information in the data file you wish to delete—i.e., the information that you do not want to include in your new template. You can delete all facts, objects, issues, questions, and research authorities and extracts. Commonly, when you create a case template, you may wish to retain some or all of the objects, issues, questions, and research authorities. Generally, but not always, you will need to create new facts. When you click Next and Finish, you are done, and CaseMap will open the new template. You can then delete any information that you do not wish to keep in your template. For example, if you have global facts that apply to all clients, but wish to have client-specific templates, you could create your template by copying one client's database and then deleting the client-specific facts and information. There are multiple other ways of adding information to and deleting information from a template, although this is probably the easiest way to do so.

Regardless, you can always edit your template simply by going to the File>Open menu and navigating to the template, which will appear as though it is a CaseMap case. You can also add additional information to a template as well. When you make changes to a template, they apply to all future cases created using that template.

Bulk Field Update

The Bulk Field Update utility (Tools>Case Tools>Bulk Field Update) updates a particular field with a specified value for all visible records in a spreadsheet. As with Bulk Field Copy, the data in the destination field will be overwritten, and you will not be able to undo any of the changes that are made. You should therefore make a backup of the case file before proceeding.

Bulk Import PDFs

Bulk Import PDFs (Tools>Case Tools>Bulk Import PDFs) is a utility that allows you to populate the Objects-Documents spreadsheet with individual PDFs one by one or to import an entire folder of documents automatically, filling in the full name and short name fields, and establishing a link in CaseMap for easy access to the PDFs on a user's system. The Bulk Import utility only works with documents in PDF format, and you must have Adobe Acrobat Standard or Professional Version 6 or higher installed on the computer on which the utility will be run. The utility, which is described in greater detail previously in this chapter, will not work with the free Adobe Reader.

Bulk Issue Linker

The Bulk Issue Linker (Tools>Case Tools>Bulk Issue Linker) allows you to link all records in a view in a Fact, Object, Question, or Research spreadsheet to one or more issues. The Bulk Issue Linker eliminates the need to make individual links.

Short Name Assistant

The Short Name Assistant (Tools>Case Tools>Short Name Assistant) reviews the entire database and automatically links all unlinked object short names in any of the description fields in a case.

Object Link Merger

The Object Link Merger (Tools>Case Tools>Object Link Merger) is used to correct the situation that arises when duplicate objects are created in the Objects spreadsheet. The Object Link Merger utility makes links between two different short names and corrects the duplication problem.

Facts Linked to Selected Objects Utility

The Facts Linked to Selected Objects utility (Tools>Case Tools>Facts Linked to Selected Objects) displays a list of the facts that are linked to the objects listed in the current spreadsheet. CaseMap then prompts you to choose whether to include facts that are linked via the Fact Text, Description, Status Description, Source(s), Potential Source(s) or Source Quote fields. This utility does not examine links in any other fields.

Change Linked File Paths Utility

The Changed Link File Paths utility (Tools>Case Tools>Facts Linked to Selected Objects) should be used when you have moved files that have been

Use the Linked File Paths Utility

If a CaseMap user is going to go to trial, it can be extremely helpful to place a replica, along with the related documents, on a laptop computer for use in the courtroom. Similarly, if you create a replica on your computer but move the replica to a laptop or another computer, you may wish to have copies of the linked document files.

Following synchronization, however, the Documents spreadsheet will continue to show links to the location specified in the second step of the Create Replica Wizard, and not to the laptop or other location to which you have moved the documents. To resolve this issue, you should review the Linked File column on either the Document or All Objects spreadsheet. Next, verify that the path for the files is different from the location at which you now are storing the files. Then perform a global search-and-replace, replacing the specified path for the current/ accurate one—e.g., replace L:\\Docs\CaseMap\Jones with C:\\Jones, or whatever other location you are using—and then open a few files to confirm that the changes were correct. By doing so, you will allow seamless integration with CaseMap and avoid any "surprises" in the courtroom.

linked to a particular case to a new location on your computer or network. You will be prompted to browse to the new location and will need to have access to that folder before continuing. If all of the linked files were previously linked in the same folder, the utility will automatically update all of the links in the current spreadsheet to the new path, regardless of any filters that may be applicable. If the linked files were originally in multiple locations, you will be prompted to select the particular path you want to change, and only linked files with that path will be updated.

Because this is a global change utility, it is recommended that you make a backup of your data before proceeding. Restoring the backup will be the only way to undo the changes.

Delete All Records in View

The Delete All Records in View utility (Tools>Cast Tools>Delete All Records in View) deletes all records *showing/on display in the current spreadsheet*. This utility should only be used on a limited basis because it makes global changes that cannot be undone unless the database is backed up and a restore is run.

Batch Processing

CaseMap includes multiple batch processing options that can perform various operations on linked files. Found at Tools>Linked Files>Batch Processing, the utility will work with Acrobat (PDFs) and Windows files that are already linked to your CaseMap database. For PDFs, you can Bates stamp, copy, print, verify, or update the files. Similarly, for Windows files, you can copy or link them. Thus, you can verify that all linked PDFs or other files are accessible to CaseMap or print all PDFs, etc.

Appendix

Default CaseMap Program Shortcut Keys

To Do This	Use the Following Keystrokes
Activate the main CaseMap menu	F10 or ALT
To display the system menu with choices to restore, move, or resize the window	ALT + Spacebar
Cancel out of message boxes	ESC
Close the application (with no open dialog boxes)	ALT + F4
Open the Link Assistant	CTRL + Spacebar

Default Shortcut Keys for Spreadsheet Views

To Do This	Press
Insert a new record	Insert
Undo changes made to a record prior to refreshing	ESC
Redo or undo changes made to a text or description type of field prior to refreshing	CTRL + Z
Find	CTRL + F
Replace	CTRL + H
Insert symbol	CTRL + Y
Refresh the spreadsheet view	F5
Open the Detail window	CTRL + F2
Open the Link Assistant	CTRL + Spacebar
Select all text in a column	CTRL + Enter
Copy selected text to clipboard	CTRL + C
Cut selected text	CTRL + X
Paste selected text	CTRL + V
Delete a record	CTRL + Delete
Post changes to a record when editing an existing record or adding a record	CTRL+ E
Run an instant filter	CTRL + I
Run an instant tag	CTRL + G
Cancel instant filter/tag	CTRL + Shift + I
Open Fact spreadsheet	CTRL + 1
Open Object spreadsheet	CTRL + 2
Open Issue spreadsheet	CTRL + 3
Open Question spreadsheet	CTRL + 4
Open Research Authorities spreadsheet	CTRL + 5
Open Research—Extract from Authorities spreadsheet	CTRL + 6

Open Research—Authorities and Extracts spreadsheet	CTRL + 7
Open Print dialog box	CTRL + P
Move from field to field (excluding read-only fields)	Tab or Enter
Move backward from field to field (excluding read-only fields)	Shift + Tab or Shift + Enter
Access edit mode within a field	F2
Display the edit shortcut menu to cut, copy, and paste (in a description field)	Shift + F10
Delete characters or contents of a selected field	Delete
Move left across fields in a spreadsheet view	The Left Arrow key
Move right across fields in a spreadsheet view	The Right Arrow key
Open the window associated with clicking	ALT + Up or Down arrow
Move to the beginning of the line of text	Home
Move to the end of the line of text	End
Select an entire word left or right of the current pointer position (in edit mode)	CTRL + Shift + Left or Right arrow
Select an entire word from the pointer up or down	Shift + Up or Down Arrow
Move the pointer one word at a time left or right from the current pointer position (in edit mode)	CTRL + Left or Right arrow
Toggle the state of check boxes or option buttons	Spacebar
Drop a list of options associated with a field into view	ALT + Down arrow or any key
Scroll through list options associated with a field	The Right arrow or Left arrow key or The Up or Down arrow key
Open online Help	F1
Add an object from the Fact Text, Source(s), or Question Text field	CTRL + A
Open the Object Detail window for the highlighted object short name in the Fact Text, Source(s), or Question Text field	CTRL + D
Insert a copy of the selected record	CTRL + Insert
Copy the contents of the above field	CTRL + '
Use spell checker	F7

The following shortcuts only work when all of the text is selected in the current field:	
Move the pointer to the first record of a column	CTRL + Home
Move the pointer to the last record of a column	CTRL + End
Move to the first or last record in view	CTRL + Up or Down arrow key
Move the pointer to the first field selected record	Home or CTRL + Left arrow
Move the pointer to the last field selected record	End or CTRL + Right arrow

Default Shortcut Keys for Dialog Boxes

To Do This	Press
Move around a dialog box (top to bottom, left to right)	Tab
Move backward within a dialog box	Shift + Tab
Redo or undo changes made to a text or description type of field prior to refreshing	CTRL + Z
Copy selected text to clipboard	CTRL + C
Cut selected text	CTRL + X
Paste selected text	CTRL + V
Scroll through a list of options associated with a field	The Right or Left arrow key Or The Up or Down arrow key
Select an entire word left or right of the current pointer position (in edit mode)	CTRL + Shift + Left or Right arrow
Select an entire line from the pointer up or down	Shift + Up or Down arrow
Move the pointer one word at a time left or right from the current pointer position (in edit mode)	CTRL + Left or Right arrow
Move to the beginning of the line of text within a multiple line field	Home
Display the edit shortcut menu to cut, copy, and paste	Shift + F10
Toggle the state of check boxes or option buttons	Spacebar
Cancel out of message boxes	ESC
Close an open dialog box	ALT + F4

Index

Selected Books from . . .
THE ABA LAW PRACTICE MANAGEMENT SECTION

The Lawyer's Guide to Collaboration Tools and Technologies: Smart Ways to Work Together
By Dennis Kennedy and Tom Mighell
This first-of-its-kind guide for the legal profession shows you how to use standard technology you already have and the latest "Web 2.0" resources and other tech tools, like Google Docs, Microsoft Office and Share-Point, and Adobe Acrobat, to work more effectively on projects with colleagues, clients, co-counsel and even opposing counsel. In *The Lawyer's Guide to Collaboration Tools and Technologies: Smart Ways to Work Together*, well-known legal technology authorities Dennis Kennedy and Tom Mighell provides a wealth of information useful to lawyers who are just beginning to try these tools, as well as tips and techniques for those lawyers with intermediate and advanced collaboration experience.

The Lawyer's Guide to Marketing on the Internet, Third Edition
By Gregory H. Siskind, Deborah McMurray, and Richard P. Klau
In today's competitive environment, it is critical to have a comprehensive online marketing strategy that uses all the tools possible to differentiate your firm and gain new clients. The Lawyer's Guide to Marketing on the Internet, in a completely updated and revised third edition, showcases practical online strategies and the latest innovations so that you can immediately participate in decisions about your firm's Web marketing effort. With advice that can be implemented by established and young practices alike, this comprehensive guide will be a crucial component to streamlining your marketing efforts.

The Lawyer's Guide to Adobe Acrobat, Third Edition
By David L. Masters
This book was written to help lawyers increase productivity, decrease costs, and improve client services by moving from paper-based files to digital records. This updated and revised edition focuses on the ways lawyers can benefit from using the most current software, Adobe® Acrobat 8, to create Portable Document Format (PDF) files.

PDF files are reliable, easy-to-use, electronic files for sharing, reviewing, filing, and archiving documents across diverse applications, business processes, and platforms. The format is so reliable that the federal courts' Case Management/Electronic Case Files (CM/ECF) program and state courts that use Lexis-Nexis File & Serve have settled on PDF as the standard.

You'll learn how to:

- Create PDF files from a number of programs, including Microsoft Office
- Use PDF files the smart way
- Markup text and add comments
- Digitally, and securely, sign documents
- Extract content from PDF files
- Create electronic briefs and forms

The Electronic Evidence and Discovery Handbook: Forms, Checklists, and Guidelines
By Sharon D. Nelson, Bruce A. Olson, and John W. Simek
The use of electronic evidence has increased dramatically over the past few years, but many lawyers still struggle with the complexities of electronic discovery. This substantial book provides lawyers with the templates they need to frame their discovery requests and provides helpful advice on what they can subpoena. In addition to the ready-made forms, the authors also supply explanations to bring you up to speed on the electronic discovery field. The accompanying CD-ROM features over 70 forms, including, Motions for Protective Orders, Preservation and Spoliation Documents, Motions to Compel, Electronic Evidence Protocol Agreements, Requests for Production, Internet Services Agreements, and more. Also included is a full electronic evidence case digest with over 300 cases detailed!

Virtual Law Practice: How to Deliver Legal Services Online
By Stephanie L. Kimbro
Virtual law practice is revolutionizing the way the public receives legal services and how legal professionals work with clients. If you are interested in this form of practice, Stephanie Kimbro will show you how to successfully set up and operate a virtual law office and responsibly deliver legal services online to your clients. This practical guide also provides case studies of individual virtual law practices along with client scenarios to show how web-based technology may be used by legal professionals to work with online clients and avoid malpractice risks.

Social Media for Lawyers: The Next Frontier
By Carolyn Elefant and Nicole Black
The world of legal marketing has changed with the rise of social media sites such as Linkedin, Twitter, and Facebook. Law firms are seeking their companies attention with tweets, videos, blog posts, pictures, and online content. Social media is fast and delivers news at record pace. This book provides you with a practical, goal-centric approach to using social media in your law practice that will enable you to identify social media platforms and tools that fit your practice and implement them easily, efficiently, and ethically.

How to Start and Build a Law Practice, Fifth Edition
By Jay G Foonberg
This classic ABA bestseller has been used by tens of thousands of lawyers as the comprehensive guide to planning, launching, and growing a successful practice. It's packed with over 600 pages of guidance on identifying the right location, finding clients, setting fees, managing your office, maintaining an ethical and responsible practice, maximizing available resources, upholding your standards, and much more. If you're committed to starting your own practice, this book will give you the expert advice you need to make it succeed.

ABA LAW PRACTICE MANAGEMENT SECTION
MARKETING • MANAGEMENT • TECHNOLOGY • FINANCE

Google for Lawyers: Essential Search Tips and Productivity Tools
By Carole A. Levitt and Mark E. Rosch
This book introduces novice Internet searchers to the diverse collection of information locatable through Google. The book discusses the importance of including effective Google searching as part of a lawyer's due diligence, and cites case law that mandates that lawyers should use Google and other resources available on the Internet, where applicable. For intermediate and advanced users, the book unlocks the power of various advanced search strategies and hidden search features they might not be aware of.

The Lawyer's Guide to Working Smarter with Knowledge Tools
By Marc Lauritsen
This ground-breaking guide introduces lawyers and other professionals to a powerful class of software that supports core aspects of legal work. The author discusses how technologies like practice systems, work product retrieval, document assembly, and interactive checklists help people work smarter. If you are looking to work more effectively, this book provides a clear roadmap, with many concrete examples and thought-provoking ideas.

The Lawyer's Guide to Microsoft Outlook 2007
By Ben M. Schorr
Outlook is the most used application in Microsoft Office, but are you using it to your greatest advantage? *The Lawyer's Guide to Microsoft Outlook 2007* is the only guide written specifically for lawyers to help you be more productive, more efficient and more successful. More than just email, Outlook is also a powerful task, contact, and scheduling manager that will improve your practice. From helping you log and track phone calls, meetings, and correspondence to archiving closed case material in one easy-to-store location, this book unlocks the secrets of "underappreciated" features that you will use every day. Written in plain language by a twenty-year veteran of law office technol-ogy and ABA member, you'll find:

- Tips and tricks to effectively transfer information between all components of the software
- The eight new features in Outlook 2007 that lawyers will love
- A tour of major product features and how lawyers can best use them
- Mistakes lawyers should avoid when using Outlook
- What to do when you're away from the office

The Lawyer's Guide to Microsoft Word 2007
By Ben M. Schorr
Microsoft Word is one of the most used applications in the Microsoft Office suite—there are few applications more fundamental than putting words on paper. Most lawyers use Word and few of them get everything they can from it. Because the documents you create are complex and important—your law practice depends, to some degree, upon the quality of the documents you produce and the efficiency with which you can produce them. Focusing on the tools and features that are essential for lawyers in their everyday practice, *The Lawyer's Guide to Microsoft Word* explains in detail the key components to help make you more effective, more efficient and more successful.

The Lawyer's Guide to Microsoft Excel 2007
By John C. Tredennick
Did you know Excel can help you analyze and present your cases more effectively or help you better understand and manage complex business transactions? Designed as a hands-on manual for beginners as well as longtime spreadsheet users, you'll learn how to build spreadsheets from scratch, use them to analyze issues, and to create graphics presentation. Key lessons include:

- Spreadsheets 101: How to get started for beginners
- Advanced Spreadsheets: How to use formulas to calculate values for settlement offers, and damages, business deals
- Simple Graphics and Charts: How to make sophisticated charts for the court or to impress your clients
- Sorting and filtering data and more

Find Info Like a Pro, Volume 1: Mining the Internet's Publicly Available Resources for Investigative Research
By Carole A. Levitt and Mark E. Rosch
This complete hands-on guide shares the secrets, shortcuts, and realities of conducting investigative and background research using the sources of publicly available information available on the Internet. Written for legal professionals, this comprehensive desk book lists, categorizes, and describes hundreds of free and fee-based Internet sites. The resources and techniques in this book are useful for investigations; depositions; locating missing witnesses, clients, or heirs; and trial preparation, among other research challenges facing legal professionals. In addition, a CD-ROM is included, which features clickable links to all of the sites contained in the book.

TO ORDER CALL TOLL-FREE:
1-800-285-2221

VISIT OUR WEB SITE:
www.lawpractice.org/catalog

30-Day Risk-Free Order Form
Call Today! 1-800-285-2221
Monday–Friday, 7:30 AM – 5:30 PM, Central Time

Qty	Title	LPM Price	Regular Price	Total
_____	The Lawyer's Guide to Collaboration Tools and Technologies: Smart Ways to Work Together (5110589)	$59.95	$ 89.95	$_____
_____	The Lawyer's Guide to Marketing on the Internet, Third Edition (5110585)	74.95	84.95	$_____
_____	The Lawyer's Guide to Adobe Acrobat, Third Edition (5110588)	49.95	79.95	$_____
_____	The Electronic Evidence and Discovery Handbook: Forms, Checklists, and Guidelines (5110569)	99.95	129.95	$_____
_____	Virtual Law Practice: How to Deliver Legal Services Online (5110707)	47.95	79.95	$_____
_____	Social Media for Lawyers: The Next Frontier (5110710)	47.95	79.95	$_____
_____	How to Start and Build a Law Practice, Fifth Edition (5110508)	57.95	69.95	$_____
_____	Google for Lawyers: Essential Search Tips and Productivity Tools (5110704)	47.95	79.95	$_____
_____	The Lawyer's Guide to Working Smarter with Knowledge Tools (5110706)	47.95	79.95	$_____
_____	The Lawyer's Guide to Microsoft Outlook 2007 (5110661)	49.99	69.99	$_____
_____	The Lawyer's Guide to Microsoft Word 2007 (5110697)	49.95	69.95	$_____
_____	The Lawyer's Guide to Microsoft Excel 2007 (5110665)	49.95	69.95	$_____
_____	Find Info Like a Pro, Volume 1: Mining the Internet's Publicly Available Resources for Investigative Research (5110708)	47.95	79.95	$_____

*Postage and Handling	
$10.00 to $49.99	$5.95
$50.00 to $99.99	$7.95
$100.00 to $199.99	$9.95
$200.00+	$12.95

**Tax
DC residents add 5.75%
IL residents add 10.25%

*Postage and Handling	$_____
**Tax	$_____
TOTAL	$_____

PAYMENT

❑ Check enclosed (to the ABA)

❑ Visa   ❑ MasterCard   ❑ American Express

_____
Account Number   Exp. Date   Signature

Name _____ Firm _____

Address _____

City _____ State _____ Zip _____

Phone Number _____ E-Mail Address _____

Guarantee

If—for any reason—you are not satisfied with your purchase, you may return it within 30 days of receipt for a complete refund of the price of the book(s). No questions asked!

Mail: ABA Publication Orders, P.O. Box 10892, Chicago, Illinois 60610-0892
♦ Phone: 1-800-285-2221 ♦ FAX: 312-988-5568

E-Mail: abasvcctr@abanet.org ♦ Internet: http://www.lawpractice.org/catalog

Are You in Your Element?

Tap into the Resources of the ABA Law Practice Management Section

ABA Law Practice Management Section Membership Benefits

The ABA Law Practice Management Section (LPM) is a professional membership organization of the American Bar Association that helps lawyers and other legal professionals with the business of practicing law. LPM focuses on providing information and resources in the core areas of marketing, management, technology, and finance through its award-winning magazine, teleconference series, Webzine, educational programs (CLE), Web site, and publishing division. For more than thirty years, LPM has established itself as a leader within the ABA and the profession-at-large by producing the world's largest legal technology conference (ABA TECHSHOW®) each year. In addition, LPM's publishing program is one of the largest in the ABA, with more than eighty-five titles in print.

In addition to significant book discounts, LPM Section membership offers these benefits:

ABA TECHSHOW

Membership includes a $100 discount to ABA TECHSHOW, the world's largest legal technology conference & expo!

Teleconference Series

Convenient, monthly CLE teleconferences on hot topics in marketing, management, technology and finance. Access educational opportunities from the comfort of your office chair – today's practical way to earn CLE credits!

Law Practice Magazine

Eight issues of our award-winning *Law Practice* magazine, full of insightful articles and practical tips on Marketing/Client Development, Practice Management, Legal Technology, and Finance.

Law Practice Today

LPM's unique Web-based magazine covers all the hot topics in law practice management today — identify current issues, face today's challenges, find solutions quickly. Visit www.lawpracticetoday.org.

Law Technology Today

LPM's newest Webzine focuses on legal technology issues in law practice management — covering a broad spectrum of the technology, tools, strategies and their implementation to help lawyers build a successful practice. Visit www.lawtechnologytoday.org.

LawPractice.news
Monthly news and information from the ABA Law Practice Management Section

LawPractice.news

Brings Section news, educational opportunities, book releases, and special offers to members via e-mail each month.

To learn more about the ABA Law Practice Management Section, visit www.lawpractice.org or call 1-800-285-2221.

MARKETING • MANAGEMENT • TECHNOLOGY • FINANCE

LawPracticeManagementSection

MARKETING • MANAGEMENT • TECHNOLOGY • FINANCE